UNITED STATES FOREIGN POLICY TOWARDS SUB-SAHARAN AFRICA

David A. Dickson

With a preface by
Kenneth W. Thompson

UNIVERSITY
PRESS OF
AMERICA

LANHAM • NEW YORK • LONDON

Copyright © 1985 by

University Press of America,® Inc.

4720 Boston Way
Lanham, MD 20706

3 Henrietta Street
London WC2E 8LU England

Co-published by arrangement with
The White Burkett Miller Center of Public Affairs
University of Virginia

Library of Congress Cataloging in Publication Data

Dickson, David, 1954-
  United States foreign policy towards sub-Saharan
Africa.

  (American values projected abroad ; v. 18)
  "By arrangement with The White Burkett Miller Center
of Public Affairs, University of Virginia"—T.p. verso.
  Bibliography: p.
  1. Africa, Sub-Saharan—Foreign relations—United
States. 2. United States—Foreign relations—Africa,
Sub-Saharan. 3. Africa, Sub-Saharan—Foreign relations—
1960-   . 4. United States—Foreign relations—
1945-   . I. Title. II. Series.
JX1417.A74 1985   vol. 18   303.4'8273 s   85-9044
    [DT353.5.U6]   [327.73067]
  ISBN 0-8191-4727-3 (alk. paper)
  ISBN 0-8191-4728-1 (pbk. : alk. paper)

AMERICAN VALUES PROJECTED ABROAD

VOLUME XVIII

A SERIES FUNDED BY THE
EXXON EDUCATION FOUNDATION

FOUNDATIONS OF AMERICAN VALUES

AMERICAN VALUES VIEWED THROUGH OTHER CULTURES

*This work is dedicated
to my mother, Vera May
Allen Dickson and my
father, David Watson
Daly Dickson. Without
their firm support and
inspiration over the years
I could not have reached
the point where this
project could be undertaken.*

ACKNOWLEDGEMENTS

Many people have assisted me in the preparation of this work. Insights into the complex world of the United States executive bureaucracy and the Congress were offered by a number of current and former governmental officials. A researcher soon gains an appreciation of the openness of our democratic system. Personnel at the Kennedy Presidential Library and the Harvard University Government Documents room displayed unending patience during the long hours I spent with them. They helped me gain access to both their own collections and those of other government document depositories around the nation. My gratitude also goes to Roger Hecht who did much of the painstaking work necessary for the completion of preliminary drafts and the final draft. Special thanks go to Professor Joseph S. Nye Jr. and Professor Martin Kilson of Harvard University. They provided critiques through the entirety of the research and writing process. Quite simply, this work could not have been completed without their unselfish assistance.

TABLE OF CONTENTS

Contents

PREFACE

Dr. David Dickson has written a work of lasting importance on African-American relations in the post-independence era. It becomes, therefore, a companion study to that of Dr. Katherine Harris on 19th century African-American relations. As the Exxon Educational Foundation Series focuses on the interaction of cultures and regions, Dr. Dickson's study is appropriately a part of that series.

What Dr. Dickson succeeds in demonstrating is the continuity of America's relations with sub-Saharan Africa during this period. He examines the factors responsible for such continuity including bureaucratic, domestic, political, geopolitical, cultural and economic factors. Such factors have provided opportunities and possibilities but as relations show are not deterministic.

This book is a critical and perceptive review of American foreign policy in sub-Saharan Africa from Kennedy to Reagan. It deals more explicitly with foreign policy than some of the Exxon volumes. However Dickson's intention throughout is to look below the surface for causative factors that have shaped the evolution of American policy. He seeks to explain the reasons American policy has developed as it has rather than merely describing facts and events. It also sets standards against which effectiveness is evaluated. It has a theoretical framework but it also looks at strategic options for the United States.

The book promises to be one of the most important treatises written on American relations with Africa.

Dr. Kenneth Thompson
Executive Director
Miller Center of Public Affairs
University of Virginia

INTRODUCTION

In the mid 1970s, after a lapse of almost a decade, sub-Saharan Africa was once again thrust into a debate over proper responses to Soviet strategic initiatives on the Continent. This followed a period during which Africa, seemingly insulated from the superpower conflict and wracked by internal ethnic quarrels and coups, had receded as a concern of American strategists. The policy debate which emerged in the 1970s and persisted into the 1980s has conventionally been treated as a struggle between globalists and regionalists. Globalists focused on the pervasiveness of the Soviet threat and often advocated a military response. Regionalists stressed that Soviet ties to African regimes would be short-lived. They argued that the most effective instrument for countering Soviet influence was the economic strength of the West.

The policy debate took place in response to a number of dramatic developments. In 1974, a right-wing Portuguese regime fell, leading to a major change in the configuration of power in the southern Africa area. Radical governments buttressed by Cuban troops rose to power in Angola and Mozambique. Simultaneously, Rhodesia was engulfed in a civil war which threatened to escalate into a confrontation between the superpowers. In the Horn of Africa, a newly Marxist Ethiopian government appeared to open up new strategic opportunities for the Soviets. Elsewhere in Africa there were fears that endemic instability would facilitate the emergence of forces hostile to the West. Outside of the Continent the Vietnam War was approaching a climax. The battle lines had already been drawn. One group felt the experience dictated a reassertion of American muscle in other parts of the globe. A contending group wished to discourage America's proclivity to use force in distant lands.

The writer concurs with the view that Africa has recently been thrust more deeply into the East-West contest. However, the purpose of this study is not to join the chorus of voices heralding the virtues of globalist or regionalist thinking. Rather, the goals of this undertaking are fourfold.

First, to trace the evolution of American foreign policy in sub-Saharan Africa from the Kennedy through Reagan administrations. Studies of the development of our African policy have been conducted by Rupert Emerson, FS Arkhurst, Jennifer Whitaker, Robert M. Price, Henry Jackson and Helen Kitchen.[1] None of these studies approached the comprehensiveness of the one undertaken here.

The second purpose of this study is to explain why America's African policy has developed as it has.

Third, an effort will be made to determine the effectiveness of this policy in meeting American security needs regionally and globally.

A final goal is to identify future strategic options for America's African policy.

The evaluation of each administration will be divided into three areas.

The first area will be devoted to an assessment of the development of our African policy. The strategic aspects of American foreign policy will be the principal concern of this assessment. Much of the information for this section will be drawn from declassified government documents and interviews. In an effort to establish elements of continuity and discontinuity between administrations, a number of issues which have played a major role in American foreign policy considerations will be dealt with in depth. They will include American approaches to the Congo crises which have occurred intermittently over the past two decades, and American relations with Rhodesia. US treatment of the Portuguese colonies of Angola and Mozambique, and the South Africa and South-West Africa issues will also be considered.

Following an overview of the evolution of each administration's policy, the reasons for this evolution will be identified. Bureaucratic, domestic non-bureaucratic, geopolitical, cultural, and economic theories will be used for this purpose.

The third area will be an exploration of the success of the policy in fostering American security interests.

A final chapter will present conclusions and offer recommendations for America's African policy. "Foreign policy is not a matter of objectives; it is a matter of strategy. Fine goals matter less than the right strategy."[2] The formulation of this strategy with ample room for tactical flexibility is a major concern of this study.

The term "strategic" will be used to encompass all policies which affect American security interests directly or indirectly. An effort will be made to avoid a narrow definition of the term. Strategic interests will not be equated exclusively to American access to minerals and important air and sea routes. A wide array of interests, which have arisen as global interdependence has grown, will be addressed.[3]

It is the central proposition of this work that the underlying tenets of America's sub-Saharan African policy have remained consistent during the post-independence era. Bureaucratic, domestic non-bureaucratic, geopolitical, cultural, and economic factors have contributed to this continuity. They have not been wholly deterministic, however. There has been room for policy innovation. The failure of American policy makers to take advantage of this potential has had a deleterious impact on both regional and global American security needs.

NOTES TO INTRODUCTION

1. Rupert Emerson, *Africa and United States Foreign Policy* (Englewood Cliffs, New Jersey: Prentice Hall, 1967); Frederick S. Arkhurst, ed., *US Policy Toward Africa* (New York City: Praeger Publishers, 1975); Jennifer Seymour Whitaker, ed., *Africa and the United States: Vital Interests* (New York City: New York University Press, 1978); Robert M. Price, *US Foreign Policy in Sub-Saharan Africa: National Interest and Global Strategy* (Berkeley: University of California Press, 1978); Henry Jackson, *From the Congo to Soweto: US Foreign Policy Toward Africa Since 1960* (New York City, William Morrow and Co., 1982); and Helen Kitchen, *US Interests in Africa* (New York City: Praeger Publishers, 1983).
2. "Carter's U Turn in Foreign Policy," *US News and World Report* 88 (28 January 1980): 3.
3. The consequences of the growth of global interdependence are explored in Robert O. Keohane and Joseph S. Nye, *Power and Interdependence* (Boston: Little, Brown, and Co., 1971), pp. 23–27.

CHAPTER ONE

United States Foreign Policy Towards Sub-Saharan Africa Prior to the Kennedy Administration: INDIFFERENCE YIELDS TO MILD CONCERN AND APPREHENSION: A Brief Overview

1. The Nature of the Policy

The United States relationship with Africa is almost as old as the nation itself. The early years following independence witnessed the establishment of bilateral diplomatic and commercial ties with a succession of North African states. Morocco recognized the United States in 1786. In

1792, in an effort to mitigate the poor treatment meted out to American sailors by North African pirates, a series of diplomatic posts were set up.[1] An American consulate was established at Algiers in 1792. Diplomatic posts were also launched at Tripoli and Tunis in 1795, and Tangier in 1797.[2] American governmental ties with sub-Saharan Africa, large portions of which remained unknown to the West well into the nineteenth century, were slower in developing. In 1799, an American post was set up at Cape Town at the southern tip of the Continent.[3] American governmental links were not extended to another sub-Saharan entity for more than a half a century. In 1853, the US initiated commercial and diplomatic relations with Portugal's territories, followed by Liberia in 1863, and the Congo in 1884.[4]

In 1884–1885, at the Berlin Conference which formulated the rules for the scramble for Africa, the US government issued its first policy statement applicable to sub-Saharan Africa as a whole. In this statement, which was a precursor of a similar stance adopted shortly thereafter for the Far East, it endorsed free access for American commerce and benevolent treatment of the Africans. Yet, this assertion was little more than a rhetorical flourish.[5] Concrete measures were not taken to ensure its implementation, and President Cleveland refused to offer it to the Senate for approval. Secretary of State Bayard declared that the United States was "unprepared to accept political engagements in so remote and undefined a region as that of the Congo Basin."[6]

Following the Berlin Conference, official American interest in sub-Saharan Africa underwent a prolonged dip until the Second World War. Neither the Boer War of 1899–1902, or the partition of German territories among the victorious European powers following the First World War aroused governmental interest.[7] Only two sub-Saharan African issues provoked curiosity in governmental circles.

The first issue involved Liberia's economic and political difficulties. Liberia, a refuge for freed American slaves, found its economic wellbeing increasingly dependent on the assistance of the United States financial community during the first quarter of the twentieth century. In 1912, it received a loan of $1.2 million from United States sources. In subsequent years, Liberia requested large credits from the Senate. By the late 1920s, an American financial expert had an influential role in the Liberian budget process. Reports of slavery in Liberia in the 1920s and 1930s also stimulated governmental scrutiny.[8]

A second pre-World War II African issue attracting United States governmental attention was the Italian invasion of Ethiopia in 1935. Congress responded to this act by barring the export of arms to the adversaries.[9]

Despite these actions, American interest in Africa prior to World War II was limited. By 1939, the United States had only "three legations, three consulates general, eight consulates, and one consular agency on the Continent."[10] More importantly, most governmental decisions dealing with Africa were made in the State Department Division of European Affairs. This was the case, though African topics had theoretically been assigned to the Near Eastern Division in 1937.[11]

African issues occupied little time among United States policy-makers in the pre-World War II period. Humanitarian rhetoric occasionally surfaced as illustrated by the Berlin Conference of 1884–1885, and the criticism of Liberian forced labor in the 1920s and 1930s. This rhetoric was not coupled with tangible policies. This period is important for two reasons.

First, for the disinclination of the United States to acquire a territorial foothold in sub-Saharan Africa with accompanying financial links (Liberia is a partial exception to this rule). This contributed to the low priority assigned African issues by the government in subsequent years. It also played a part in the failure of the US for many years to develop a sizable group of African experts in the governmental and academic communities capable of formulating policies which combined an understanding of internal African realities, and global conditions. This state of affairs, corrected only partially in the post-World War II period, was to have an adverse impact on America's African policies during and following the early 1960s rush to independence.

Second, as a partial consequence of the first factor, the United States allowed the Europeans to take the lead in Africa. The United States seldom questioned the legitimacy of European initiatives on the Continent. While understandable in light of America's pre-occupation with the Western Hemisphere and the Pacific, this too was ultimately to have a negative effect on American global and African strategic interests.

Inattention to the internal dynamics of African affairs and an acquiescence to European actions on the Continent was the legacy of American behavior prior to World War II.

For a period of time following the outbreak of World War II, it appeared that a more active and independent American African policy might emerge. The war increased the Continent's strategic importance. North Africa faced the soft underbelly of Europe and provided a place for Allied troops to regroup. Central and southern Africa offered vital minerals such as uranium. West Africa, particularly Senegal and Liberia, straddled important Atlantic sea routes. Liberia attracted a sizable American military contingent. Fear of an invasion of the Western Hemisphere from West Africa was a serious concern in the war's early stages.[12]

Africa assumed a more important status in the State Department in 1943 when an African section was organized in the Near Eastern Division.[13] Moreover, US officials, led by President Franklin D. Roosevelt, began to challenge European colonialism. On July 23, 1942, Secretary of State Cordell Hull stated: "In this vast struggle, we Americans stand united . . . with those who are fighting for the opportunity to achieve freedom."[14] Then, on August 19, 1943, Henry Villard, assistant chief of the Division of Near Eastern Affairs, asserted that the United States had a political and economic stake in Africa.[15] In early 1944, Secretary Hull reiterated his call for self-determination in ex-enemy territories declaring that "there rests upon independent nations a responsibility to . . . help the aspiring peoples . . . to self-government."[16] There was ambivalence in the American approach to the issue of decolonization in Africa. For at the same time Federal officials expressed their support of the principle, they were assuring the allies of American backing of their positions in the colonies.[17] Nonetheless, the outlines of a new assertive American African policy appeared to be taking shape.

Such a policy did not materialize, however. The years immediately following the Second World War were characterized by increasing tension between the United States and the Soviet Union. The bold cries for self-determination of the World War II period were largely subordinated to a preoccupation with the containment of the Soviets. In Africa, this meant that the colonial powers, bastions against Soviet expansionism, were not to be undermined. The United States did support a timetable for independence for what was formerly Italian Somaliland. However, this was an unusual case.[18] The Truman presidential years of 1945–1952 can best be described as a period during which the philosophical basis for containment was formulated, and early efforts at implementing this philosophy initiated. Despite the designation of an Office of African Affairs in the Near Eastern Division of the State Department, Africa largely lost the importance it was assigned during the Second World War.[19] The Continent was to remain a preserve of the Europeans.

The first half of the Eisenhower administration retained continuity with the Truman administration in terms of America's African policy. Stalin's death, one month after Eisenhower made his first foreign policy address to the Congress, gave hope in limited segments of the American foreign policy community that a thaw in the cold war might be in store. This illusion was shattered in the fall of 1953 when the Soviets exploded a hydrogen bomb. The American governmental reaction to this event, and perceived Soviet inspired aggression in Korea and elsewhere was to build upon the Truman administration's policy of containment. It did so by placing less of an emphasis on its economic component. Secretary of

State John Foster Dulles frequently expressed his disdain for neutral Afro-Asian states which refused to accept American leadership in an anti-Communist coalition. Nor was he tolerant of Socialist experiments in the third world which rejected the ethos of private enterprise. The atmosphere in the early 1950s was hardly ripe for the emergence of a creative African policy.

An examination of speeches and policy pronouncements yields the following conclusions about the Eisenhower administration's African policy during its first term.

First, a stress would be placed on military-security issues as opposed to issues related to economic and political development. Underlying the administration's African policy as well as its third world policy in general was a desire to preclude any growth in Soviet influence. It must be kept in mind, however, that much of the European economic aid to its colonies during this period was indirectly extracted from Marshall Plan funds.

Second, European interests would assume primacy over African interests. This meant that little effort would be expended by the US to promote decolonization in Africa.[20]

Yet, the Eisenhower administration's early policy on Africa did not go unchallenged. Perhaps the most thoughtful and comprehensive critique of America's African policy was provided by Chester Bowles, whose work *Africa's Challenge to America,* appeared in 1957. Bowles argued first of all for a coherent US policy in Africa. He contended that "the most powerful nation in the world . . . cannot declare itself to be a non-participant in the affairs of a Continent boiling with change without abdicating its position of leadership."[21] He then made a plea for the injection of moral principles into America's African policy.

Bowles considered these principles to be major weapons in the battle against Soviet penetration of the Continent. They were to be incorporated into American policy through economic and political measures. Bowles argued for large amounts of economic aid to Africa without political conditions, and for a high profile anti-colonial policy with target dates for independence.[22]

Bowles was not the only critic of America's African policy. In a July 2, 1957 speech, then Senator John F. Kennedy charged that the administration's policy had a pro-colonial bias. The focus of this speech was on the American position on the Algerian independence drive. However, it was interpreted by many Americans as a general critique of the administration's colonial policy.[23]

The Eisenhower administration did not respond directly to these voices of dissent, but it could not avoid a response to a rapid series of events which were sweeping the third world in the mid 1950s. These events forced a reassessment of the administration's African policy. First, decolonization was picking up momentum. The Bandung Conference of Afro-Asian states took place in 1955, and British and French colonies in sub-Saharan Africa were beginning their march toward independence.[24] Second, the US was experiencing increasing tensions with its European allies as exhibited by the split over the Suez invasion in 1956.[25] Finally, the Russian economic and political presence in Africa was growing by the mid 1950s.[26]

The Eisenhower administration's reaction to these events was to send Vice President Richard Nixon on a trip to eight African states in February and March of 1957 to investigate conditions. Nixon's subsequent recommendations included an increase in the United States consular representation, a cautious commitment to decolonization, and an enhancement of both private and governmental aid.[27]

Hence, 1957 marks a watershed in the Eisenhower administration's African policy. After this date it began to adopt a more sophisticated multi-dimensional approach to Africa.

First, an institutional setting for the handling of African policy was established. On July 8, 1958, a Bureau of African Affairs with its own assistant secretary was authorized by Congress.[28]

Second, loans and grants in Africa from the Mutual Security Act, which had totaled $120.3 million in the fiscal years 1953–1957, were enlarged. In 1958, $82.4 million was provided to the Continent, and in 1960 this figure rose to $169.7 million.[29]

Third, in 1958 the United States supported UN proposals to accelerate the movement of UN Trust Territories on the Continent toward independence.[30]

Fourth, an assortment of US governmental agencies expanded their activities in Africa in the late 1950s.[31]

These innovations in America's African policy did not erase the administration's focus on the United States-Russian rivalry. This rivalry often contributed to administration postures in the late 1950s which resembled its stances during the first term. On February 26, 1957, the US opposed resolutions which would have hastened the independence process for the Cameroons.[32] Moreover, some State Department officials began to once again utter a warning about the perils of a precipitous rush toward independence.[33]

Nonetheless, one can see a subtle change in the Eisenhower administration's policy in the late 1950s. The changes were accompanied by an ambivalence which sometimes resulted in contradictory policy pronouncements confusing both Africans and Europeans alike. The policy changes were not motivated by abstract moral considerations. Instead, they were based on the cold calculation that Soviet bloc inroads could best be opposed by a varied policy which did not relegate itself to the military card.

2. Main Premises of the Policy

Thus, on the verge of the emergence of the Kennedy administration, a discernible American approach to sub-Saharan Africa was emerging. Its chief premises can be identified.

First, Soviet bloc influence in African should be limited as must as possible. Its member states were to be kept out of Africa, or at least they were to be prevented from exerting a sway over the policy decisions of individual regimes. A corollary of this was that Africa should be encouraged to retain strong bonds to the West, both diplomatically and economically.

The final two premises of America's posture on African affairs were holdovers from an earlier era, though world conditions had changed radically.

The second element was that Africa would continue to possess a low status globally in terms of an American commitment of physical and human resources.

Finally, the United States would continue to adjust its policy to European concerns on African issues. This approach was illustrated by the United States position on decolonization in sub-Saharan Africa. The United States did not become an assertive advocate of decolonization until the French, British and Belgians were devoted to this process and it appeared irreversible.

These premises were far from complementary. On the contrary, the final two premises made the first one difficult to achieve. This was particularly the case when the prevention of Soviet bloc encroachments required appropriate resources, and policies which conflicted with those of the Europeans. As we shall see in subsequent chapters, the United States could have cleansed itself of any major concern about African events. As it was, it retained a concern over the outcome of events in Africa. It seldom, however, acquired the capabilities or demonstrated the will to exert a major impact on these outcomes. In Africa, unlike most other parts of the globe, the US would not vacillate between the poles of intervention and withdrawal from events. Here the norm was withdrawal. Such an orientation rendered the achievement of American goals in Africa difficult, and in some instances impossible.

NOTES TO CHAPTER ONE

1. G. Mennen Williams, *Africa for the Africans* (Grand Rapids, Michigan: William B. Eerdmans Publishing Co., 1969), p. 163.
2. Ibid.
3. Ibid.
4. Ibid.
5. Emerson, *Africa and United States Policy*, p. 16.
6. Ibid.
7. Ibid.
8. Ibid., pp. 17–18.
9. Ibid., p. 18.
10. Vernon McKay, "The African Operations of United States Government Agencies," in *The United States and Africa*, ed. Walter Goldschmidt (New York City: Frederick A. Praeger Publishers, 1963), p. 275.
11. Williams, *Africa for Africans*, p. 164.
12. Rupert Emerson, "The Character of American Interests in Africa" in *The United States and Africa*, ed. Walter Goldschmidt (New York City: Frederick A. Praeger Publishers, 1963), p. 28.
13. Williams, *Africa for Africans*, p. 164.
14. Waldemar A. Nielsen, *The Great Powers and Africa* (London: Pall Mall Press, 1969), p. 247.
15. Ibid., pp. 248–49.
16. Ibid., p. 249.
17. Ibid., pp. 247–50.
18. Emerson, *Africa and United States Policy*, p. 22.
19. Williams, *Africa for Africans*, p. 164.
20. The best analysis of the Eisenhower administration's African policy during its first term is provided by Nielsen, *Great Powers and Africa*, pp. 259–82. One of the most important speeches on Africa by an official of the administration during its first term was delivered by Henry A. Byroade, the assistant secretary of state in charge of the Bureau of Near Eastern, South Asian, and African Affairs, on October 30, 1953. Excerpts from this speech can be found in Nielsen, *Great Powers and Africa*, pp. 260–62.
21. Chester Bowles, *Africa's Challenge to America* (Westport, Connecticut: Negro Universities Press, 1956), pp. 96–97.
22. Ibid., pp. 107–24.
23. Nielsen, *Great Powers and Africa*, pp. 268–70.
24. Ibid., p. 262.
25. Ibid., pp. 264–65.
26. A detailed breakdown of the increased Soviet presence in Africa from the mid-1950s through the early 1960s is provided by Vernon McKay, "Changing External Pressures on Africa," in *The United States and Africa*, ed. Walter Goldschmidt (New York City: Frederick A. Praeger Publishers, 1963), pp. 89–97.
27. Nielsen, *Great Powers and Africa*, pp. 265–67.
28. McKay, "African Operations of United States Agencies," p. 275.
29. Emerson, *Africa and United States Policy*, p. 26.
30. Nielsen, *Great Powers and Africa*, p. 271.
31. A list of United States agencies involved in Africa by the late 1950s can be found in

McKay, "African Operations of United States Agencies," pp. 273–93.
32. Nielsen, *Great Powers and Africa,* p. 267.
33. Ibid., p. 270.

CHAPTER TWO

The Kennedy Administration:
EARLY EXUBERANCE AND A RETURN TO NORMALCY:
January 20, 1961
Through
November 22, 1963

1. Strategic Importance of Sub-Saharan Africa and the Nature of Soviet Activity on the Sub-Continent in the Early 1960s

On January 20, 1961, John Fitzgerald Kennedy was sworn in as the thirty-fifth president of the United States. Before examining his administration, two questions must be addressed. First, what was the strategic importance of sub-Saharan Africa during the early 1960s? Second, what was the nature of Soviet activity in the area at this point?

Few governmental officials deemed sub-Saharan Africa a vital interest of the United States in the early 1960s. An administration memorandum addressed to Secretary of Defense McNamara put it quite succinctly: "Sub-Saharan Africa is of secondary importance to United States military strategy . . . There is, however, a need to deny it to the Sino-Soviet bloc because of the natural resources and the flanking geographical position of Africa" in relation to Europe, the Middle East, and South America.[1] Wayne Fredericks, deputy assistant secretary of state for African affairs during the Kennedy administration in a March 1982 interview with the author was equally frank in his appraisal of American security interests in sub-Saharan Africa. According to Fredericks, when he entered office sub-Saharan Africa wasn't particularly important strategically.[2]

Nonetheless, American strategic interests in Africa can be identified as the 1960s unfolded. These interests were threefold.

First, the area commanded sea and air passages which affected the West's economic and military wellbeing. Evidence of explicit Soviet plans to disrupt these passages was lacking, and therefore many analysts felt this would only occur in the context of a full-scale conflict with the Soviets. During such a conflict, Soviet control of airfields, ports, and support facilities in the Horn of Africa or the western bulge of Africa could jeopardize communication between the Persian Gulf area, North America, and Western Europe.[3]

Moreover, the Cape Route off the coast of the Republic of South Africa had assumed importance. It facilitated the passage of raw materials to the United States including oil, copper, and manganese.[4] The precarious nature of the Suez Canal, dramatically displayed during the 1956 Middle Eastern crisis, enhanced the status of the Cape Route.[5] Militarily, this route was a passageway from the South Atlantic to the Indian Ocean.[6] The diminishing ability of the British to project their seapower was contributing to a focus of American military analysts on this consideration.[7]

A second strategic concern of the United States in the early 1960s was a string of tracking stations and bases. Space tracking facilities existed in Nigeria, Zanzibar, South Africa, and Madagascar. The State Department felt these facilities were vital to the NASA (National Aeronautics and Space Administration) space research program.[8] Their military usage was uppermost in the minds of American governmental officials. One such facility was the Atlantic missile range tracking station near Pretoria. As expressed in an internal Kennedy administration memorandum, the station contributed greatly to American missile development and would continue to be important in the future, "though not vital."[9] The Kagnew communications and intelligence gathering center in Ethiopia monitored Middle Eastern events.

In addition, America possessed mineral interests in sub-Saharan Africa. The importance of these mineral interests was lessened by the existence of strategic stockpiles in the United States, alternative sources of supply, and the availability of substitutes. Worst case scenarios as embodied in radical regime changes on the sub-Continent, an accompanying denial of minerals to the West, and the formation of mineral cartels were highly improbable in the early 1960s. Soviet power projection capabilities, a helpful condition if not a prerequisite for the emergence of Marxist regimes in sub-Saharan Africa, were weak during this period. Moreover, the nexus of economic ties between the mineral producing states of sub-Saharan Africa, and the Western powers and Japan was of such a magnitude that even a radical state would have felt compelled to sell minerals to the West. Only these states could buy the minerals in adequate quantities to produce the revenue necessary to sustain a modern welfare state.[10]

A cartel of mineral producers was an even less likely scenario as the Kennedy administration began. This could be attributed to the youthful nature of African states, their reliance on export markets in the West, and the implausibility of any states joining the Republic of South Africa in such a venture.

Did high Kennedy administration officials share these doubts about the degree of American dependence on major sub-Saharan African mineral producers? An examination of memoranda circulating among top administration figures in the early 1960s reveals that their assessment of the degree of dependence was modest. A memorandum to Secretary of State Rusk, entitled "US and South African Economic Leverage on Each Other," puts United States and South African mineral relations into perspective. The memorandum yields the following information. From 1957–1961, 21 percent of United States uranium imports came from South Africa, though a 100 percent increase in domestic production during this period had significantly lessened its dependence on the Republic.[11] In 1961, South Africa was the sole supplier to the United States of amosite, which was used for high temperature insulation. The US, however, had a strategic stockpile of the commodity and substitutes existed. America in 1961, was somewhat more dependent on chromium imports from South Africa. Forty-four percent of this substance, which was used in steel alloys, came from South Africa. The US had only minor domestic sources of this ore, and no substitutes could be found. Its stockpile in chromium was adequate, and alternative sources in the Philippines, Turkey, and Southern Rhodesia could have met a sizable portion of US needs.[12] In 1961, 72 percent of the mineral thorium, which was used in power reactors in the United States, came from South Africa. American stockpiles in this mineral were large, and there were

13

exploitable resources available at home. Finally, 23 percent of US germanium needs came from South Africa, though replacements were readily available. Germanium's chief application was in electronic devices.[13] According to a Department of State Policy Planning Staff memorandum, South Africa also produced over 50 percent of the world's gold during the Kennedy years.[14] Furthermore, it exported manganese, platinum, antimony, vanadium, and asbestos to the United States.[15]

An additional mineral source for the United States was the Congo, which in 1960, provided three-quarters of the cobalt imported into the country and one-half of the tantalum. Both minerals had strategic uses in aerospace production. In addition, 80 percent of the industrial diamonds — as well as copper and tin — utilized by the US came from the Congo.[16] Gabon provided manganese, and Nigeria furnished columbium.[17]

Hence, the US had strategic interests in sub-Saharan Africa in the early 1960s. These interests were very limited, however, relative to American strategic interests elsewhere in the world. In the hierarchy of American concerns, Africa ranked below most inhabited parts of the globe. On a few occasions, a small commitment of American troops to the Congo was contemplated in the middle echelons of the bureaucracy. Such thoughts were soon squelched by upper level officials or overtaken by events. Sub-Saharan Africa's significance in the early 1960s derived from political and psychological factors rather than concrete strategic factors. Many American policy makers had been shaken by the recent Soviet penetration of the Western Hemisphere through the establishment of a Communist regime in Cuba, and were wary of growing Communist threats in Asia. They felt Communist successes in Africa would contribute to its momentum around the world. As in the Eisenhower administration, the concept of containment was to be applied to Africa. This was not done because of its minerals or its sea lanes. It was done because of Africa's role in the global battle with communism.

By the beginning of the 1960s, the Soviet presence in sub-Saharan Africa was increasing but was small relative to that of the West. Much of it consisted of legitimate bilateral ties.

In 1958, a department responsible for African affairs had been created in the Russian Foreign Ministry. Within four years, the Soviet bloc had eighty diplomatic posts in Africa. In contrast, in 1954, there were only Soviet diplomatic posts in Ethiopia and Egypt, and a Czech consular mission in South Africa.[18]

Soviet economic ties with Africa expanded in the early 1960s. By 1961, eighty-five Eastern Bloc trade delegations had negotiated trade agreements with African states. Russian exports to Africa were $94 million at this time, and her imports from the Continent were $148 million. These figures appeared small relative to American exports of $827 million, and imports of $583 million. Yet, the 1961 Soviet trade figures must be compared to the 1956 figures when she exported $24 million and imported $29 million.[19] Moreover, the number of African students in Soviet bloc universities doubled to nearly 1,200 between 1960 and 1961. However, there were 2,831 African students enrolled in schools in the United States, from 7,000 to 9,000 in France, and 17,000 in the United Kingdom at the inception of the Kennedy administration.[20]

United States governmental officials charged, as the 1960s began, that the Communists had set up several trade union organizations that served as fronts. By mid 1962, African trade unions identified as having connections with the Communist dominated World Federation of Trade Unions included the following units: The General Confederation of Cameroon Trade Unions, the Mauritius Trade Union Federation, the Sudanese Workers Trade Union Federation, and four branches of the General Confederation of African Workers in French Equatorial Africa.[21]

Yet, by mid 1962, there were only two Communist parties operating in Africa which were defined as such by Communist states. These were the parties in South Africa and the island of Réunion.[22] The Soviet influence outside of the Ghana-Guinea-Mali axis, and the Republic of the Congo was limited. Even in these states, the governments—and in the Congo a political faction—were run by men whose ties to the Soviets were motivated largely by pragmatism. The Soviets recognized this reality, and a survey of the literature published by Soviet ideologists and academicians confirms these observations.[23]

In the early 1960s, the potential for Soviet influence in sub-Saharan Africa, outside of the Congo (Leopoldville), was not contingent on the feeble efforts of Soviet backed trade unions or indigenous revolutions in a region with few proletarians. Nor was it contingent on cultural exchanges. Rather, it was dependent largely on the ability of the West to forge policies which restricted Soviet opportunities. It is to these policies, and the issues underlying them that we now turn.

2. Background to Principal Issues Dealt With by the United States Government in Sub-Saharan Africa

Several issues were the centerpiece of the Kennedy administration's policy in sub-Saharan Africa. They included the Congo (Leopoldville), Angola, Mozambique, and the South Africa and South-West Africa issues. Southern Rhodesia did not command much attention from American governmental officials at this point, but will be dealt with briefly because of its importance in subsequent administrations. A few words must be said about the background of these issues.

The Congo was perhaps the most urgent African issue facing the Kennedy administration during its early days. Less than a week after its independence from Belgium on June 30, 1960, the Congo began a descent into chaos. Portions of the Congolese army mutinied in Leopoldville and Thysville, and the country was swept by violence. The United States declined an invitation from Congolese President Kasavubu and Prime Minister Lumumba to send troops. Instead, the US suggested that a UN force be sent to restore order.[24] In July and August 1960, the United Nations Security Council gave permission to Secretary General Dag Hammarskjöld to assist the Congolese government. While this was taking place, Katanga province under provincial President Moise Tshombe, declared its independence on July 11, 1960 and asked Belgium for help.[25] United States alarm was aroused by the Soviet Union's introduction of planes and equipment into the country by August 1960. This precipitated a clash between Prime Minister Lumumba, who favored Soviet military assistance, and President Kasavubu, who did not. In ensuing months, President Kasavubu and Prime Minister Lumumba dismissed one another, and General Joseph Mobutu proceeded to place Lumumba under arrest.[26]

By the inception of the Kennedy administration, Lumumba had been murdered, and a radical government in Stanleyville challenged the central government in Leopoldville. Moreover, the provinces of Katanga and South Kasai were in a state of revolt.[27]

The South African—South-West Africa issue also captured the attention of the Kennedy administration. This issue had two components.

The first component concerned the Republic of South Africa's continued control over the territory of South-West Africa. Following World War I, the League of Nations granted South Africa a mandate over South-West Africa. In 1946, the United Nations General Assembly suggested that South-West Africa become a United Nations trusteeship. This recommendation was repudiated by the South African government, but it did agree "to administer the territory in the spirit of the mandate."[28] In 1950, the UN General Assembly requested that the International Court of Justice offer an opinion on South-West Africa's status. The court concluded that any UN management of the territory should follow the procedures of the League. However, it also ruled that unilateral revisions of South-West Africa's status by South Africa would not be permitted. The South African government did not accept these conclusions.[29]

South-West Africa was a volatile issue by the time the Kennedy administration assumed office. It was faced by calls for sanctions in the United Nations and a threat by the South African foreign minister to use force to prevent UN supervision. Moreover, Liberia and Ethiopia brought a suit against South Africa in the International Court of Justice. They argued that South Africa's efforts to institute apartheid in South-West Africa contravened the League of Nations mandate that the administering power enhance the welfare of all the inhabitants.[30]

A second component of the South African issue was the question of apartheid in the Republic of South Africa itself. Apartheid, the doctrine of racial separation, received its chief impetus in 1948 when the Afrikaner settlers rose to power in South Africa under the banner of the Nationalist Party. In subsequent years, restrictions on the freedom of non-whites were intensified. These restrictions included the elimination of the franchise on a national level, and the institutionalization of a pass system limiting the access of non-whites to white areas. They also involved the subjection of non-whites to arbitrary arrest for security violations.[31]

By the early 1960s, calls for the international isolation of South Africa for its apartheid policy had multiplied. The internal debate in the Kennedy administration over this issue and the strategic repercussions of various policy options was intense.

A third issue of concern to the Kennedy administration was that of Angola and Mozambique. Angola and Mozambique entered the 1960s as colonies of Portugal. The Portuguese had maintained a presence in these colonies since the late fifteenth century. The 90 percent of the populace categorized as indigenous by the Portuguese had few rights, and were subjected to forced labor and imprisonment without trial. The Portuguese paid little attention to improving the internal infrastructure of the colonies, and by 1958 less than 1 percent of the indigenous population had received three years of education.[32]

The colonial status of Angola and Mozambique was not unchallenged, however. In February 1961, police stations and prisons in Luanda, the capital of Angola, were attacked by members of the Popular Movement for the Liberation of Angola (MPLA). This rebellion was easily suppressed, but only a month later the National Front for the Liberation of Angola (FNLA) launched a massive assault on northern Angola. Hundreds of Europeans were killed in a two day period.[33] The forces of revolution in Mozambique would lag behind those in Angola, but the revolt against Portuguese rule had begun.

The causes of this revolt were threefold. First, longstanding social and economic grievances. Second, in the case of northern Angola, a major decline in the price of coffee in the late 1950s and early 1960s.[34] Finally,

17

the rising expectations of the non-Portuguese populace of the colonies as a result of the emergence of independent states elsewhere on the Continent. In short, an increasingly mobilized black African population, without institutional channels for the expression of grievances, turned to violence. The Portuguese response to the rebellion was fierce. In subsequent months, they destroyed entire villages and killed up to 50,000 Africans.[35]

Therefore, the Kennedy administration in its early days was confronted by the question of how it would respond to the conflict in Angola. A crucial element in the equation was that Portugal, one of the parties in the conflict, was a member of NATO. Moreover, the agreement which allowed the US to use an airbase on the Portuguese controlled Azore islands was to lapse on December 31, 1962.[36]

A final issue to be dealt with is that of Southern Rhodesia. Starting in 1923, it had largely been self-governing. Power, however, was monopolized by the small white minority, and the black population had minimal electoral clout. When, in 1961, white Rhodesians formulated a constitution which allowed a limited number of black Africans to qualify, black leaders resisted. They contended that the constitution was intended to sustain minority rule indefinitely. The Kennedy administration was to grapple with the problem of self-determination for Southern Rhodesia raised by black Africans, and the extent to which the United States would accept British initiatives on the Rhodesian question.[37]

An analysis of the policy which actually did emerge over the approximately one thousand days of the Kennedy administration awaits us.

3. The Nature of the Policy

In the early days of the administration, it appeared there might be a major departure from the premises of America's African policy which had emerged by the end of the Eisenhower presidency.

In numerous rhetorical pronouncements, Kennedy administration officials seemingly challenged what had heretofore been the chief premise of America's policy. This premise was that Africa should be tightly bound to the West, therefore precluding Communist gains. A new slogan arose which soon found its way into many administration statements. This slogan was that the cold war was to be kept out of Africa. Africa was to be free to follow its own destiny removed from the manipulation of the superpowers. A few examples will suffice.

On February 13, 1961, Walter Kotsching, director of the State Department's Office of Economic and Social Affairs, stated that the United States did "not want to see African progress impeded by conflicts . . .

18

between powers outside the African Continent."[38] This theme was reiterated three months later by Assistant Secretary for African Affairs G. Mennen Williams. He proclaimed that America supported independent Africa governments where men had "the opportunity to choose their own national course free from the dictates of any other country."[39] In December 1962, Chester Bowles, the president's adviser on African, Asian and Latin American affairs, asserted that "African nations . . . have no desire to be Russianized, Sinocized, or even Americanized."[40]

If judged by the rhetoric which emanated from the executive branch on Africa, the administration had adopted a benign attitude toward the concept of neutrality. Nor was this approach wholly without substance. The neutralist states of Guinea and Ghana were the objects of administration economic and diplomatic initiatives. Aid programs to these states were stepped up, and they were not written off because of their proclaimed neutrality.[41]

A second premise of America's African policy, namely that Africa would possess a low status globally in terms of an American commitment of physical and human resources, was also challenged at the inception of Kennedy's presidency. Africa's new-found prominence on the American foreign policy agenda was illustrated by the fact that the first State Department appointee was the assistant secretary for African affairs. This post was given to G. Mennen Williams, governor of Michigan, and an aggressive advocate of civil rights.[42] Care was also given to other African-related appointments. They were indeed the best and the brightest. As described by former Ambassador to Guinea, William Attwood, many of them were younger people from outside the government who had political experience. This enabled them to establish a rapport with African leaders.[43] This group included Philip Kaiser, a former Rhodes Scholar, who was appointed to Senegal, liberal activist James Loeb, who was sent to Guinea, and Edmund Gullion, who was placed in the Congo (Leopoldville).[44] Higher level appointees were also of a high quality. Wayne Fredericks, whose tenure with the Kellogg Company in South Africa had given him a strong antipathy toward apartheid, became deputy assistant secretary of state for African affairs.[45] Liberals Chester Bowles and Adlai Stevenson became undersecretary of state and ambassador to the United Nations, respectively. The post of assistant secretary of state for international organization affairs went to Harlan Cleveland who, as an administrator at Syracuse University, had endorsed increased economic and administrative aid to less developed countries.[46]

Africa's newly acquired high profile was also reflected in President Kennedy's willingness in the first days of his administration to meet frequently with African leaders. The president's tenure as head of the

Senate Foreign Relations Subcommittee on Africa had apparently whetted his appetite for African issues. Former Deputy Assistant Secretary for African Affairs Wayne Fredericks noted that the president was often eager to see African visitors. The United Nations was in plenary session in 1961 when Kennedy assumed the presidency. When informed that the Africans wanted to meet him, he invited them to the White House.[47] Many came, the meeting went well, and the administration was off to a good start.[48] According to Assistant Secretary Williams, on the first African Freedom Day in 1961, President Kennedy held a reception for Africans in the State Department. A speech he delivered at the reception was received enthusiastically.[49] There were other meetings between the president and Africans in the following months. At this point few would have debated former Ambassador to Guinea William Attwood's observation that President Kennedy had "an understanding of what the non-aligned nations wanted . . . and was able to make the leaders of these new nations feel that he was interested in them . . . "[50]

Africa's improved status was not to be relegated to increased attention on the part of the executive branch, and the assignment of highly qualified personnel to African issues. Kennedy administration officials gave the impression that new physical resources and aid would be forthcoming from the United States. An early expression of this commitment can be found in the president's Inaugural Address. President Kennedy was addressing himself to the people of Africa as well as those of Latin America and Asia when he proclaimed in this address: "To those people in the huts and villages of half the globe struggling to break the bonds of mass misery, we pledge our best efforts to help them help themselves, for whatever period is required—not because the Communists may be doing it . . . but because it is right."[51] Other officials joined the chorus for greater economic assistance to Africa. On June 21, 1961, at a commissioning ceremony for Operation Crossroads Africa, Assistant Secretary G. Mennen Williams pledged that the United States would "extend practical help in educational and economic development to Africa."[52] Government memoranda and documents testify to the fact that increased economic help for Africa was a goal of Kennedy administration officials in the early 1960s. Many of these officials hoped that grants, loans, and Food for Peace assistance would be accompanied by an increase in self-sufficiency by African states. One aspect of self-sufficiency was to be an enhancement of multilateral market opportunities for African exports.[53]

An issue over which the administration initially defied the premise that the United States would devote minimal resources to Africa was the Congo. The human resources devoted to the Congo were not inconsiderable. It commanded a significant amount of attention from high level officials. Numerous Congo related memoranda circulating among top officials, including Secretary of State Rusk, and the president to a lesser extent, can be found at the John F. Kennedy Presidential Library in Boston, Massachusetts.

US military assistance to the Congo, largely under the auspices of the United Nations, was significant. In March 1961, the US announced to the United Nations General Assembly that it would make a contribution to the United Nations operations in the Congo over its share of the total of $120 million.[54] Following the death of UN Secretary Hammarskjöld in September 1961, the United States, sensing a potential for greater instability and Communist penetration of the Congo, increased its military aid program. The US agreed to send four transport planes immediately. It also promised to give eight jet fighter planes to the UN if other states did not do so.[55] By early December 1961, American planes were carrying United Nations troops from Leopoldville to Katanga province. Twenty additional transport planes were also offered.[56] Furthermore, US military aid was instrumental in the suppression of the Katanga independence movement by the UN in December 1962 and January 1963. This assistance was offered despite US ambivalence about the use of force by the UN in Katanga.[57]

The Kennedy administration also gave a good deal of economic aid to the Congo. It supported the UN economic stabilization plan of June 1961 by sending surplus agricultural goods and grants to the Congo. By 1962, US economic aid to the Congo totaled $55 million, and by 1963 it surpassed Belgian aid.[58]

Moreover, there were signs, as the Kennedy administration began, that the US might distance itself somewhat from the European states in its African policy. In so doing it would jeopardize the third premise of U.S. policy in Africa: that the US would adapt this policy to European predispositions on the Continent. America, in the words of one official, "began to talk to Africa about Africa as Americans and not as junior partners of France and England."[59] This transformation was reflected in the administration's rhetoric on decolonization. Administration figures made bold statements on behalf of decolonization on the Continent. Perhaps the most noteworthy of these statements was that of G. Mennen Williams. Just a short time after President Kennedy assumed office, Williams declared his support of the concept of "Africa for the Africans." This comment aroused heated criticism from American conservatives. There were even calls for William's resignation. At a news conference in March 1961, President Kennedy defended Williams and his statement on self-determination, though he emphasized that "Africa for the Africans" meant all those who felt that they were Africans whatever their color might be.[60] William's statement on behalf of self-determination was only one of a long string of such statements by administration members. They often pointed out that the chaos which accompanied the independence of the Congo was atypical. Most African states could achieve independence peacefully in their estimation. Assistant Secretary Williams made this point on August 25, 1961, in Rhodesia, a state whose passage to self-determination and majority rule over the next two decades would be arduous and bloody.[61] American officials rhetorically supported eventual self-determination as an inalienable right of people on the Continent.[62]

As time elapsed, there were officials who argued that the US should give economic assistance to African states to provide them with an alternative to continued dependence on the former colonial metropoles.[63] They suggested that aid should go directly to African states, as opposed to being channeled through the former colonial powers.[64]

More concretely, the US took actions against Portugal following its suppression of the Angolan uprising in 1961. They included a cut in the US military program from $25 million to $3 million, and a ban on the commercial sale of arms to Portugal. Moreover, the US supported a resolution in the UN on behalf of reforms in Angola.[65] It was during the Kennedy administration that the US, to the dismay of Portugal, established contact with the anti-colonial rebels of Holden Roberto.[66]

Hence, in the early days of the Kennedy administration there were indications that a new African policy might be taking shape. In accordance with this policy, Africa would not be viewed exclusively through the prism of the cold war, and would be the object of major increases in American aid and attention.

As the Kennedy administration progressed, however, it became increasingly clear that the premises of America's African policy, which had appeared during the Eisenhower administration, would not undergo extensive revisions. This development and the forces behind it will now be explored.

As befit an administration headed by a man who had accused the previous Republican administration of a lack of vigor and imagination in opposing the Communist threat, there was to be no lapse in the struggle with communism. The analyst, John Gaddis, differentiates between administrations following a selective (asymmetrical) pathway to containment and those adopting a near universal (symmetrical) approach.[67] The Kennedy administration falls into the latter category.[68]

The chief premise on which US foreign policy operated was to be a commitment to prevent Communist inroads on the Continent. Its economic ties to the West, and if necessary military ties, were to be strengthened. Administration pronouncements that the cold war was to be kept out of Africa were fundamentally for public consumption. In reality, members of the Kennedy administration considered Africa a battleground in the cold war, though a secondary one relative to other sectors of the world community. They were not about to accept a draw in this battle. Declassified government documents bear this out. A 1962 State Department document entitled "Africa: Department of State Guidelines for Policy and Operations" presented a framework for American policy in sub-Saharan Africa accepted by most elements of the administration. It offered a series of short-term and long-term goals for American foreign policy in Africa. These goals included the prevention of Soviet and Communist Chinese military gains in Africa, and the achievement of limited military cooperation between the United States and African states.[69] An important objective was to be the encouragement of the emergence of a number of strongly pro-Western African states capable of exerting leadership on the Continent. Among the countries mentioned as possible candidates for this role were Nigeria, Tunisia, Tanganyika, the Ivory Coast, the Sudan, and Senegal.[70] As articulated in the 1962 State Department document on policy guidelines and reflected in the actions of the administration, America's chief goal in Africa was clear. It was the emergence of African states cognizant of the threat from the Sino-Soviet bloc and unambiguously leaning toward the West. Formal alignment with the West was not to be actively sought in the short term, though it was not ruled out as an option if circumstances changed.[71]

Nor did the Kennedy administration's tolerance of neutrality by Ghana and Guinea carry over to other issues.

In the Congo, the pre-eminent sub-Saharan issue of this period, the administration's policy was geared to preventing a growth in Communist influence. At his first news conference, on January 25, 1961, Kennedy referred to the Congo, in addition to Cuba and Laos, as an area threatened by communism.[72] Early addresses by Undersecretary of State George Ball and Assistant Secretary Williams also highlighted the administration's goal of precluding Communist successes in the Congo. In Los Angeles, California, on December 19, 1961, Ball asserted that the "immediate objective" of US policy in the Congo was to stabilize the country and prevent its conversion into a Soviet stronghold. He added that it was imperative that the Congo maintain major ties to the West.[73] Williams commented a few months later that the US desired a strong Congo which could stand up against the blandishments of communism.[74]

On a substantive level, the US policy in the Congo was designed to promote ties with the West. US support of the government of Prime

Minister Cyrille Adoula, starting in the first year of the administration, was hailed as a symbol of its acceptance of neutralism. Yet, the US hoped to induce Adoula to move closer to the West, as clarified in the following document. In a telegram addressed to the State Department in early 1962, Edmund Gullion pointed out that efforts had been made to "encourage the Adoula government formed on the basis of positive neutrality" to establish better relations with the US.[75] A focus on the need to counter Soviet initiatives was to remain the key element of the administration's Congo policy for its duration. This approach was reinforced by intelligence reports which spoke of Communist destabilization efforts. A January 1963 Central Intelligence Agency memorandum contended that the Soviets, despite setbacks, still viewed the Congo as a favorable target for exploitation.[76] As the administration headed into its final months, the dual themes of cutting down on Soviet penetration and promoting a central government sympathetic to the West dominated its policy. These themes constituted the heart of a February 1963 State Department document entitled "US Policy in the Congo: A Plan of Action."[77]

Similarly, the administration endeavored to prevent Communist gains in the Republic of South Africa. Two schools of thought on how best to achieve this goal arose within the administration.

On one side stood the voices of caution, represented most prominently by Secretary of State Rusk and US Ambassador to South Africa Satterthwaite. They stressed the importance of maintaining reasonably good relations with South Africa because of its important role as a regional ally in the global struggle with communism. They warned that excessive pressure on South Africa to change its policies would only provoke greater intransigence on its part.[78]

On the other side stood UN Ambassador Adlai Stevenson, Undersecretary of State and Special Representative for Asia and Africa Chester Bowles, and G. Mennen Williams. Deputy Assistant Secretary for African Affairs Wayne Fredericks can also be placed in this group. They were no less concerned than their colleagues about the global Communist threat. They felt, however, that unless South Africa was compelled to change its policy on South-West Africa and its internal policies, new opportunities for the Soviets would open up.[79]

The policy which emerged from the interplay of these schools of thought had four elements. First, stern public rebukes of South Africa for its South-West Africa and internal policies. This was done at the United Nations and elsewhere.[80] Second, concrete measures directed against South Africa to convince it that the costs of maintaining its policies were unacceptable. An embargo on the shipment of US arms to

South Africa was the most prominent of these measures. It was to go into effect at the end of 1963.[81] A third element of US policy toward South Africa was to avoid a breach which would damage American strategic connections with the Republic. Thus, the US opposed UN resolutions requiring economic sanctions against South Africa, or the use of force.[82] Moreover, it discouraged the expulsion of South Africa from the United Nations.[83] Finally, loopholes were created in the embargo on arms sales to South Africa.[84]

Towards the end of the Kennedy administration, a consensus was developing on behalf of an increasingly firm policy toward South Africa. We learn from a memorandum addressed to McGeorge Bundy, President Kennedy's national security adviser, in early November 1963, that segments of the administration, particularly in the State Department, favored cutting off US government loans and credits to South Africa. They also endorsed discouraging private investors from entering the Republic.[85] The common denominator of these varied facets of America's South African policy was that they were all intended to avert Communist encroachments into the area.

As will be clarified shortly, the administration was also riven by divisions over what policy to pursue toward the Portuguese colonies. Yet, all officials accepted the premise that Western influence of one form or another should be fostered in the area and Soviet influence discouraged.

A second premise of America's African policy, that the Continent would not be the recipient of a major commitment of American human and physical resources, reemerged during Kennedy's tenure.

A spate of attention to African issues as the administration entered office was soon overwhelmed by events in other areas of the world. Competition with the Soviet Union remained at center-stage, but the regional focus for this competition shifted to Cuba, Southeast Asia, and elsewhere. Sub-Saharan Africa, with the partial exception of the Congo, did not become a major arena for the American-Soviet rivalry. An American ambassador to Africa during the administration acknowledged in an interview conducted after it had left office that the president had "many . . . greater foreign policy problems" than Africa.[86]

In addition, hopes for a major increase in American economic aid to Africa were eventually dashed. In a report on a recent trip to Africa in mid 1962, Assistant Secretary Williams expressed his disappointment over the level of aid. He noted gloomily that "unless we can provide more aid, . . . I foresee unhappy relations ahead in two or three years. To meet this challenge, I believe it is most important to expedite such aid as has been scheduled and to make such reasonable increases as we can."[87]

25

The next year, Deputy Assistant Secretary Wayne Fredericks, speaking in Minnesota, urged that Europe continue to assume principal responsibility for assisting Africa financially.[88] An appraisal of aid figures reveals that this was indeed the case during the Kennedy era.

The US channeled $276 million into Africa between July 1959 and June 1960.[89] At the height of the Kennedy administration, US economic aid to Africa had increased to only $215 million annually. This contrasted with the $700 million worth of aid provided to Africa by the French and British.[90]

The Congo was somewhat of an exception to the maxim that the US would not make a large commitment of resources to Africa. Even here, however, despite the existence of contingency plans for direct US military intervention involving troops, this never transpired.

Requests for military intervention by second echelon officials, as exemplified by Ambassador to the Congo Timberlake in March 1960, were rebuffed by Rusk and the president.[91]

Finally, impressions that the administration would establish an African policy largely independent of those policies implemented by its European allies were slowly dispelled.

On a rhetorical level, administration officials endorsed the decolonization process. On a confidential level, however, they were calling for a retention of European influence in key areas of the national life of the emerging nation-states. G. Mennen Williams was articulating this approach in late 1961 when he asserted in a report following a trip to Africa that the maintenance of a major French presence in its former dependencies was essential for their survival.[92] In early 1962, a State Department document reflecting American policy officially stated that the European metropoles would be urged to meet the military and economic requirements of their former colonies. The US was to supplement European efforts in these areas.[93] In a candid interview conducted after he had left office, G. Mennen Williams stated that US policy looked sympathetically upon a role for the European powers in Africa. He explained that the US, on a number of occasions, told the Europeans that it hoped to "give them an opportunity to maintain their influence."[94]

American policy in the Congo embodied its tendency to not initiate policies which conflicted seriously with its European allies. A great deal of American attention in the Congo was devoted to the Katanga secession. One learns from an overview of American conduct on this issue that the US seldom strayed very far from Western European opinion, especially that of Belgium and Britain. American policy on the Katanga secession can be divided into five stages.

The first stage encompassed the first few months of the administration.

During this period, the US, along with its Western European allies, favored negotiations between the central government and the authorities in Katanga. In so doing it was hoped that Tshombe, the pro-Western secession leader, would maintain power, and the Belgian economic position would be preserved. This contrasted with the position of the Soviet bloc and the black Africans who advocated force to suppress the rebellion.[95] US opposition to the use of force by the United Nations was illustrated by its repudiation of a UN request for American transport planes to carry troops to Katanga.[96]

During the second stage, which followed UN Secretary Hammarskjöld's death on September 17, 1961, the US stepped up its military supplies to the UN forces. On September 17, 1961, the US increased its military supplies to these forces. On September 19, it told the UN it would give them fighter planes if necessary.[97] Yet, negotiations continued to be the US government's heavily preferred option in subsequent months. Belgium by this point had cast its lot with negotiations. The US feared that Belgium, Britain and other Europeans would be alienated by any major use of military power.[98] One of the most powerful expressions of the administration's support of negotiations can be found in a memorandum addressed to the president from Secretary of State Dean Rusk on November 11, 1961. In this memorandum, Rusk asserts that the US will resist any effort in the Security Council to promote the reintegration of Katanga through force. He continues that such an approach would provoke civil war. He advocated a peaceful solution.[99] Three months later, the administration's position had not changed. During Congolese Prime Minister Adoula's February 1962 trip to the US, he was informed by Undersecretary of State Hull that the Katanga issue should not be resolved with force.[100]

A third stage in America's Katanga policy arose in February 1962 when, under State Department prodding, the US government endorsed economic sanctions against Tshombe and Katanga.[101] Again, the US did not differ greatly with the Belgian stance by promoting this approach. A Department of State Bureau of Intelligence and Research memorandum in March 1962 noted that most of the members of the Belgian government now supported a unified Congo.[102] American policy was still to be designed and implemented in collaboration with Belgium.[103]

A fourth stage emerged when the United States gave the United Nations material support to put down the Katanga rebellion, starting in December 1962. Belgium and Britain did not object strenuously to this strategy. Britain, and Belgium under Foreign Minister Paul Henri Spaak, had concluded that force might be necessary. The US, nonetheless, mindful of the sensitivities of its allies, conveyed to the UN its reservations about the use of force. The UN went ahead with military measures, and the rebellion was crushed by January 1963.[104]

In the months that followed the suppression of Katanga, the US adopted the goal of maximizing the role of Belgium in the Congo and minimizing its own role.[105] Belgium, in the eyes of US officials, was to become the dominant partner in the Congo.[106]

An internal government document of February 1963 vividly expresses the nature of US policy in the Congo during Kennedy's term. According to this document, the US had pursued its Congo policy "in association with M. Spaak [of Belgium], and even avoided any irreparable parting with the British."[107]

America's South African policy went beyond a conscious concern for European feelings. America's emphasis on sustaining its European ties caused it to place parameters on how aggressively it would pursue measures directed against South Africa. It was particularly cognizant of British reservations about stern measures. The British had closer economic ties with South Africa than any other power and did not want to endanger them. Hence, when the State Department Planning Group met to consider an embargo of arms intended for South Africa, it was warned by one member that it should coordinate its policy with Britain.[108] A subsequent meeting, of what was labeled the State Department Tuesday Planning Group, decided to follow this course of action.[109] The failure of the most ardently anti-South African members of the administration to prevail in the internal policy debate can, in part, be attributed to the primacy placed on European ties and initiatives.

The US approach to the Portuguese colonies of Angola and Mozambique was also affected profoundly by US relations with the metropole. After an initial period of firm measures in response to Portuguese conduct in Angola, US policy softened considerably. US concern over access to the Portuguese controlled Azore islands contributed to a diminishment of its support for anti-Portuguese UN resolutions.

In addition, the administration did not provide an explicit definition of ultimate self-determination for the Portuguese colonies, thereby allowing the metropole to largely formulate its own definition. Adlai Stevenson, in an address in March 1961, spoke of the dangers of early independence for Angola and the need for Angola to attain political maturity before independence could be realized.[110] Subsequent addresses by other high echelon administration officials reiterated this theme.[111] A 1962 memorandum addressed to McGeorge Bundy, provides evidence of how the Kennedy administration policy on the Portuguese colonies question evolved from a virtual confrontation with the metropole to what was largely an accomodation to its desires. In the memorandum, it is suggested that the US should convey to the Portuguese that it "fully supports continued Portuguese influence in Africa."[112]

On the issue of Southern Rhodesia, the US also accepted the initiatives of its European partner. In this case it was Britain. While urging Britain to be cognizant of the wider strategic implications of its policy in Southern Rhodesia, the US openly supported Britain's right to determine the destiny of its colony. This position was articulated most clearly at the sixteenth session of the United Nations General Assembly in June 1962. At a late June meeting, the United States representative stated that Rhodesia was Britain's responsibility.[113] This view conflicted with that of the black African states, who advocated immediate independence for Rhodesia. At a State Department Planning Group meeting in mid 1962, it was emphasized that the British, not the US, should "take the lead" in Rhodesia.[114] The administration's policy did not stray from this principle.

Thus, the Kennedy administration promised a major overhaul of America's African policy during its first few months in office. This did not occur. It returned to the policy assumptions which had emerged during Eisenhower's presidency. Why was this so? Why did the policy of an administration heralded by its liberal supporters as a new and daring experiment adhere to the policy preferences of an administration they scorned? The reasons for this evolution will now be explored.

4. Theories for Analyzing the Development of United States Policy

In light of the inadequacy of single-factor analysis, a number of theories must be employed to explain why the Kennedy administration African policy developed as it did. Five have been chosen. They will also be used for subsequent administrations.

First, cultural theory will be utilized. This theory operates on the assumption that individual states are bestowed with distinctive cultures which influence the way in which they view the world, and therefore, their international conduct. Cultural disparities between states or regions may result in misperceptions and conduct which conflicts with a state's interests.[115]

Second, bureaucratic theory is helpful. It views foreign policy outcomes as the result of bargaining between discrete components or agencies within the government. It is used here to encompass interaction between units of the executive branch which deal with foreign policy, including the White House. In some cases, a bureaucratic unit is able to establish primacy on an individual issue and dictate the manner in which it is handled.[116]

Third, the impact of domestic nonbureaucratic groups on America's African policy will be touched on. Lobby groups, congressional input, and the role of the general public will be dealt with.

Two other modes of analysis will be used by the author, despite reservations about their use.

Geopolitical theory often postulates that nation-states, as unified actors, attempt to maximize their interests abroad in terms of power. The advantage of this approach is that it recognizes that states respond to external variables. A weakness it shares with some other theories is that it does not acknowledge the salience of internal and bureaucratic cleavages in influencing foreign policy outcomes.[117]

Economic paradigms run the gamut from those which argue that a state's external behavior is a direct derivation of explicit class interests to those which assert that domestic and global economic cycles shape state actions abroad. Many operate on the assumption that the economic interests of states have primacy over non-economic interests.[118]

5. Factors Behind the Policy

The reasons that the Kennedy administration ultimately treated African events as a component of the East-West contest, assigned Africa a low status, and adjusted its policy to European concerns, were multifaceted.

Bureaucratic factors made a major contribution to the developments just outlined. In the beginning of the administration, it appeared that its most liberal members might dictate the shape of America's African policy. Assistant Secretary Williams, Undersecretary of State Bowles, and UN Ambassador Stevenson were outspoken in their support of a new, and what they deemed a progressive African policy. Their public and private comments, as delineated earlier, on topics ranging from the Portuguese possessions to South Africa, seemed to indicate a new policy course.

Within a short period, however, the influence of these men was surpassed by a coalition of Europeanists and globalists. While ultimately divided on such questions as Vietnam, they joined forces in rebuffing African regionalist precepts.[119] Bowles was replaced by the Europeanist, George Ball. Ball was a supporter of the proposition that American security ties with European states must take precedence over African concerns.[120] Moreover, Secretary of State Rusk privately began to assert himself as a relatively conservative figure within the administration. We have seen how he attempted to discourage the use of force in the Congo. Rusk also proclaimed that strategic necessities made a consideration of loopholes in the arms embargo against South Africa necessary.[121]

The president himself eventually gravitated toward Rusk's view on the arms embargo.[122]

Another bureaucratic factor which influenced the shape of the administration's African policy was the increasingly prominent role played by divisions of the government which regarded sensitivity to black African concerns as a distraction from American responsibilities elsewhere. Stephen Weissman, in his study of America's Congo policy, and Deputy Assistant Secretary Wayne Fredericks, contend that governmental departments are not monolithic. It is their belief that a search for intra-administration cleavages should focus on individuals.[123] This is fundamentally correct. Yet, patterns of thinking can be found within various governmental departments or their sub-divisions. It was the Defense Department, along with the armed forces, and the European Bureau of the State Department whose opposition to an over-emphasis on African regional concerns struck a responsive chord in the latter stages of the administration. Both stressed the overriding importance of maintaining close ties to America's NATO allies, even if this meant riding roughshod over black African interests. They were successful in this regard. An illustration of this approach was the Defense Department's discouragement of continued pressure on Portugal to revise its Angolan policy. It did so because of its deep concern about American ties to Portugal, and access to the Portuguese controlled Azores. A mid 1963 memorandum to Secretary of Defense Robert McNamara from the chairman of the Joint Chiefs of Staff, Maxwell Taylor, captures the significance assigned to the Azores by the military. It is observed in this memorandum that

> "the importance of Portugal lies primarily in US base rights in the Azores and secondarily in the membership ... of Portugal in NATO. Loss of the Azores would seriously degrade the responsiveness, reliability, and control of major US forces. With regard to transportation to Europe, the Middle East and Africa costs in tonnage and time would be raised appreciably with a direct effect on limited war or contingency actions."[124]

Similarly, members of the European Bureau argued that the Azores were vital to US security interests, and that we should avoid alienating Portugal.[125] The postures of the Defense Department and European Bureau on the Azores were essentially adopted.

Had liberal domestic American groups been better organized and more sophisticated in their lobbying techniques, it is probable that the administration's African policy would not have swung as far as it did away from the liberal end of the political spectrum. This was not to be, however. A natural constituency for a liberal input into America's African policy was black Americans. It would be fair to state that early administration rhetorical statements on behalf of self-determination and racial justice were influenced by the existence of a sizable American black community with electoral clout in the major urban centers of the East and Midwest. Certainly, there were not a dearth of officials willing to speak to black audiences on African issues. It is difficult, however, to find any major correlation between concrete administration African policies and black input. Black lobbying efforts were cursory and ineffective. In 1962, major American black civil rights leaders tried to change this pattern by forming the American Negro Leadership Conference on Africa (ANLCA). Its purpose was to both achieve civil rights gains in the US, and self-determination in Africa. Its members included Roy Wilkins of the National Association for the Advancement of Colored People; Reverend Martin Luther King of the Southern Christian leadership Conference; Whitney Young, head of the National Urban League; and A. Philip Randolph of the AFL-CIO's Brotherhood of Sleeping Car Porters.[126] There is little evidence that the ANLCA had any affect on America's African policy. The chief concern of its members, and the black populace at large, continued to be the yet unfinished business of securing civil rights within the United States. Radical blacks who reached out to the diaspora, as Malcolm X of the Nation of Islam, had no legitimacy among administration officials and were also ineffective.[127]

Nor were multiracial liberal groups, such as the American Committee on Africa (ACOA) started in the early 1950s by George Houser, able to exert a major impact on America's African policy. The failure of the ACOA lay not only in its inability to establish ties to major American domestic constituencies, but in its naivete about the lobbying process. It concentrated much of its lobbying effort on the State Department's Bureau of African Affairs. This bureau had little leverage within the administration, and was made up of individuals who often agreed with ACOA positions anyhow.[128]

In contrast to their liberal counterparts, conservative domestic groups had a visible and ongoing impact on America's African policy. One of the most prominent of these groups was the Katanga lobby. It received financial support from both American and Belgian sources and consisted of a wide gamut of conservatives, whose chief spokesman was Senator Dodd of Connecticut. They opposed UN efforts to suppress the rebellion of the rightist Moise Tshombe in the Congo. Memoranda exchanged among Kennedy administration officials reveal that the administration was conscious of the political strength of the Katanga lobby. G. Mennen Williams stressed this fact following his departure from the federal government. In Williams' words: "People like Senator Thomas J. Dodd of Connecticut and that clique were in favor of Moise Tshombe . . . so I imagine it was incumbent upon the president to move carefully in these areas to accomplish his essential purpose."[129] The slowness with which the US moved toward support of the military suppression of the Katanga rebellion can in part be attributed to the existence of the Katanga lobby.

Portuguese and South African positions were also supported by efficient American lobbying bodies. Adlai Stevenson, in a 1962 memorandum to the president, expressed concern over the influence of the pro-Portuguese public relations firm of Selvage and Lee.[130]

Congressional opinion on behalf of a liberal African policy was spearheaded by Senator Hubert Humphrey of Minnesota.[131] A powerful array of individuals, however, lined up on the conservative side of the congressional debate. Senator Dodd channeled energy into discussions of the Congo.[132] Southern senators, including Richard Russell of Georgia, also aligned themselves with Tshombe and cast their lot with the colonial and white regimes.[133] President Kennedy was sufficiently concerned with Russell's critiques of US Congo policy to dispatch a high ranking administration member to inform him of the rationale of the administration's position.[134] Hence, what non-bureaucratic domestic input there was into America's African policy emanated largely from conservative sources.

The continuity of the Kennedy administration's African policy with its predecessor was also a derivation of cultural factors. The intensity of its focus on averting communist successes can be understood by using cultural theory. Key policy makers possessed what Robert Packenham, in a work published in the mid 1970s, deemed the liberal ethos. They were convinced that radicalism was bad. Moreover, the primacy they placed on European as opposed to African interests was affected by their cultural affinity to Western Europe.[135]

The administration's African policy was also a response to geopolitical factors. There were numerous examples of assertive behavior by Communist states abroad, from Eastern Europe to Southeast Asia. Berlin remained a symbol of Western vulnerability. The caldron boiled in Vietnam and Laos. An alien system was brought into America's backyard, as a pro-Soviet regime emerged in Cuba. In Africa itself, there were moderate efforts by Communist powers to acquire influence. This state of affairs prevailed in the Congo (Leopoldville), Ghana, Mali, and Guinea. It was hardly surprising, in light of these events, that Africa would be treated as part of the global East-West conflict. The dominant role of NATO in American strategic plans made it imperative, from the perspective of many, for the US to not introduce policies into Africa which conflicted dramatically with those of its allies.

Finally, the absence of major American economic interests in Africa played a part in its refusal to assign the Continent a high priority, and to allow Europe to assume much of the responsibility. Less than 3 percent of American investments and trade abroad were with the Continent at the inception of the administration. US investments were heavily skewed toward the Republic of South Africa and North Africa.[136] European economic ties with the Continent were stronger. A number of analysts have argued that while American economic interests in Africa are not large in a global context, ties between America officials and companies with American economic interests have affected our continental policy. Stephen Weissman, in a work on American foreign policy in the Congo, lists ties between American governmental figures and corporations with investments in the Congo.[137] Others have done so for the Republic of South Africa. This explanatory framework should not be wholly dismissed. It does not, however, adequately explain how these business ties correlate to policy outcomes.

Thus, the dynamics of the bureaucracy which composed the Kennedy administration had a major impact on the nature of its African policy. Non-bureaucratic domestic input was discernible, if limited. Geopolitical, cultural, and economic factors reinforced the patterns which arose within the bureaucracy.

6. The Effectiveness of the Policy

We are left with a final question to be addressed. Was the United States policy in Africa during the Kennedy administration compatible with American strategic interests on both a regional and a global level? Two interests will be examined. They have been pursued by every administration in the post World War II era. First, resisting the spread of Soviet influence. A corollary of this is the maintenance of the independence of the US in its own affairs. A second US interest is the preservation of an orderly international system. This is a core concern of the US in light of its status as a non-revolutionary power. An orderly system is one which does not pose a threat to its political or economic system. Many additional interests can be identified, but this scheme is adequate for the purposes of this work.[138]

In the short term, the Kennedy administration's African policy was a success. In the Congo, the central government which eventually emerged had strong ties to the West. The power behind the scenes continued to be the pro-Western army general Mobutu despite changeovers in the government's personnel. As the administration approached its final months, the Katanga rebellion had been crushed. Moreover, the continuation of insurgencies could not hide the fact that the Soviets had failed to establish a permanent foothold in the country. On the South African and South-West Africa issues, the US forged a reasonably independent policy through its early support of the arms embargo. Nonetheless, it had not lost access to missile and space tracking facilities in the Republic. Nor had the US been ejected from bases on the Portuguese controlled Azores. US security interests in Africa did not appear to be in immediate jeopardy when the administration's term was cut short.

Yet, an assessment of the long-term implications of the Kennedy administration African policy leads to a more sober assessment of its effectiveness. In Mobutu, the administration fostered the rise of a man unable to sustain a strong popular base in the country. His survival in future years would be contingent on the use of white mercenaries and direct military intervention by Western powers. It is questionable whether the administration's initiatives increased the probability of a pro-Western government maintaining power over the long haul. Moreover, it failed to adequately divorce the US from the South African government in the eyes of much of the world community, with unforeseen future consequences. A cautious exertion of pressure in the economic realm may have helped facilitate this goal. Perhaps the least farsighted Kennedy administration policy was that relating to the Portuguese. It did not follow up on the firm measures it instituted during its first months in office. If the US had stepped up pressure on the Portuguese to accelerate the movement toward independence for its colonies, it is possible it would have lost the Azores. Such a loss, however, pales in comparison to the strategic setback for the West which occurred less than a decade and a half later when it witnessed the emergence of leftist regimes in the former Portuguese colonies. These regimes were pragmatic, initially, in their policies toward the West on economic issues. Yet, they did usher in new opportunities for the Soviets and their allies to enlarge their political and military presence on the sub-Continent. An American sponsored package of incentives and penalties for Portugal in the early 1960s, designed to convince it to adjust to desired policy objectives, may have averted such an outcome. Such a package was, in fact, considered by segments of the State Department during the waning months of the administration.[139] It did not become a part of US policy.

The success of the Kennedy administration in improving the global image of the US proved to be ephemeral. Its substantive policies in Africa did not contribute, in the long run, to a stable world order more resistant to the rise of anti-Western forces.

Could the Kennedy administration, beset by bureaucratic inertia in some governmental divisions, conservative elements at home, and strategic ties with its European allies, have followed a different policy course? The answer is a qualified yes. It would be naive to argue that it could have initiated revolutionary changes in US policy, nor would such changes have been desirable. Yet, the administration did have room to maneuver in light of the absence of major external and domestic constraints on its policy initiatives. African policy, to a greater extent than that for any other region, was an outgrowth of bureaucratic interaction. There were elements within the bureaucracy who called for a gradualistic disassociation from South Africa if it did not alter its policies.[140] Others argued for a tougher approach to Portugal on the Angolan question.[141] Furthermore, the Central Intelligence Agency and individuals in the State Department informed other members of the administration on a number of occasions that the Portuguese government was weak politically. They did not rule out the possibility of a regime change.[142]

There are major limitations on the ability of the US to produce desired policy outcomes abroad. The omnipotence attributed to it by leftist critics and right-wing nationalists alike ignores this reality. Yet, it is likely that moderate changes in America's African policy, establishing in some cases an independent course from Europe, would have enhanced American security requirements regionally and globally.

NOTES TO CHAPTER TWO

1. Memorandum for Secretary of Defense McNamara, "US Policy Toward Portugal and the Republic of South Africa," 10 July 1963, National Security File, John F. Kennedy Presidential Library, Boston, p. 2.
2. Personal Interview, Wayne Fredericks, Ford Motor Company, New York City, 23 March 1982.
3. Geoffrey Kemp, "US Strategic Interests and Military Options in Sub-Saharan Africa," in *Africa and the United States: Vital Interests,* ed. Jennifer Whitaker (New York City: New York University Press, 1978), p. 123.
4. Ibid., p. 124.
5. US, Department of State, Bureau of Public Affairs, Address by G. Mennen Williams, "Change and Challenge in Africa," 29 March 1962, *Department of State Bulletin* 46 (30 April 1962): 719.
6. Kemp, "US Interests and Options in Africa," p. 127.
7. Ibid., pp. 123–40.
8. Williams, "Change and Challenge in Africa," p. 719.
9. Robert McNamara, Memorandum for Secretary of State Dean Rusk, National

Security File, 11 July 1963, John F. Kennedy Presidential Library, Boston, p. 1.

10. Susan Gilpin, "Minerals and Foreign Policy," *Africa Report* 27 (May–June 1982): 19–20.

11. Thomas Hughes, Memorandum for Secretary of State Dean Rusk, "US and South African Economic Leverage on Each Other," 12 August 1963, National Security File, John F. Kennedy Presidential Library, Boston, p. 5.

12. Ibid., p. 6.

13. Ibid.

14. Waldemar B. Campbell and William Duggan, Department of State National Strategy Series Memorandum, "South Africa: Background and Policy Recommendations," 28 October 1963, National Security File, John F. Kennedy Presidential Library, Boston.

15. Gordon Bertolin, "US Economic Interests in Africa: Investment, Trade, and Raw Materials," in *Africa and the United States: Vital Interests,* ed. Jennifer Whitaker (New York City: New York University Press, 1978), pp. 42, 44, 47.

16. Stephen Weissman, *American Foreign Policy in the Congo: 1960–1964* (Ithaca, New York: Cornell University Press, 1974), pp. 28–29.

17. Bertolin, "US Interests in Africa," pp. 42, 44.

18. Vernon McKay, "Changing Pressures on Africa," p. 89.

19. Ibid.

20. Ibid., pp. 95–96.

21. Ibid., pp. 62–64.

22. Ibid., p. 90.

23. See Milene Charles, *The Soviet Union and Africa: The History of the Involvement* (Lanham, Maryland: University Press of America, 1980); and Robert Legvold, *Soviet Policy in West Africa* (Cambridge: Harvard University Press, 1970).

24. US, Department of State, Bureau of Public Affairs, Address by G. Mennen Williams, "An Overview of US Policy in the Congo," 25 April 1965, *Department of State Bulletin* 52 (25 May 1965): 797.

25. Ibid.

26. Ibid., pp. 798–99.

27. Ibid., p. 799.

28. State Department Memorandum, "The South-West Africa Issue in the United Nations," 19 April 1963, National Security File, John F. Kennedy Presidential Library, Boston, p. 2.

29. Ibid., pp. 2–3.

30. Ibid., pp. 3–4.

31. A comprehensive analysis of the evolution of apartheid and a delineation of its principal features is provided by the Foreign Policy Study Foundation, *South Africa: Time Running Out: The Report of the Study Commission on US Policy Toward Southern Africa* (Berkeley: University of California Press, 1981), pp. 25–167.

32. John Stockwell, *In Search of Enemies: A CIA Story* (New York City: W. W. Norton and Co., 1978), p. 50.

33. H. Mark Roth, "Historical Setting," in *Angola: A Country Study,* ed. Irving Kaplan (Washington DC: American University, 1979), pp. 46–47.

34. Ibid., p. 47.

35. Estimates of the casualties vary widely. The number is put at 50,000 black Africans killed by Rene Pelissier and Douglas Wheeler in *Angola* (Westport, Connecticut: Greenwood Press, 1971), p. 191. The figure of 20,000 black Africans killed is provided by John Marcum in, *The Angolan Revolution: Vol. 1: The Anatomy of an*

Explosion (Cambridge, Massachusetts: The MIT Press, 1969), p. 144.

36. Stockwell, *A CIA Story,* p. 51.

37. A comprehensive analysis of American foreign policy in Rhodesia through the mid-1970s can be found in the following work: Anthony Lake, *The Tar Baby Option: American Policy Toward Southern Rhodesia* (New York City: Columbia University Press, 1976).

38. US, Department of State, Bureau of Public Affairs, Statement by Walter M. Kotsching, "The United States and Africa: Common Goals," 13 February 1961, *Department of State Bulletin* 44 (13 March 1961): 377.

39. US, Department of State, Bureau of Public Affairs, Statement by G. Mennen Williams, "United States and Africa: A Common Tradition," 19 April 1961, *Department of State Bulletin* 44 (15 May 1961): 731.

40. US, Department of State, Bureau of Public Affairs, Address by Chester Bowles, "A Close Look at Africa," 14 December 1962, *Department of State Bulletin* 47 (31 December 1962): 1006.

41. Insights into the Kennedy administration's policy toward neutralist governments can be found in Donald Lord, *John Kennedy: The Politics of Confrontation and Conciliation* (Woodbury, New York: Barrons Educational Series, 1977), p. 229; Transcript of Interview with William Attwood, US ambassador to Guinea, Nairobi, Kenya, 8 November 1965, Oral History Collection, John F. Kennedy Presidential Library, Boston, pp. 4-7; and Transcript of Interview with Walt Rostow, special assistant to the president for national security affairs, State Department, Washington, DC, 11 April 1964, Oral History Collection, John F. Kennedy Presidential Library, Boston, pp. 57-58.

42. Weissman, *American Policy in the Congo,* p. 122.

43. Interview, Attwood, p. 8.

44. Weissman, *American Policy in the Congo,* p. 117.

45. Ibid., p. 130.

46. Ibid., p. 129.

47. Interview, Fredericks.

48. Williams, *Africa for Africans,* p. 161.

49. Ibid.

50. Interview, Attwood, p. 11.

51. Nielsen, *Great Powers and Africa,* p. 25.

52. US, Department of State, Bureau of Public Affairs, Remarks by G. Mennen Williams, "Operation Crossroads Africa," 21 June 1961, *Department of State Bulletin* 45 (24 July 1961): 153.

53. A comprehensive statement of the goals of US economic aid to Africa is provided by the Department of State, Memorandum, "Africa: Department of State Guidelines for Policy and Operations," March 1962, National Security File, John F. Kennedy Presidential Library, Boston, pp. 29-37.

54. US, Department of State, Bureau of Public Affairs, Statement by Philip M. Klutznick, US representative to the United Nations General Assembly, "Financing the UN Military Operation in the Congo," 30 March 1961, *Department of State Bulletin* 44 (17 April 1961): 566.

55. Madeline Kalb, *The Congo Cables: The Cold War in Africa from Eisenhower to Kennedy* (New York City: MacMillan Publishing Co., 1982), pp. 302-3.

56. Ibid., p. 314.

57. Ibid., pp. 367-70.

58. Ibid., pp. 4-7.

59. Interview, Attwood, p. 8.
60. US, President, *Public Papers of the Presidents of the United States* (Washington, DC: Government Printing Office), John F. Kennedy, 1961, p. 139.
61. US, Department of State, Bureau of Public Affairs, Address by G. Mennen Williams, "Basic United States Policy in Africa," 25 August 1961, *Department of State Bulletin* 45 (9 October 1961): 602.
62. US, Department of State, Bureau of Public Affairs, Address by G. Mennen Williams, "The Future of the Europeans in Africa," 28 June 1962, *Department of State Bulletin* 47 (16 July 1962): 108.
63. US, Department of State, Bureau of Public Affairs, Address by J. Wayne Fredericks, "Our Policy Toward Africa," 18 July 1963, *Department of State Bulletin* 49 (19 August 1963): 284.
64. Transcript of Interview with G. Mennen Williams, assistant secretary of state for African affairs, Grosse Pointe Farms, Michigan, 28 January 1980, Oral History Collection, John F. Kennedy Presidential Library, Boston, p. 61.
65. Stockwell, *A CIA Story,* p. 51.
66. References to contacts between the US and Holden Roberto can be found in the following source: Elbrick, Telegram to Secretary of State Dean Rusk, 22 February 1962, John F. Kennedy Presidential Library, Boston, pp. 1-3.
67. John Gaddis, *Strategies of Containment: A Critical Appraisal of Post-War American National Security Policy* (New York City: Oxford University Press, 1982), pp. 352-57.
68. Ibid., p. 214.
69. State Department, "Africa: Department of State Guidelines," pp. 13-14.
70. Ibid., pp. 14, 19.
71. Ibid., p. 14.
72. Public Papers of the Presidents, John F. Kennedy, 1961, pp. 12-23.
73. US, Department of State, Bureau of Public Affairs, Address by George Ball, "The Elements in Our Congo Policy," 19 December 1961, *Department of State Bulletin* 46 (8 January 1962): 43.
74. US, Department of State, Bureau of Public Affairs, Address by G. Mennen Williams, "The United Nations Plan for the Congo," 30 August 1962, *Department of State Bulletin* 47 (17 September 1962): 420.
75. Edmund Gullion, Telegram for Dean Rusk, "Problems and Accomplishments in 1961," 27 January 1962, National Security File, John F. Kennedy Presidential Library, Boston, pp. 1-3.
76. Sherman Kent, Memorandum for the Director of the CIA Office of National Estimates, "Soviet View of the Congo," 27 January 1963, National Security File, John F. Kennedy Presidential Library, Boston, p. 2.
77. State Department, Memorandum, "US Policy in the Congo: A Plan of Action," 20 February 1963, National Security File, John F. Kennedy Presidential Library, Boston, pp. 1-28.
78. The chief arguments of this group on the South African question are found in the following documents located in the National Security File at the John F. Kennedy Presidential Library in Boston: Dean Rusk, Outgoing State Department Telegram, 20 January 1963, pp. 1-2; Joseph Satterthwaite, Memorandum to Dean Rusk, 16 May 1963, pp. 1-2; Dean Rusk, Memorandum for Mr. Johnson, Mr. Williams, et al., 15 June 1963: pp. 1-3; and William Brubeck, Memorandum for Mr. Bundy, 12 September 1963, p. 1.
79. The principal arguments of this group are captured in the following documents located at the John F. Kennedy Presidential Library in Boston: G. Mennen Williams,

"US Policy Toward South Africa," 12 June 1963, National Security File, p. 2; and Adlai Stevenson, Memorandum for Dean Rusk, 21 August 1963, National Security File, pp. 5, 6, 9.

80. A representative US critique of apartheid can be found in the following source: US, Department of State, Bureau of Public Affairs, Address by J. Wayne Fredericks, 23 October 1963, "Nations in the Making in Africa," *Department of State Bulletin* 49 (18 November 1963): 784.

81. An announcement of the arms embargo can be found in the following source: US, Department of State, Bureau of Public Affairs, Statement by Adlai Stevenson, "Security Council Calls for Ban on Sale of Arms to South Africa," 2 August 1963, *Department of State Bulletin* 49 (26 August 1963): 335. Dialogue among government officials on the wisdom of imposing the arms embargo can be found in the following documents located at the John F. Kennedy Presidential Library in Boston: Henry Owen, Memorandum for State Department Policy Planning Group meeting, "The White Redoubt," 10 July 1962, National Security File, p. 21; and Memorandum of Conversation between Secretary of State Dean Rusk, W. C. Naude, Ambassador of Republic of South Africa, et al., "South Africa and the Security Council," 17 July 1963, National Security File, pp. 1-2.

82. Dean Rusk, Memorandum for the President, 6 November 1963, National Security File, John F. Kennedy Presidential Library, Boston, p. 1.

83. Opposition to the expulsion of South Africa from the United Nations is expressed in the following government document: Rusk, Outgoing Telegram, 20 January 1963, pp. 1-2.

84. References to loopholes in the arms embargo can be found in the following documents located at the John F. Kennedy Presidential Library in Boston: Draft Security Council Statement on Apartheid, 6 August 1963, National Security File, pp. 1-2; and Memorandum for the President, "Sale to South Africa of Submarines and Spare Parts for C-130s," 28 August 1963, National Security File, pp. 1-2.

85. William H. Brubeck, Memorandum for Mr. Bundy, "Rostow's South African Study," 1 November 1963, National Security File, John F. Kennedy Presidential Library, Boston, p. 1.

86. Interview, Attwood, p. 8.

87. G. Mennen Williams, Report on his Fourth Trip to Africa, April 13, 1962 through May 14, 1962, National Security File, John F. Kennedy Presidential Library, Boston, p. 1.

88. Fredericks, "Our Policy Toward Africa," p. 284.

89. Kotsching, "The United States and Africa: Common Goals," p. 377.

90. US, Department of State, Bureau of Public Affairs, Address by G. Mennen Williams, "The Challenge of Africa to the Youth of America," 10 March 1962, *Department of State Bulletin* 46 (2 April 1962): 549.

91. Kalb, *Congo Cables,* pp. 240-41.

92. G. Mennen Williams, Memorandum, "Additional Comments of Governor Williams on Specific Countries and Problems During His Third Trip to Africa," September 29–October 26, 1961, 26 October 1961, National Security File, John F. Kennedy Presidential Library, Boston, p. 5.

93. State Department, "Africa: Department of State Guidelines," pp. 27-30.

94. Interview, Williams, p. 62.

95. Kalb, *Congo Cables,* p. 290.

96. Ibid., p. 295.

97. Ibid., p. 303.

98. A reference to Belgium's acceptance of the negotiation option can be found in the following document: George Ball, Memorandum for the President, "US Policy Toward the Congo-Katanga Problem," 23 September 1961, National Security File, John F. Kennedy Presidential Library, Boston, pp. 4-5.

99. Dean Rusk, Memorandum for the President, "Next Steps in the Congo," 11 November 1961, National Security File, John F. Kennedy Presidential Library, Boston, pp. 1-2.

100. Kalb, *Congo Cables,* pp. 335-36.

101. A discussion of the potential efficacy of economic sanctions can be found in the following document: Proposal for discussion by NSC Standing Group, "Proposed Action Program for Congo," 9 February 1962, National Security File, John F. Kennedy Presidential Library, Boston, pp. 1-2.

102. Roger Hilsman, Department of State Bureau of Intelligence and Research, Memorandum to Dean Rusk, "Policy Alternatives in the Congo," 29 March 1962, National Security File, John F. Kennedy Presidential Library, Boston, p. 5.

103. George Ball, Outgoing State Department Telegram, "Talks on Congo with UK and Belgium," 11 May 1962, National Security File, John F. Kennedy Presidential Library, Boston, p. 1.

104. Kalb, *Congo Cables,* pp. 367-71.

105. Rusk, "Next Steps in Congo," p. 1.

106. Thomas Hughes, Memorandum to Dean Rusk, "The West at a New Congo Crossroads," 19 April 1963, National Security File, John F. Kennedy Presidential Library, Boston, p. 1.

107. "US Policy in the Congo: Summary: A Plan of Action," 20 February 1963, National Security File, John F. Kennedy Presidential Library, Boston, p. 18.

108. Owen, "White Redoubt," p. 21.

109. Memorandum discussed at Tuesday Planning Group Meeting, "Problems of South Africa," 4 October 1962, National Security File, John F. Kennedy Presidential Library, Boston, p. 28.

110. US, Department of State, Bureau of Public Affairs, Statement by Adlai Stevenson, "US Supports Afro-Asian Resolution on Angola," 15 March 1961, *Department of State Bulletin* 44 (3 April 1961): 497-99.

111. US, Department of State, Bureau of Public Affairs, Address by G. Mennen Williams, "The United Nations and the New Africa," 29 March 1963, *Department of State Bulletin* 48 (22 April 1963): 604-5; and Fredericks, "Our Policy Toward Africa," p. 286.

112. David Klein, Memorandum for McGeorge Bundy, "Portugal and the Azores Base," 26 May 1962, National Security File, John F. Kennedy Presidential Library, Boston, p. 1.

113. US, Department of State, Bureau of Public Affairs, Statement by Jonathan Bingham, "UN General Assembly Debates Question of Southern Rhodesia," 22 June 1962, *Department of State Bulletin* 47 (20 August 1962): 300.

114. Owen, "White Redoubt," p. 15.

115. For an illustration of cultural theory see Robert Packenham, *Liberal America in the Third World: Political Development Ideas in Foreign Aid and the Social Sciences* (Princeton, New Jersey: Princeton University Press, 1975).

116. For illustrations and examinations of bureaucratic theory see the following works: Graham Allison, "Conceptual Models and the Cuban Missile Crisis," *American Political Science Review* 63 (September 1969): 689-718; and S. Krasner, "Are Bureaucracies Important?" *Foreign Policy,* no. 7 (Summer 1972), pp. 159-79.

117. For illustrations and examinations of geopolitical theory see the following works:

Inis Claude, *Power and International Relations* (New York City: Random House, 1962); Keohane and Nye, *Power and Interdependence;* Graham Allison, *Essence of Decision: Explaining the Cuban Missile Crisis* (Boston: Little, Brown and Co., 1971); and Hans Morgenthau, *Politics among Nations: the Struggle for Power and Peace* (New York City: A. A. Knopf, 1948).

118. For illustrations and critiques of economic theory see the following works: V. I. Lenin, *Imperialism: The Highest Stage of Capitalism* (Peking: Foreign Languages Press, 1965); Harry Magdoff, *The Age of Imperialism* (New York City: Monthly Review Press, 1969); and Benjamin Cohen, *The Question of Imperialism: The Political Economy of Dominance and Dependence* (New York City: Basic Books, 1973).

119. For a delineation of George Ball's foreign policy philosophy, see George Ball, *The Past Has Another Pattern* (New York City: W. W. Norton and Co., 1982).

120. Ibid.

121. Dean Rusk, Memorandum to the President, "South African Interest in Purchase of US Submarines," 16 March 1963, National Security File, John F. Kennedy Presidential Library, Boston, pp. 1-2.

122. References to the President's belief that there were loopholes in the arms embargo can be found in the following government document: McGeorge Bundy, Memorandum for Dean Rusk and Robert McNamara, 23 September 1963, National Security File, John F. Kennedy Presidential Library, Boston, p. 1.

123. Weissman, *American Policy in the Congo,* pp. 297-98; and Interview, Fredericks.

124. Maxwell Taylor, Memorandum for Robert McNamara, "US Policy Toward Portugal and the Republic of South Africa," 10 July 1963, National Security File, John F. Kennedy Presidential Library, Boston, p. 1.

125. Interview, Attwood, p. 42.

126. Jackson, *Congo to Soweto,* pp. 145-46.

127. An examination of the impact of blacks on America's African policy can be found in the following works: Donald McHenry, "Captive of No Group: African Policy and Black Americans," *Foreign Policy,* no. 15 (summer 1974), p. 142; and Jackson, *Congo to Soweto,* pp. 121-68.

128. A history of the American Committee on Africa can be found in the following pamphlet distributed by its headquarters in New York City: George Houser, *Meeting Africa's Challenge: The Story of the American Committee on Africa (ACOA)* (New York City: ACOA), pp. 1-11.

129. Interview, Williams, p. 45.

130. Adlai Stevenson, Memorandum to the President, 26 April 1962, National Security File, John F. Kennedy Presidential Library, Boston, p. 3.

131. Interview, Fredericks.

132. Ball, *Past Has Another Pattern,* p. 234.

133. Ibid.

134. Ibid.

135. See Packenham, *Liberal America in Third World.*

136. African Policy Information Center of African American Institute, "African Updates Exclusive Review of Economic Relations between the US and Africa," *Africa Report* 20 (January–February 1975): 24.

137. Weissman, *American Policy in the Congo,* pp. 48-51.

138. For a more comprehensive list of US foreign policy interests see Seyom Brown, *The Faces of Power: Constancy and Change in United States Foreign Policy from Truman to Johnson* (New York City: Columbia University Press, 1968), pp. 7-27.

139. Chester Bowles, Memorandum for Dean Rusk, "Proposal for a Breakthrough in US-Portuguese Relations in Regard to Africa," 10 January 1963, National Security File, John F. Kennedy Presidential Library, Boston, pp. 1-10.

140. Memorandum discussed at Tuesday Planning Group Meeting, "Problems of South Africa," pp. 28-29.

141. Endorsements by administration members of a tougher approach to the Portuguese concerning their African colonies can be found in the following sources available at the John F. Kennedy Presidential Library in Boston: Samuel Belk, Memorandum for Mr. Bundy, "Angola," 29 June 1961, pp. 1-2; Adlai Stevenson, Memorandum for the President, "Apartheid and Portuguese Colonies," 26 June 1963, National Security File, pp. 1-3; and Thomas Wright, American consul in Lourenço Marques, Telegram to State Department, "An Assessment of the Situation in Mozambique," 16 September 1963, National Security File, p. 24.

142. CIA office of National Estimates, Memorandum, "Prospects for Nationalism and Revolt in Mozambique," 30 April 1963, National Security File, John F. Kennedy Presidential Library, Boston, p. 10; and Owen, "White Redoubt," p. 10.

CHAPTER THREE

The Johnson Administration:
INERTIA TAKES HOLD:
November 22, 1963
Through
January 20, 1969

1. Opening Observations
and the Nature of the Policy

Lyndon Baines Johnson assumed the presidency on November 22, 1963, following the death of John F. Kennedy. It was a dangerous world that he inherited. The American-Soviet contest with its potential for a nuclear holocaust continued to cast a shadow over the world community. Instability was pervasive among the nation-states which had emerged during the post-World War II era. Tragically, America was involved in a military adventure in Southeast Asia which would break up the national foreign policy consensus which had accompanied its rise to power during the previous two decades. The youthful African states proved themselves no more capable of humane behavior internally than the older nation-states

45

had been at a comparable historical stage. The Congo seethed with violence, and the Horn of Africa witnessed early signs of instability fostered largely by Somali irredentism.

Moreover, the southern tier of the Continent, still under the control of European colonialists or white settlers, was wracked by discord.

Lyndon Johnson's reaction to these world conditions was conditioned in part by the legacy left by John F. Kennedy. On one level, Kennedy's death and the residual sympathy for his former vice president contributed to a national mandate which initially gave Johnson more room to maneuver politically than any president since Franklin Roosevelt. However, the romanticism which surrounded the Kennedy legend created expectations for Johnson's presidency which no man could achieve.

In the foreign arena, Johnson was ill-equipped for the formidable task that he faced. In the context of American politics, he was a master of backroom machinations. Moreover, his formative experiences during the New Deal had endowed him with a basic decency which allowed him to rise above his parochial background, and embrace human rights at home for black and white alike. Foreign affairs made him uncomfortable, however. On more than one occasion, he remarked that foreigners just weren't like the folks back home. He saw the world almost exclusively through the lens of his American experiences. He went so far as to suggest that the quintessential American project—the Tennessee Valley Authority—was applicable to the Mekong River Delta in Vietnam.[1] Africa was particularly alien to the new president. Johnson did visit Africa as vice president.[2] Yet, his interest in the Continent was limited. Johnson's intentions were benevolent, as exhibited in a 1966 speech in which he called for an expanded program for Africa.[3] Nonetheless, the Continent occupied a low status in his consciousness of world affairs. In addition, as the years passed by, Vietnam would increasingly preclude a focus of the president upon peripheral issues.

In examining the Johnson administration's African policy, some analysts have argued that it can be divided into three stages. This interpretation is presented cogently in Waldemar Nielsen's 1969 work, *The Great Powers and Africa.*[4]

According to Nielsen's interpretation, the first period of the Johnson administration extended from Kennedy's assassination through Johnson's election in 1964. During this period, it strayed very little from the policy which had characterized the latter stages of the previous administration. Lacking a mandate for any clear policy departures, and intent on reassuring the world that American policy was stable, few initiatives were undertaken.[5]

The second period is ushered in by Johnson's crushing defeat of Barry

Goldwater in the 1964 presidential election. Confident of America's role abroad, a vigorous policy with a distinctive character is launched by the administration. A new assertiveness accompanies its actions on a number of issues, including that of South-West Africa.[6] Then, in 1966, the president delivers the second comprehensive speech ever delivered by a chief executive on Africa. He contends that the Continent will be the recipient of new economic assistance.[7] Around this time, however, the Vietnam War introduces new cleavages into American society. Domestic pressures from the right and left sap the administration's foreign policy efforts of their vitality.

The final two years of the Johnson administration's African policy are marked by a reluctance to break new ground. The US acquiesces to European sensitivies on African questions. This is particularly true in the southern African area encompassing the Republic of South Africa, Rhodesia, and the Portuguese colonies.[8]

The approach just outlined implies that three distinctive African policies can be identified during the administration. In reality, there was consistency in the Johnson administration's African policy. The stages laid out by Nielsen obscure the underlying continuity of its policy, which followed premises established previously. What was this policy?

The Johnson administration did not abandon the main premise of America's African policy. Anti-communism as a component of a universal strategy continued to be the centerpiece of this policy. Public speeches by administration officials made frequent allusions to the Communist threat. In his first State of the Union address, Johnson, like John Kennedy, was not sparing in his references to the challenge posed to the West by communism. Economic aid to Africa and elsewhere was seen as a tool in the East-West struggle. Johnson expressed this view when he stated: "We must strengthen the ability of free nations everywhere to develop their independence . . ."[9] Assistant Secretary Williams later repeated this theme in an address before the House of Representatives Committee on Foreign Affairs. Williams observed that communism feeds on the frustrations generated by poor conditions. Economic aid, he stressed, could mitigate such conditions.[10] President Johnson's emphasis on the need for economic assistance in his major speech on Africa in May 1966 was in part motivated by Cold War considerations.[11] Moreover, Williams articulated the position that keeping Africa out of the Communist orbit was connected to the well-being of the North Atlantic Treaty Organization. He asserted, in an address, that "a friendly Africa provides a protective flank to Europe and is important to the success of the Atlantic alliance . . ."[12]

Concrete evidence of the prominence played by anti-communism in the Johnson administration's approach to Africa was provided by the proliferation of confidential administration studies on Communist en-croachments on the Continent. A 1964 State Department Bureau of Intelligence and Research study, while discounting the possibility of a Communist takeover of the Continent in the near-term, identified areas of opportunity for the Communists. It warned that nationalist move-ments could be subverted, particularly in the southern Africa region.[13] A 1965 CIA study delineated Chinese Communist efforts in Africa. The study concluded that despite a short-term pragmatism, Peking ulti-mately desired to foster regimes controlled by pro-Chinese Communist parties.[14]

Hence, a desire to enhance ties between African states and the West, at the expense of the Soviet bloc and Communist China, was the driving force of the Johnson administration's African strategy. An assessment of its stance on individual issues clarifies this posture.

The Johnson administration did not alter the Congo's status as a focal point of America's anti-Communist efforts in Africa. The common thread in the administration's Congo policy over a five year period was its support of Congolese unity. This commitment emanated largely from the hardnosed judgment of administration policy-makers that a disunified Congo opened up opportunities for the Soviet Union and Communist China. This judgment was reinforced by their belief that the Communist powers were actively engaged in supporting Congolese rebels. Reports to this effect circulated freely among government officials. A few exam-ples may be offered. An August 15, 1964 memorandum from Secretary of State Rusk notes that the Chinese Communists in Congo (Brazzaville) and Burundi were supporting rebels in the western Congo.[15] A CIA report of January 5, 1965, points out that Communist manufactured arms had been discovered in the northeast.[16] In September 1965, US Ambassador to the Congo McMurtrie Godley, in a telegram addressed to the State Department, reported the presence of Russian technicians and Cubans in rebel areas.[17]

Cognizant of the Communist threat, the administration supported the central authorities in Leopoldville. Starting in its initial stages, assistance was given to suppress a series of leftist uprisings around Stanleyville and elsewhere. These efforts were marred in the eyes of even sympathetic black Africans in 1964 when the US, in a joint operation with Belgium, rescued hostages held by leftist rebels in Stanleyville.[18] Nonetheless, US assistance continued.[19] In 1967, the Johnson administration provided help for putting down a right-wing rebellion in the eastern Congo.[20] Officials worried that the national deterioration which would flow from the success of this rebellion would play into the hands of anti-Western elements.

America's South African policy during the Johnson administration was also formulated within the context of the East-West conflict. Despite stirrings on a few occasions that a dramatic policy change might occur, the basic ingredients of its South African policy remained intact for the duration of Johnson's tenure. These ingredients included the following.

First, rhetorical opposition to the South African government's policies. Second, the continuation of old measures directed against the Republic. Third, the implementation of new measures if they were primarily diplomatic, and not overly confrontational. Fourth, an opposition to the initiation of economic or forceful military measures.

The first two ingredients need no elaboration. The administration was not hesitant to declare its abhorrence of South African internal and external policies. Furthermore, it continued the arms embargo started during the Kennedy administration. In December 1963, it was broadened to include materials and equipment for the maintenance and manufacture of ammunition and arms.[21]

An examination of the final two ingredients requires a brief description of the evolution of the Johnson administration's South African policy.

The administration frequently displayed a willingness to support diplomatic steps intended to convince South Africa to loosen its hold on South-West Africa, and improve the condition of its own non-white populace. Yet, this stance was seldom accompanied by a promotion of the firm nondiplomatic measures which would have given it credibility. This pattern of behavior begins in early 1964. At that time, South Africa appeared to be moving toward the adoption of the Odendaal Commission recommendations involving the formal extension of apartheid to South-West Africa.[22] This aroused concern among many members of the international community. The United States, however, urged caution in the UN, stating that no action should be taken against South Africa over the South-West Africa issue until the International Court of Justice ruled on the status of the territory.[23] Nonetheless, by June 1964 the US had endorsed a UN Security Council resolution to set up a committee to study measures which could be implemented against South Africa if its South-West Africa policy persisted.[24] Simultaneously, it rejected calls for economic sanctions. The United States asserted that sanctions were not justified because South Africa posed no threat to the peace. Ambassador to the UN Adlai Stevenson stated on June 16, 1964, that the US "government continues to believe that the situation in South Africa, though charged with . . . dangerous implications, does not . . . provide a basis under the charter for the application by the Security Council of coercive measures."[25] Almost two years later, the US reaffirmed its opposition to economic sanctions. It questioned the legal basis for such a step, and its economic and psychological efficacy.[26] In July 1966, the International Court of Justice refused to make a definitive ruling on the South-West Africa case. The UN General Assembly subsequently, with US support, declared South Africa's mandate over the territory to be terminated.[27] The US went a step further in October 1966, when it supported the formation of a UN commission which was to facilitate South-West Africa's move toward self-determination.[28] Little came of this, and the 1967 UN General Assembly session was characterized by a split between the third world, and the United States and Western Europe over how to assert its will on the South-West Africa question.[29] The latter group favored softer tactics. This split did not deter the US, in 1967 and 1968, from voting for UN resolutions which condemned South Africa's decision to bring thirty-seven South-West Africans to trial under the Terrorism Act. United Nations Ambassador Arthur Goldberg proclaimed in December 1967 that South Africa had used the "atrocious Terrorism Act to bring these individuals to trial under conditions which are repugnant to all who believe in justice under law."[30] However, in December 1968, the US opposed efforts to bar South Africa from membership in the UN Commission on Trade and Development. This step, in the estimation of the administration, would have damaged the UN as an institution by undermining the principle of rights for all members.[31] Thus, the Johnson administration sought to demonstrate its disenchantment with South African policy, while avoiding a break which would harm its status as a Western ally.

Global strategic concerns also dictated the administration's attitude toward Portugal's African colonies. Continuing a trend which had developed in previous administrations, a primacy was placed on American access to the Azores. The focus was on their utility as a base of operations for Europe in the event of a Soviet invasion, and for the Middle East.

Lip service was paid to the concept of self-determination for Angola, Mozambique, and Portuguese Guinea. But little effort was devoted to defining what this would entail. An administration memorandum designed to prepare officials for an upcoming NATO meeting did not rule out a continued association with Portugal, or another political arrangement as acceptable political options for the colonies.[32] Moreover, pressure was not exerted on Portugal to speed up the movement of its colonies toward independence. The Johnson administration did not repeat the early Kennedy administration policy of reducing arms deliveries to Portugal. The energy exerted on behalf of self-determination was primarily diplomatic in nature. The usual declarations on behalf of self-determination were issued intermittently. A characteristic statement was made by Williams. On April 18, 1964, he observed that the UN says the Africans "should have the right to self-determination. The US fully agrees."[33] Furthermore, the United States encouraged third parties to talk to Portugal's leaders on the desirability of some form of self-determination for its colonies. In 1964, for instance, it tried to arrange discussions between the Ivory Coast's conservative leader Houphouet Boigny and representatives of Portugal. An internal administration document of this period indicates that officials hoped that talks about ties between the Ivory Coast and France would convince the Portuguese that a close relationship could be maintained "between African states and a former metropole."[34] They were disappointed when the Portuguese did not accept the idea. Telegrams from the American ambassador to Portugal to the State Department, in late January and mid February 1964, confirm the refusal of Portugal's leaders to respond positively to the American proposal.[35]

Yet, as the 1960s wore on, the fate of the Portuguese colonies faded as a concern of American policy makers. By the time Johnson left office in January 1969, American policy was clearly a captive of the desire to have access to the Azores and maintain good relations with a NATO ally.

The Johnson administration's Rhodesian policy differed in form, but not in substance, from its policy on the Portuguese colonies. On Rhodesia, unlike the Portuguese colonies, the administration's commitment to a greater voice for the black majority was accompanied by stiff economic and diplomatic sanctions. Both policies, however, were predicated on a desire to preclude the growth of Soviet influence. Concern about the Portuguese colonies, as we have seen, was subordinated to an emphasis on the role of the Portuguese controlled Azores in the Western alliance. Similarly, the importance of Britain in the alliance was the determining factor in America's Rhodesian policy.

When President Johnson assumed office, Rhodesia was divided between factions with conflicting views of its future. One faction consisted of a white minority which largely favored independence from Britain and a minority controlled government. Another faction incorporated blacks who opposed independence without majority rule, though they differed on tactics. By April 1964, a right-wing white group led by Ian Smith had gained ascendance and begun a push for independence through negotiations.[36] In November 1965, the Ian Smith led government issued a Unilateral Declaration of Independence.[37] In subsequent years, the Johnson administration conducted its Rhodesian policy in accordance with the parameters laid down by Britain.[38] The most fundamental premise for America's African and global policy, strengthening the West in the face of the Communist threat, was preserved.

A second premise continued to guide America's African policy. This premise was that Africa would occupy a low status, relative to the rest of the world, as an object of American attention and aid.

The Kennedy administration had been characterized by an initial spurt of interest in Africa, and then a precipitous drop off as other issues rose to prominence. During the Johnson years, African issues were overwhelmed in high policy circles by a gathering storm known as Vietnam. Such events as the Stanleyville airlift in November 1964, and the American reaction to the Unilateral Declaration of Independence in Rhodesia only briefly increased the profile of African issues. Even more so than in the previous administration, policy debates on Africa were carried out principally in the middle levels of the bureaucracy. Africa's limited role in the context of American global interests was reflected dramatically by the low level of aid channeled to the Continent. Assistant Secretary for African Affairs Joseph Palmer, who acquired his post in 1966, stated in an interview that "foreign aid funds were more plentiful" during the Kennedy years than the Johnson years.[39] This is borne out by a review of aid during the Johnson administration. In fiscal 1964 and fiscal 1965, President Johnson submitted foreign aid requests lower than the previous administration. These requests were cut further by Congress.[40] Developments in 1965 and 1966 proved to be a watershed in US aid to Africa.

In May 1965, President Johnson asked Assistant Secretary Williams to assess America's African policy and formulate a program with which the president could be "associated."[41] A short time later Williams called a meeting of African chiefs of mission in Addis Ababa, Ethiopia, to offer recommendations for this program. A principal recommendation which emerged from the meeting was to use economic aid to serve political purposes as well as developmental goals.[42] In ensuing months there were a series of meetings between Williams, Secretary of State Rusk, the incoming Assistant Secretary Joseph Palmer, and the president on the need for new initiatives in America's African policy. At one juncture, President Johnson suggested that an African version of the Latin American Alliance for Progress should be started.[43] Despite months of planning, the president's May 1966 speech on Africa, delivered at a reception commemorating the third anniversary of the founding of the Organization of African Unity, offered little of a concrete nature in the economic realm. A continuation of American developmental aid for Africa was mentioned.[44] The speech was followed by a more significant development. This was the designation of Edward Korry, US ambassador to Ethiopia, to study US economic aid policy. The Korry Report on economic aid, which was approved by the president in October 1966, proposed that US economic assistance emphasize regional development. Some strictly bilateral projects with individual states were to be terminated.[45]

The aftermath of the Korry Report was characterized by a major overhaul of US aid programs. Liberal opponents of large scale US intervention abroad and fiscal conservatives combined to limit the number of countries in the world eligible for technical assistance to forty, and for developmental loans to twenty. Latin America was an exception to these guidelines. The impact on Africa was devastating. Agency for International Development (AID) bilateral programs were scheduled to be ended in twenty-five African states.[46] Overall funding levels for AID had declined from $200 million per year in the period from 1961–1966, to $181 million in fiscal year 1967.[47] The president's entire foreign aid request in 1968 was $2.5 billion. This was the smallest figure since America had acquired a world-wide role in the post-World War II era.[48] The hopes of liberals in the early 1960s that Africa would be the recipient of major programs of development had been dashed by 1968. A president caught in the morass of Vietnam had lost much of his base of support. He could do little to foster the passage of foreign aid programs.

An assessment of US policy on specific African states also discloses a pattern of limited involvement as the Johnson years elapsed. This contrasts with the escalation of US involvement in Vietnam, the commitment of troops to the Dominican Republic in 1965, and a higher US profile in the Middle East.

By the mid 1960s, the US had largely washed its hands of any concrete involvement in the issues of self-determination for the Portuguese colonies, and South-West Africa. Weak diplomatic initiatives could not erase this fact. In March 1966, G. Mennen Williams, testifying before the House Foreign Affairs Subcommittee on Africa, was deeply critical of South Africa's policies. Close observers noted, however, that he did not recommend any measures for diminishing US nuclear or economic cooperation with the Republic.[49] Two years later, this stance remained the same.

On the issue of Rhodesia, two principles dominated US policy. The first was to adhere to the British policy line as long as it consisted of reasonably painless economic and diplomatic sanctions. The second was to refrain from any steps which would entail a US military role in Rhodesia. These principles were enunciated in a December 1, 1965 classified government document entitled "Guidelines to US Policy on Rhodesia." According to this document, the Unilateral Declaration of Independence was "primarily a United Kingdom problem and the US should follow and not lead in taking measures."[50] It goes on to state that

American assistance to the United Kingdom should avoid the use of US forces in Africa.[51] A December 22, 1965 memorandum addressed to President Johnson acknowledges that the British sponsored economic sanctions will not restore its authority.[52] The memorandum observes, however, that the British "cannot count on . . ." American troops.[53] America's apprehensions about getting dragged into a conflict abroad while the Vietnam conflagration continued were expressed in a speech by Secretary of Defense McNamara in May 1966. He asserted that the "US had no mandate to police the world and no inclination to do so." He continued that "there have been classic cases in which our deliberate nonaction was the wisest course of all." This was construed by African representatives as implying that the US would not assist Britain if it used military force in Rhodesia.[54]

The administration's behavior during the Nigerian Civil War of the late 1960s was a vivid example of conflict avoidance. In 1966 Nigeria was torn asunder by coups and ethnic violence. This culminated in late 1966 with a slaughter of Ibo tribesmen in northern Nigeria, and a secession by the Ibo controlled region of Biafra in mid 1967.[55] In the ensuing civil war, the US supported Nigerian unity, but refrained from any active form of intervention or military and economic assistance. Humanitarian aid was given, however. This approach was adopted despite Soviet bloc aid to the central government.[56] Assistant Secretary Palmer, speaking before the House of Representatives Subcommittee on Africa in July 1968, explained US policy. He emphasized that it was not the US intention to interfere in Nigerian military or political affairs.[57] Two months later Palmer reiterated the theme that the US supported a peaceful resolution of Nigeria's problems and advocated Nigerian unity.[58]

The pattern of a lack of commitment of human physical resources to African issues during the Johnson administration was not unqualified. Former Assistant Secretary Williams, in an interview in the mid 1970s, recalled how Johnson would visit African ambassadors on the presidential yacht and at White House luncheons.[59] Williams' successor, Joseph Palmer, related in 1969 how, in his three years as assistant secretary, there were fifteen visits by African heads of government.[60] In 1967 and 1968, Undersecretary of State Katzenbach and Vice President Humphrey made trips to Africa.[61]

More important than these symbolic gestures, American assistance to the Congo was not inconsiderable. This differed from most other parts of Africa.

We close our analysis of how the Johnson administration adhered to the premise that African issues should possess a low status in the hierarchy of American foreign policy priorities with the Congo. We do so because even here, there were narrower parameters on the degree of involvement that the administration would sanction than in Europe, Southeast Asia or Latin America.

The Johnson administration did not abandon the Kennedy administration's practice of providing assistance to the Congo to put down insurgencies. After the departure of US troops in June 1964, much of this assistance was bilateral. In August 1964, Under-Secretary of State for Political Affairs Averell Harriman informed Special Assistant to the President for National Security Affairs McGeorge Bundy that the arrival in the Congo of four C-130s, three helicopters, and other equipment would contribute to the defeat of anti-government rebels.[62] In November 1964, thirteen US planes helped to ferry Belgian paratroopers into Stanleyville to rescue hostages held by leftist insurgents. Three of these planes were then sent to the capital at Leopoldville along with a number of jeeps to help in other operations.[63] US military assistance to the Congo during the early stages of the Johnson administration can best be described as modest. Congolese requests for sophisticated weapons were often turned down. This was embodied by US Ambassador Godley's negative reaction to Prime Minister Adoula's request for fighter aircraft in 1964.[64] At no time did US assistance include the direct introduction of combat troops. Efforts were made to encourage US allies, as the Belgians in the case of the Stanleyville airdrop—or, on a number of occasions, white mercenaries—to assume the burden of fighting in the countryside.[65] The US had fewer reservations about introducing US troops into trouble spots in the Western Hemisphere as exemplified by the Dominican Republic in 1965, or Southeast Asia. Europe still had a large contingent of US troops manning North Atlantic Treaty Organization positions.

US reticence about taking major military steps in the Congo continued for the duration of Johnson's presidency. The factors precluding such actions were evident in the summer of 1967 when a revolt by white mercenaries against the central government broke out in the eastern Congo. The US promptly sent three aircraft and one hundred and fifty operating personnel who helped to put down the rebellion.[66] Yet, a timetable with deadlines accompanied the supply of these planes. Moreover, bureaucratic elements and congressional and domestic pressure groups raised such a furor over this limited use of American military aid that an escalation of US involvement would have been difficult if not impossible. The constraints on the use of US forces in the Congo will be detailed later in this chapter.

Thus, the Johnson administration did devote human and physical resources to Africa. Nonetheless, the administration followed the premise that this commitment would be very limited relative to US efforts elsewhere in the world.

We are now brought to the third premise of America's African policy. The Johnson administration consciously avoided most policy positions which conflicted with those of its European allies.

Johnson administration officials often spoke bluntly of how United States policy incorporated a recognition of Europe's unique historical relationship to Africa. In July 1964, Deputy Assistant Secretary Wayne Fredericks noted in an address at the University of Minnesota that the US had "no desire to replace the mutually beneficial relationship existing between African and European nations in many parts of the African Continent."[67] He added that the US sought to coordinate its aid with that of the European states.[68] In early 1965, Assistant Secretary Williams stated that a fundamental tenet of US African policy was to urge the Europeans to assume their responsibilities in Africa.[69] This tenet was incorporated into US handling of individual issues.

In the Congo, US-Belgian cooperation, which had grown during the Kennedy administration, reached an even higher level during the Johnson years.

In April 1964 a US State Department official observed that the Belgian leader Spaak had almost always responded favorably to US proposals on the Congo.[70] US-Belgian collaboration reached a peak with the November 24, 1964, paratrooper drop on Stanleyville. In early November, the Central Intelligence Agency and the State Department Division on Intelligence and Research warned that the collapse of the leftist rebel insurrection in the Stanleyville area could lead to the slaughter of Europeans being held captive.[71] The CIA claimed that the best method for saving the hostages would be a paratroop assault on Stanleyville.[72] On November 13, Secretary of State Rusk, in a State Department outgoing telegram, alluded to joint contingency planning with the Belgians for a rescue attempt.[73] The successful rescue effort on November 24 combined over a dozen American planes and Belgian paratroopers.[74] The reaction of most black African states to the rescue mission was highly negative, but this did not discourage the United States from working with the Belgians for the remainder of the administration.[75] It sought to consult with Belgium and occasionally Britain when it took major initiatives on the Congo. The US also urged the Belgians to accept greater responsibility in many facets of Congolese affairs.

In early February 1965, Under-Secretary George Ball, in an internal administration document, spoke of the need to talk to the Belgians and British about US efforts to foster better relations between the Congolese government and the Organization of African Unity.[76] This call for greater communication with America's allies was picked up by US Ambassador Godley in a late February 1965 telegram to the State Department. He contended that this communication could help the US to avert an escalation of its military role in the country.[77] In 1965, talks did take place between Ambassador at Large Averell Harriman and Belgian Foreign Minister Spaak concerning military aid.[78] The CIA Directorate of Intelligence concluded thereafter that the Belgians had increasingly filled the void left by the departure of US troops in June of 1964 by moving aggressively into the areas of military training and management.[79] US policy in the final years of Johnson's tenure was deeply sensitive to Belgian interests in the Congo.

On the South Africa-South-West Africa issue, the administration never quite achieved the level of agreement with interested European parties that it did on the Congo issue. An early administration document reveals that some of its members expressed high hopes that a South African regional policy could be formulated in conjunction with Britain. In this document, which was a briefing paper to assist in preparations for the visit of British Foreign Secretary Gordon Walker, the goal of continuing close consultation on South African problems was articulated.[80] This was accompanied by an expressed desire that the policies of the United States and its allies on these problems be compatible. The administration's performance on these goals in subsequent years was mixed. Consultation was maintained, but policy disagreements between the US and the Europeans did appear.

One area of disagreement stemmed from a belief by elements of Johnson's administration that the Europeans were not taking an active enough role in resolving South Africa area issues. In July 1966, Thomas Hughes, State Department director of intelligence and research, in a memorandum to Dean Rusk, lamented the fact that the British were seemingly disengaging from the area's problems. In Hughes' words, Britain was avoiding commitments that might involve confrontations.[81]

Other policy disparities were more substantive. The US, during Johnson's presidency, observed the arms embargo against South Africa more scrupulously than a number of European allies. A July 1966 State Department memorandum observed matter of factly that the United Kingdom would not follow the embargo as closely as the US.[82] A few months later, a State Department paper noted that France, Italy and to a "lesser extent the United Kingdom had not interpreted the arms embargo resolution" directed at South Africa as strictly as the US.[83] Moreover, a split developed over an October 22, 1966 United Nations resolution revoking South Africa's mandate over South-West Africa. The US supported the resolution, whereas Britain and France abstained. Portugal opposed it.[84] Nor did the US find many European allies rallying to its support in 1966 of the establishment of a UN commission to prepare South-West Africa for self-determination.[85]

However, the most important components of the administration's South African policy coincided with that of its allies. The US, along with Britain and France, felt that most coercive measures directed against South Africa would be counter-productive. They all opposed economic sanctions and the expulsion of South Africa from the UN. Instead, they preferred the use of diplomatic channels to encourage modifications of its policies.[86]

The Johnson administration's policy on the Portuguese colonies was predicated on the primacy it placed on US relations with the metropole. This emanated largely from the significance it attached to the Azores, but other strategic factors were part of the equation. Among these factors, as we learn from a 1964 memorandum addressed to the Secretary of the Navy, was a desire to place new intelligence gathering stations in Portugal.[87] Accordingly, America adjusted its policy to Portuguese concerns. A flexible interpretation of self-determination for African colonies was adopted and arms sales were maintained. In 1964 for instance, a sale of guns for use on Portuguese frigates was approved.[88]

Administration officials continued contacts with Holden Roberto's rebels in Angola, which had begun during the previous administration.[89] It also communicated with Eduardo Mondlane, a major figure in the movement against Portuguese colonialism in Mozambique.[90] These contacts did not alter the pro-Portuguese tenor of the administration's policy.

Johnson administration officials did not stray from the position of the Kennedy administration that Rhodesia was a British responsibility. A September 1965 White House memorandum expressed the view that the US backed the British stance of no independence without majority rule, and economic sanctions in the event of an illegal declaration of independence by the whites.[91] In mid October 1965, Rusk told an American representative in Southern Rhodesia to inform the government that the US support for the United Kingdom was a "firm commitment."[92] This commitment was not abandoned as the US initiated limited sanctions in November 1965 following the Unilateral Declaration of Independence, and more rigorous measures starting in 1966.[93] A State Department document in December 1966 stated that the US still considered Southern Rhodesia a British colony.[94] This theme is repeated in a February 1967 background paper for Special Assistant to the President for National Security Affairs Walt Rostow's upcoming trip to the United Kingdom. It is mentioned here that the US believes Britain has responsibility for

Rhodesia, and that the US should provide the British with "maximum leverage to use with the regime."[95]

Hence, as long as Britain did not call on the administration to provide military assistance, United States policy on Rhodesia was largely risk free. A fellow member of NATO was backed, and an encumbering involvement was averted.

Thus, the Johnson administration departed little from the African policy of its predecessors. The lines of continuity between this administration, and the latter half of the Kennedy administration in particular were visible and strong. Even after it was firmly entrenched, the Johnson administration did not establish an independent identity for its policy. Its chief premises were unchanged. An explanation is in order.

2. Factors Behind the Policy

Bureaucratic factors exerted a major impact on the shape of the Johnson administration's African policy. The most important pattern within the bureaucracy was the consolidation of the authority of the globalists, who placed a primacy on the East-West conflict. This was the continuation of a trend which had accelerated during the latter part of the Kennedy administration. It was manifested in the establishment of policy dominance by both individuals and bureaucratic units who almost invariably interpreted regional events in the context of the cold war, and felt that Africa's importance in this struggle was secondary relative to other areas. They also often felt that US security concerns dictated an adjustment of US African policy to the interests of America's European allies, even when this conflicted with the ideals of self-determination and majority rule. There was a corresponding diminishment of the influence of those administration officials and bureaucratic units who consistently questioned their maxims.

Waldemar Nielsen, in his work, *The Great Powers and Africa,* correctly observed that President Johnson allowed the old line professionals to increase their control over African issues.[96] This was symbolized by Averell Harriman's assumption of the post of ambassador at large with special responsibility for Africa in April 1964, and the continuing eclipse of G. Mennen Williams as an influential actor on African issues. Harriman was a liberal. However, his direct experience with the Soviet Union as US ambassador and other posts made him more attuned than Williams to the globalist interpretation of US security interests which monopolized post World War II thinking among America's policy elite. Williams was one of the most outspoken advocates in Washington of treating African issues on their own merits, and placing somewhat more distance between US policy and that of the Europeans. His star had already declined considerably during the Kennedy administration. During the Johnson presidency, he found his influence fading to the point where he was replaced by a career Foreign Service officer, Joseph Palmer, in 1966.[97] The ascendancy of such globalist oriented thinkers as Robert McNamara and Dean Rusk, and Europeanists as George Ball during the Johnson administration also contributed to the shape of its African policy.

Among bureaucratic units, the African and International Organization bureaus in the State Department swam against the policy currents of the administration. They found their advocacy of increasing the responsiveness of US policy to African regional needs largely overwhelmed by the contrary views of more powerful units. These units included the European Bureau, the Defense Department, the Central Intelligence Agency, and the Commerce and Treasury departments. The configuration of power among bureaucratic units during the Johnson years differed little from what it had been during the Kennedy years. President Johnson pre-occupied with Vietnam, however, intervened in African affairs even less than his predecessor. He allowed the power imbalance among his administration's bureaucratic divisions to play themselves out.

A few illustrations of how the bureaucratic factors just outlined affected individual issues will be helpful.

On the Congo, a powerful array of individuals and divisions including Secretary of State Dean Rusk, the European Bureau, and the Defense Department favored working closely with Belgium to preclude Communist successes. They also preferred to avoid any major US presence in the country or massive deliveries of aid. These positions were captured in a telegram to the State Department from Ambassador Godley in February 1965. He observed that US cooperation with the Belgians would avoid a situation where "by default we will have to assume even larger military responsibilities in the Congo . . . and even undertake crash deliveries."[98] This approach, due in part to the bureaucratic balance of power, prevailed.

On the South Africa-South-West African issue we have seen how the Johnson administration differed with its chief European allies on a few questions, but sided with them on the crucial issue of economic sanctions. South Africa's behavior in South-West Africa had internally convinced such disparate figures as conservative US ambassador to South Africa Satterthwaite, and the liberal G. Mennen Williams to proclaim that sanctions might be necessary. Satterthwaite did so in a December 14, 1963 telegram to the State Department. He pointed out that economic sanctions may be helpful if US diplomatic overtures were rebuffed.

Satterthwaite also asserted that they should be applied before South Africa slid into racial chaos.[99] Williams, in a May 1964 memorandum to Averell Harriman, called for a marshalling of domestic and foreign pressures on South Africa "spearheaded by Great Power firmness."[100] Satterthwaite, Williams, and the African Bureau were confronted by much of the European Bureau, the Defense Department, and the Central Intelligence Agency. The European Bureau, and the Defense Department worried that sanctions could open up cleavages in the Western Alliance. The CIA, in classified studies completed in September 1965 and June 1966, questioned the efficacy of sanctions.[101] The Agency, in the 1966 study, proclaimed that sanctions would be "difficult to enforce" without the use of military force, and that it was unlikely that a key actor, England, would participate.[102] Moreover, Secretary of State Rusk was highly unenthusiastic about the prospect of implementing sanctions against South Africa.[103] The greater bureaucratic weight carried by those divisions and individuals who opposed economic sanctions prevented this source of leverage from becoming a tool of US policy for South Africa.

On most issues relating to the Portuguese colonies, the most influential components of the executive branch favored the Portuguese.[104] This stance grew more pronounced as the years progressed.

On the issue of Rhodesia, bureaucratic factors contributed to a pragmatic alliance between strange bedfellows. Elements in the State Department European Bureau who did not want to embarrass the British, found themselves in agreement with members of the African Bureau. The latter group felt an endorsement of economic sanctions would at least prevent a full break with black African states. Williams, the defender of African interests, in November 1965 told Rusk that America must support the United Kingdom in its positions on Southern Rhodesia in the Security Council.[105] In this case, Williams was not outgunned. The big guns were on his side, despite the apprehension about moving on to mandatory sanctions voiced by Rusk and the Central Intelligence Agency.[106] The administration followed the British sanctions policy.

Domestic non-bureaucratic factors played a more prominent role in America's African policy during Johnson's tenure than they had during the Kennedy period.

Some factors were unchanged. The disorganization and general ineffectiveness of liberal lobby groups on African issues remained a feature of the political scene. The American Negro Leadership Conference on African was but a shell of an organization. Its members concentrated almost all of their energies on the amelioration of America's internal racial inequities. They had the will and energy to do little else.

61

The American Committee on Africa, though sincere in its efforts to encourage a progressive policy, had few resources and was still unschooled in sophisticated lobbying techniques. Two additional groups, the National Conference on the South African Crisis, and American Action articulated liberal positions during the Kennedy administration. Despite a March 1965 meeting with officials who included Dean Rusk, they had little discernible influence on US policy.[107] Even the competent Biafra lobby, an array of secular and religious groups with liberal leanings, was not able to seriously dent US support of Nigeria's central government.[108] An argument could be made, however, that its existence was among the factors which prevented the US from assisting that government more vigorously.

The weakness of liberal pressure groups ensured that the administration would not move beyond its emphasis on anti-communism on the Continent. This orientation was reinforced by the pre-eminence of the conservative lobby groups, which were still more potent than their liberal foes. This was particularly the case with the Congo. Wary allusions to the influence of the Katanga lobby can be found in many internal administration documents. Officials found it necessary to talk with its members. On January 21, 1965, White House official R. W. Komer had a confidential discussion with Senator Dodd of the lobby in an effort to convince him that the current policy was correct.[109] In Komer's words: "I had a good half hour with Senator Dodd on the Congo . . . I told him I was there with the president's OK because Mr. Bundy (National Security Adviser) and I thought it would be easier to clarify our policy and problems on the Congo face to face."[110] In October 1965, in a memorandum for Averell Harriman, Komer expressed anxiety about the difficulties Dodd could cause for the United States Congolese policy.[111] The limitations on US assistance to the Congo were in part a derivation of the strength of the Katanga lobby.

Conservative lobby groups concerned with South Africa, the Portuguese colonies, and the Rhodesian issue also proliferated. On the latter issue they did not have any solid successes until the Nixon years.

In Congress the power of conservatives on African issues ebbed somewhat. The most recalcitrant on racial issues suffered a setback when the administration endorsed economic sanctions against Rhodesia following its Unilateral Declaration of Independence and adhered to them.[112] There was minimal Congressional input on the Rhodesian issue for the duration of the Johnson administration. Rhetorical thunder emanated from conservatives such as Senator Eastland of Mississippi, who supported the breakaway regime of Ian Smith. However, they had little of a concrete nature to show for their efforts beyond keeping the public relations Rhodesian Information Office open.[113] Nor were liberals such as Representative Donald Fraser of Minnesota, and Senator Edward Brooke of Massachusetts able to convince the administration to adopt sterner measures against the Rhodesian government.[114] On other southern African issues, the conservative tenor of a segment of Congress marginally affected the caution with which the administration dealt with them.

An amorphous but important domestic factor during the Johnson administration was American public opinion. Looming over its approach to foreign affairs was Vietnam. Vietnam altered American policy in Africa through the lens of American public opinion in a number of ways. First, it bred a disillusionment with American involvement abroad among liberal Americans. This group then joined with traditional conservative opponents of foreign aid to damage an instrument of American foreign policy which could have influenced policy outcomes in Africa. The administration's foreign aid requests for Africa were slashed massively as time wore on.[115] Moreover, the administration found itself unable to even seriously consider a military option for African issues because of opposition from opponents and supporters of US policy in Vietnam. Opponents of the policy wanted to avoid a similar adventure elsewhere. Its supporters, particularly in the post 1965 period, did not want to divert needed military resources from Southeast Asia. In addition, Johnson's need to garner support for his Vietnam initiatives from American conservatives discouraged any serious effort to change the status quo in the southern African area.

In light of the existence of this odd coalition, it was little wonder that two of the chief premises of America's policy continued to be to avoid a commitment of resources to the Continent, and to leave its affairs largely in the hands of the Europeans. Groups which could have swayed the administration toward a more active course on the Continent, such as blacks, were largely quiescent on continental affairs during the Johnson years, as they had been during the previous administration.

The geopolitical imperatives which had influenced US African policy during the Kennedy presidency made themselves felt after Johnson assumed power. If Africa had been viewed largely within a regional context by the Johnson administration, geopolitical developments would have encouraged it to place less of an emphasis on US competition with the Soviet Union and Communist China. For the Soviets had exhibited the characteristics of a paper tiger in sub-Saharan Africa. After an initial period of activity in the early 1960s in Guinea, Mali, the Congo and Ghana, they had lost their status as a force in the area. Guinea sought to increase its contacts with the West, and Soviet opportunities in the

Congo had largely slipped away. Moreover, Ghana's charismatic leader, Kwame Nkrumah, who had shown signs of falling under the tutelage of the Soviets, was overthrown in 1966. Finally, Nikita Khrushchev's replacement by a collective leadership which included Leonid Brezhnev in 1964, contributed to a less adventuristic Soviet foreign policy. Its principal focus was on the consolidation of the Soviet controlled areas in Eastern Europe and Asia. Khrushchev's bold efforts in the Congo, as the 1960s began, would not be repeated by the conservative men who followed him during Johnson's term in office. Soviet literature on Africa in the mid 1960s is not optimistic about serious movement on the Continent toward the Soviet model in the short term.[116]

However, the powers in the Johnson administration interpreted African affairs within a global context. It was a global context in which the US rivalry with the Communist powers was a pervasive factor. Administration officials could claim that communist expansionism continued unabated in Southeast Asia and to a lesser degree in the Western Hemisphere through sputtering insurgencies. How could one then avoid in their eyes treating Africa as a component of the struggle with the East? Yet, the escalating US role in Vietnam after 1965, and a commitment to Europe drained the scarce resources available for the foreign arena away from Africa. A recognition of this state of affairs, and NATO's enduring strategic significance prevented the US from doing much to defy European policy on the Continent.

Nor did cultural and economic factors undergo a transformation which would have altered America's African policy under Johnson. The men who ran the Johnson foreign policy apparatus were still immersed in cultural norms which precluded the emergence of a more independent and multi-dimensional policy, less absorbed with the Communist threat. They were largely tied to a post World War II tradition which neglected the non-cold war components of world politics.[117] Such concepts as "flexibility" in dealing with the third world, and "regime maintenance" were not a major part of their world outlook.[118]

American economic activity grew at a faster pace in black Africa than in the Republic of South Africa during the Johnson years.[119] Yet, this growth was not large enough to dictate a change in policy. Other factors rendered America's meager economic interests in sub-Saharan Africa of little importance as a determinant of policy.

Hence, during the Johnson administration, bureaucratic factors continued to play a salient role in the formulation of African policy. This role, however, was somewhat smaller than it was during the Kennedy administration as domestic non-bureaucratic and geopolitical forces rose to prominence. Cultural and economic factors again had only a secondary impact on policy.

3. The Effectiveness of the Policy

The issue of the efficacy of America's African policy in meeting its security interests during the Johnson period arises once more.

Waldemar Nielsen asserts that the Johnson administration had a surprising number of achievements in Africa in light of the "intractability" of the crises it faced.[120] He cites the US role in the removal of the South African mandate over South-West Africa, support of Britain on Rhodesia, and assistance to Ghana following Nkrumah's overthrow. He also refers positively to US military assistance to the Congo in 1967, and its refusal to interfere in the Nigerian Civil War.[121]

The record does divulge ad hoc and partial successes by the administration. Its continuation of the arms embargo against South Africa could be added to Nielsen's list.

Yet, an assessment of the Johnson administration's African policy in the larger context of history, almost fifteen years after it left office, does not yield a favorable judgment. It did not meet our two criteria for an effective policy. Little was done to contribute to the long-term survival of governments sympathetic to US interests. The probability that regimes friendly to Moscow would eventually emerge was not significantly reduced. Nor were steps taken which could have helped facilitate the maintenance of an orderly international system.

In the Congo, Mobutu was now the principal occupant of the throne as opposed to his previous status as the power behind it. Unabashedly pro-American, he nonetheless demonstrated an inability to construct a stable political base among members of the indigenous population. US Congolese policy was little more that a series of stop-gap measures to help shore up the government when it appeared to be on the verge of collapse.

On the South African-South-West Africa issue, the Johnson administration refused to bite the bullet on the question of limited and gradualistic economic sanctions. Its opposition to South African policies outside of the arms embargo, and its diplomatic position on the status of South-West Africa were polemical. In the absence of firmness, US rhetoric fell upon deaf ears.

On Rhodesia, the administration did adhere to concrete sanctions. Yet, this policy was not an adequate mechanism for restoring British authority to its colony, and averting a civil war with a potential for increasing Eastern Bloc influence in the area.

The Johnson administration's approach to the Portuguese colonies

65

was myopic, and compounded the errors of the latter part of the Kennedy administration. The American policy pendulum moved toward an acquiescence to Portuguese initiatives and remained ensconced there until a revolution in Portugal in 1974 awakened top US policy makers.

The Johnson administration had less room for policy innovation in Africa than the previous one. Vietnam undermined the US consensus on foreign affairs, and largely robbed the administration of two mechanisms for influencing policy outcomes. Stepped up economic and military aid were no longer acceptable options to a wide spectrum of American opinion. Other weapons in the US diplomatic arsenal remained intact, however. Interest group activity on African issues was still considerably less than it was on issues in other regions of the globe. There were no African interest groups comparable in strength to the Chinese, or Israeli lobbies. If administration members had possessed the will to do so, they could have lifted Africa from the realm of American inaction and contributed to long-term US security interests. How could this have been done?

First, more emphasis could have been placed in the late 1960s on encouraging Mobutu to expand his political base. Second, gradualistic and limited economic sanctions against South Africa, such as a halt on new investments, would not have reaped immediate dividends. Yet they would have conveyed a message to Pretoria that a continuation of its policies would have negative repercussions. While it would have been unrealistic to expect a moderation of its internal policies as a result of this approach in the short run, it would have begun the process of detaching the US from a pariah regime. South Africa possessed few forms of retaliation that could have rendered unacceptable damage to US strategic interests. As explicated in a March 13, 1964 briefing paper for the National Security Council standing group, even US missile and space-tracking facilities in South Africa could have been replaced within a short period of time by alternate sites.[122]

In Rhodesia, a direct application of US military force would have been unfeasible. However, high diplomatic channels could have been used to urge Britain to be somewhat more forceful in the resolution of its disputes with the breakaway colony.

Finally, the US could have followed a three pronged policy in its dealings with the Portuguese with the intention of accelerating the movement of its colonies toward independence. Threatened military aid reductions could have been combined with promises of additional economic aid. Moreover, aid could have been extended clandestinely to moderate anti-colonial elements in the colonies through third parties in Africa. G. Mennen Williams made such a proposal in an April 29, 1964 memorandum addressed to Dean Rusk.[123] These steps were largely ignored by high ranking administration figures. Moreover, they treated Central Intelligence Agency reports on the weaknesses of the Portuguese regime and the difficulties it faced in suppressing the colonial rebellion with indifference. A May 1964 CIA intelligence report alluded to "discontent on the part of some upper echelon officers" in the Portuguese armed forces.[124] A December 18, 1964 CIA report concluded that even though the Portuguese would succeed in putting down the colonial rebellions in the short-run, their prospects for success in the long-term were highly questionable.[125]

Thus, it was the innate conservatism and lack of imagination of American policy-makers during the Johnson years which prevented them from developing a more vigorous American African policy attuned to America's global strategic needs over the long-haul. Bureaucratic constraints proved once again to be the principal villain in precluding moderate policy breakthroughs on the Continent.

NOTES TO CHAPTER THREE

1. For additional insights into how Lyndon Johnson's background affected his view of the world see Doris Kearns, *Lyndon Johnson and the American Dream* (New York City: Harper and Row, 1976).
2. Interview, Williams.
3. Nielsen, *Great Powers and Africa,* pp. 312–13.
4. Ibid., pp. 305–26.
5. Ibid., pp. 306–7.
6. Ibid., pp. 308–12.
7. Ibid., pp. 312–13. The first comprehensive speech by a US president on sub-Saharan Africa was made by President Eisenhower in 1960. Ibid., pp. 274–75.
8. Ibid., pp. 313–26.
9. US, Department of State, Bureau of Public Affairs, Address by G. Mennen Williams, "Promising Trends in Africa," 15 February 1964, *Department of State Bulletin* 50 (9 March 1964): 373.
10. US, Department of State, Bureau of Public Affairs, Statement by G. Mennen Williams, "US Program of Economic Assistance to Africa," 10 February 1965, *Department of State Bulletin* 52 (8 March 1965): 353–54.
11. Transcript of Interview with Joseph Palmer, assistant secretary of state for African affairs, Department of State, Washington, DC, 8 January 1969, Lyndon Baines Johnson Presidential Library, Austin, Texas, pp. 5–6.
12. US, Department of State, Bureau of Public Affairs, Address by G. Mennen Williams, "Africa's Problems and Progress," 1 March 1964, *Department of State Bulletin* 50 (30 March 1964): 502.
13. Thomas Hughes, Memorandum for Dean Rusk, "An Outline Guide to Communist

Activities in Africa," 15 May 1964, Lyndon Baines Johnson Presidential Library, Austin, Texas, pp. 9–10.

14. Central Intelligence Agency Directorate of Intelligence, Memorandum, "Chinese Communist Activities in Africa," 30 April 1965, Lyndon Baines Johnson Presidential Library, Austin, Texas, annex.

15. Dean Rusk, Outgoing Telegram, "Congo Situation," 15 August 1964, Lyndon Baines Johnson Presidential Library, Austin, Texas, p. 1.

16. Central Intelligence Agency Directorate of Intelligence, Memorandum, "The Situation in the Congo," 5 January 1965, Lyndon Baines Johnson Presidential Library, Austin, Texas, p. 1.

17. McMurtrie Godley, Telegram to State Department, 21 September 1965, Lyndon Baines Johnson Presidential Library, Austin, Texas, p. 1.

18. A good account of the negative reaction of black Africans to the rescue mission can be found in the following source: Central Intelligence Agency Directorate of Intelligence, "The Situation in the Congo," 1 December 1964, Lyndon Baines Johnson Presidential Library, Austin, Texas, p. 1.

19. For a detailed account of US policy in the Congo through 1964 see Weissman, *American Policy in the Congo.*

20. Nielsen, *Great Powers and Africa*, p. 322.

21. US, Department of State, Bureau of Public Affairs, Statement by G. Mennen Williams, "United States Policy Toward South Africa," 1 March 1966, *Department of State Bulletin* 54 (21 March 1966): 436.

22. Briefing for National Security Council Standing Group, "South Africa and South-West Africa," 10 March 1964, Lyndon Baines Johnson Presidential Library, Austin, Texas, p. 3.

23. US, Department of State, Bureau of Public Affairs, Address by G. Mennen Williams, "African Issues at the United Nations," 18 April 1964, *Department of State Bulletin* 50 (11 May 1964): 754.

24. Nielsen, *Great Powers and Africa*, pp. 306–7.

25. US, Department of State, Bureau of Public Affairs, Statement by Adlai Stevenson, "UN Security Council Condemns Apartheid in South Africa; Sets Up Committee to Study Sanctions," 16 June 1964, *Department of State Bulletin* 51 (6 July 1964): 31.

26. Williams, "US Policy Toward South Africa," pp. 436–37.

27. Nielsen, "Great Powers and Africa," pp. 315–17.

28. US, Department of State, Bureau of Public Affairs, Statement by Arthur Goldberg, "United States Urges Concrete UN Action on South-West Africa," 12 October 1966, *Department of State Bulletin* 55 (31 October 1966): 691.

29. Background paper for Visit of United Kingdom Prime Minister Wilson, "South-West Africa," June 1967, Lyndon Baines Johnson Presidential Library, Austin, Texas, pp. 1–2.

30. US, Department of State, Bureau of Public Affairs, Statement by Arthur Goldberg, "UN Condemns South Africa's Violation of Rights of South-West Africans," 14 December 1967, *Department of State Bulletin* 58 (15 January 1968): 92; and US, Department of State, Bureau of Public Affairs, Statement by Arthur Goldberg, "Security Council Censures South Africa for Defiance of UN Authority," 14 March 1968, *Department of State Bulletin* 58 (8 April 1968): 476–77.

31. US, Department of State, Bureau of Public Affairs, Statement by James Wiggins, US Representative to the UN General Assembly, "UN General Assembly Rejects Move to Bar South Africa from Membership in UNCTAD," 13 December 1968, *Department of State Bulletin* 60 (6 January 1969): 9–10.

32. Bilateral Paper on Portugal from North Atlantic Treaty Organization Ministerial meeting, 3 December 1966, Lyndon Baines Johnson Presidential Library, Austin, Texas, p. 2.
33. Williams, "African Issues at the United Nations," p. 753.
34. L.M. in Abidjan, Telegram to State Department, 22 January 1964, Lyndon Baines Johnson Presidential Library, Austin, Texas, p. 1.
35. Ambassador Anderson, Telegram to State Department, 31 January 1964, Lyndon Baines Johnson Presidential Library, Austin, Texas, p. 1; and Ambassador Anderson, Telegram to State Department, 14 February 1964, Lyndon Baines Johnson Presidential Library, Austin, Texas, p. 1.
36. US, Department of State, Bureau of Public Affairs, Address by G. Mennen Williams, "Southern Rhodesia Today," 15 June 1965, *Department of State Bulletin* 53 (12 July 1965): 72-73.
37. Lake, *Tar Baby Option*, p. 1.
38. Lake, *Tar Baby Option*, pp. 60-122.
39. Interview, Palmer.
40. Nielsen, *Great Powers and Africa*, p. 320.
41. G. Mennen Williams, Memorandum for Dean Rusk, "Strengthened Africa Program," 17 September 1965, Lyndon Baines Johnson Presidential Library, Austin, Texas, p. 1.
42. State Department, Memorandum, Conference of Ambassadors and Principal Officers, Addis Ababa, Ethiopia, May 22-26, 1965, Lyndon Baines Johnson Presidential Library, Austin, Texas, p. 2.
43. Benjamin Read, executive secretary of State Department, Memorandum for Joseph Palmer, Lyndon Baines Johnson Presidential Library, Austin, Texas, 23 April 1966, p. 1.
44. Nielsen, *Great Powers and Africa*, p. 313.
45. Information on the recommendations of the Korry Report can be found in Nielsen, *Great Powers and Africa*, p. 321. Formal presidential approval of the Korry Report is expressed in the following document: Lyndon Johnson, National Security Action Memorandum 356, "Implementation of the Korry Report and Development Policies and Programs in Africa," 5 October 1966, Lyndon Baines Johnson Presidential Library, Austin, Texas, p. 1.
46. Nielsen, *Great Powers and Africa*, p. 321.
47. US, Department of State, Bureau of Public Affairs, Address by Joseph Palmer, "Africa: Continent of Change," 5 December 1968, *Department of State Bulletin* 59 (30 December 1968): 701.
48. Nielsen, *Great Powers and Africa*, p. 326.
49. Ibid., p. 312.
50. US, State Department, Memorandum, "Guidelines to US Policy on Rhodesia," 1 December 1965, Lyndon Baines Johnson Presidential Library, Austin, Texas, p. 1.
51. Ibid.
52. Thomas Mann, Memorandum for Lyndon Johnson, "Rhodesian Crisis," 22 December 1965, Lyndon Baines Johnson Presidential Library, Austin, Texas, p. 2.
53. Ibid., p. 7.
54. Nielsen, *Great Powers and Africa*, pp. 313-14.
55. Ibid., p. 323.
56. Ibid., pp. 323-34.
57. US, Department of State, Bureau of Public Affairs, Statement by Joseph Palmer, "Assistant Secretary Palmer Reports on Recent Visit to Africa," 23 July 1968, *Department of State Bulletin* 59 (19 August 1968): 206.

58. US, Department of State, Bureau of Public Affairs, Statement by Joseph Palmer, "Magnitude and Complexity of the Nigerian Problems," 11 September 1968, *Department of State Bulletin* 49 (7 October 1968): 360.
59. Interview, Williams.
60. Interview, Palmer.
61. Nielsen, *Great Powers and Africa,* p. 325.
62. Averell Harriman, Memorandum for McGeorge Bundy, "The Congo," 17 August 1964, Lyndon Baines Johnson Presidential Library, Austin, Texas, p. 1.
63. Central Intelligence Agency Directorate of Intelligence, Memorandum, "The Situation in the Congo," 24 November 1964, pp. 1–3.
64. American Embassy, Leopoldville, Congo, Telegram for State Department, "Congo," 23 May 1964, Lyndon Baines Johnson Presidential Library, Austin, Texas, p. 1.
65. McMurtrie Godley, Telegram to State Department, 30 October 1965, Lyndon Baines Johnson Presidential Library, Austin, Texas, pp. 1–3.
66. Nielsen, *Great Powers and Africa,* p. 322.
67. US, Department of State, Bureau of Public Affairs, Address by J. Wayne Fredericks, "American Policy in Africa," 7 July 1964, *Department of State Bulletin* 51 (10 August 1964): 198.
68. Ibid.
69. US, Department of State, Bureau of Public Affairs, Address by G. Mennen Williams, "United States Policy in Africa," 18 March 1965, *Department of State Bulletin* 52 (12 April 1965): 547.
70. MaCarthur, Telegram to State Department, "Harriman-Spaak Meeting," 30 April 1964, Lyndon Baines Johnson Presidential Library, Austin, Texas, p. 1.
71. Central Intelligence Agency, "Situation in Congo," 24 November 1961, p. 1; Central Intelligence Agency, Directorate of Intelligence, Memorandum, "The Situation in the Congo," 10 November 1964, Lyndon Baines Johnson Presidential Library, Austin, Texas, p. 2; and Thomas Hughes, Memorandum for Dean Rusk, "The Rebels and the Hostages: an Assessment," Lyndon Baines Johnson Presidential Library, Austin, Texas, p. 3.
72. Central Intelligence Agency, "Situation in Congo," 10 November 1964, p. 2.
73. Dean Rusk, Telegram to US Embassy, Brussels and US Embassy, Congo (Leopoldville), 13 November 1964, Lyndon Baines Johnson Presidential Library, Austin, Texas, p. 1.
74. Central Intelligence Agency "Situation in Congo," 24 November 1964, p. 1.
75. Central Intelligence Agency Directorate of Intelligence, Memorandum, "The Situation in the Congo," 1 December 1964, Lyndon Baines Johnson Presidential Library, Austin, Texas, pp. 1, 5.
76. George Ball, Telegram to US Embassy, Brussels and US Embassy, Congo (Leopoldville), "Congo," 6 February 1965, Lyndon Baines Johnson Presidential Library, Austin, Texas, pp. 1, 7.
77. McMurtrie Godley, Telegram to State Department, 27 February 1965, Lyndon Baines Johnson Presidential Library, Austin, Texas, p. 3.
78. Central Intelligence Agency Directorate of Intelligence, Memorandum, "The Situation in the Congo," 17 March 1965, Lyndon Baines Johnson Presidential Library, Austin, Texas, p. 1.
79. Central Intelligence Agency Directorate of Intelligence, Memorandum, "The Situation in the Congo," 7 April 1965, Lyndon Baines Johnson Presidential Library, Austin, Texas, p. 5.
80. State Department, Talking Points Paper for Visit of British Foreign Secretary Gordon

Walker from October 26–27, 1964, Lyndon Baines Johnson Presidential Library, Austin, Texas, p. 1.

81. Thomas Hughes, Memorandum to Dean Rusk, "Implications of UK Disengagement from South Africa," 26 July 1966, Lyndon Baines Johnson Presidential Library, Austin, Texas, p. 1.

82. Ibid., p. 5.

83. State Department, Background Paper on South Africa and South-West Africa in Preparation for North Atlantic Treaty Organization Meeting from December 14-17, 1966, 3 December 1966, Lyndon Baines Johnson Presidential Library, Austin, Texas, p. 1.

84. Nielsen, *Great Powers and Africa,* pp. 315–17.

85. Interview, Palmer.

86. See US, Department of State, Bureau of Public Affairs, *Department of State Bulletin* (1963–1968).

87. Richard Craighill, Politico-Military Policy Division of the Department of Naval Operations, Memorandum for the Secretary of the Navy, 1964, Lyndon Baines Johnson Presidential Library, Austin, Texas, p. 1.

88. Ibid.

89. Telegram to Department of State, 17 July 1964, pp. 1–2.

90. Leonhart from Dar es Salaam, Tanzania, Telegram to State Department, "Talk with Mondlane," 10 May 1964, Lyndon Baines Johnson Presidential Library, Austin, Texas, p. 1.

91. Rick Haynes, White House Memorandum, "Possible Speeding up of Southern Rhodesia Unilateral Declaration of Independence," 13 September 1965, Lyndon Baines Johnson Presidential Library, Austin, Texas, p. 2.

92. Dean Rusk, Telegram to US Embassy, Salisbury, Southern Rhodesia, 12 October 1965, Lyndon Baines Johnson Presidential Library, Austin, Texas, p. 1.

93. Gordon Chase, Memorandum for Mr. Bundy, "Southern Rhodesia Security Council Statement," 12 November 1965.

94. State Department, Background Paper on Southern Rhodesia in Preparation for North Atlantic Treaty Organization Meeting from December 4-17, 1966, 3 December 1966, Lyndon Baines Johnson Presidential Library, Austin, Texas, p. 1.

95. State Department, Background Paper on Southern Rhodesia for Walt Rostow's trip to the United Kingdom, February 1967, Lyndon Baines Johnson Presidential Library, Austin, Texas, pp. 15–16.

96. Nielsen, *Great Powers and Africa,* p. 307.

97. Ibid., p. 314.

98. McMurtrie Godley, Telegram to the State Department, 27 February 1965, Lyndon Baines Johnson Presidential Library, Austin, Texas, p. 3.

99. Joseph Satterthwaite, Telegram to the State Department, 14 December 1963, Lyndon Baines Johnson Presidential Library, Austin, Texas, pp. 1–2.

100. G. Mennen Williams, Memorandum for Averell Harriman, "Significance of Odendaal White Paper," 13 May 1964, Lyndon Baines Johnson Presidential Library, Austin, Texas, pp. 1–2.

101. Central Intelligence Agency Office of Research and Reports, Memorandum, "Sanctions and the South African Economy," 3 September 1965, Lyndon Baines Johnson Presidential Library, Austin, Texas, p. 1; and Central Intelligence Agency Directorate of Intelligence, Memorandum, "Some Implications of Economic Sanctions Against South Africa," June 1966, Lyndon Baines Johnson Presidential Library, Austin, Texas, p. 1.

102. Central Intelligence Agency, "Implications of Sanctions," p. 1.
103. An illustration of Rusk's skeptical view of sanctions can be found in the following source: State Department, Memorandum of Conversation, "Dean Rusk's Meeting with Delegation from National Conference on the Southern African Crisis and American Action," 23 March 1965, p. 5.
104. Nielsen, *Great Powers and Africa,* pp. 310-11.
105. G. Mennen Williams, Memorandum to Dean Rusk, "Southern Rhodesia Unilateral Declaration of Independence: US Policy and Initial Actions," November 1965, Lyndon Baines Johnson Presidential Library, Austin, Texas, p. 3.
106. Apprehensions about the impact of sanctions can be found in the following documents: State Department, Outgoing Telegram, 15 December 1965, Lyndon Baines Johnson Presidential Library, Austin, Texas, p. 2; and Central Intelligence Agency Director-ate of Intelligence, Memorandum, "Rhodesia and Zambia: From Voluntary to Mandatory Sanctions," January 1967, Lyndon Baines Johnson Presidential Library, Austin, Texas, pp. 1-9.
107. State Department, Rusk's Meeting with Delegation on Southern African Crisis, p. 5.
108. Nielsen, *Great Powers and Africa,* p. 324.
109. R. W. Komer, Memorandum of Record, "Congo," 21 January 1965, Lyndon Baines Johnson Presidential Library, Austin, Texas, pp. 1-3.
110. Ibid., p. 1.
111. R. W. Komer, Memorandum for Averell Harriman, "Congo," 21 October 1965, Lyndon Baines Johnson Presidential Library, Austin, Texas, p. 1.
112. Lake, *Tar Baby Option,* pp. 81-82, 85-87, 91-92, 102-3.
113. Ibid., pp. 107, 117-20.
114. Ibid., p. 119.
115. Nielsen, *Great Powers and Africa,* pp. 320, 326.
116. See Charles, *The Soviet Union and Africa,* pp. 115-16, et al.
117. A deeper understanding of the men who ran the Johnson administration foreign policy apparatus is provided by the following sources: John Donovan, *The Cold Warriors: A Policy Making Elite* (Lexington, Massachusetts: Heath, 1974); and David Halberstam, *The Best and the Brightest* (New York City: Random House, 1972).
118. Joseph S. Nye, "US Power and Reagan Policy," *Orbis: A Journal of World Affairs* 26 (Summer 1982): 403-9.
119. US, Department of State, Bureau of Public Affairs, Address by Arthur Goldberg, "The United States, the United Nations, and Southern Africa," 27 January 1967, *Department of State Bulletin* 56 (20 February 1967): 291.
120. Nielsen, *Great Powers and Africa,* p. 305.
121. Ibid., p. 327.
122. Supplementary Briefing Paper for National Security Council Standing Group, "Steps to be Taken by NASA and Department of Defense to Reduce Dependence on Republic of South Africa," 13 March 1964, Lyndon Baines Johnson Presidential Library, Austin, Texas, pp. 1-4.
123. G. Mennen Williams, Memorandum for Dean Rusk, "Portuguese Colonies," 29 April 1964, Lyndon Baines Johnson Presidential Library, Austin, Texas, pp. 1-9.
124. Central Intelligence Agency Office of Current Intelligence, Report, "Portuguese Economic Outlook and its Political Implications," 22 May 1964, Lyndon Baines Johnson Presidential Library, Austin, Texas, p. 3.
125. Central Intelligence Agency Office of Current Intelligence, "Anti-Portuguese Campaign in Africa Shifts to Mozambique," 18 December 1964, Lyndon Baines Johnson Presidential Library, Austin, Texas, pp. 1, 7.

CHAPTER FOUR

The Nixon and Ford Administrations:
COMPLACENCY, DISASTER AND THE NEW REALISM:
January 20, 1969
Through
January 20, 1977

1. Kissinger's World View

The Nixon and Ford administrations which spanned the period from 1969 through the beginning of 1977 were characterized by both stability and change. The stability was provided by the presence of Henry Kissinger whose world vision and predilection for the centralization of authority was a major factor in the foreign policy making process. The changes of the Nixon-Ford era were embodied by Nixon's ignominious fall from power in 1974, and the policy revisions which followed the Portuguese coup of April 1974, and the subsequent American debacle in Angola.

Henry Kissinger served as assistant to the president for national

73

security affairs from 1969 through 1974, and secretary of state from 1973 through 1977. During his tenure he attempted to impose his world view on American foreign policy. He was reasonably successful in doing so. His administrative approach, a consolidation of authority and vision, had major ramifications for America's African policy.

Both Kissinger and President Nixon were critical of the foreign policy bureaucracy. It was cumbersome and sometimes defied the initiatives of the White House. Their response was to centralize foreign policy making power in the White House, circumventing State Department channels. Furthermore, they often conducted negotiations on two levels. Negotiations for public consumption were carried out by subordinates. On a second level, secret negotiations where substantive issues were dealt with, were conducted by Kissinger and his staff.[1]

The implications of this approach were two-fold. First, White House decisions on African issues often ignored the empirical evidence that could have been acquired from closer consultation with specialists on Africa. Second the predominance of the globalist perspective in the White House ensured that it would prevail over Africanist views in the treatment of major African issues.

Kissinger's world view also influenced African policy. A chief component of this view was his deemphasis on ideology and emphasis on power factors and state behavior as the chief determinant of policy.[2] This allowed him to pursue a policy of detente with countries which had formerly been deemed America's ideological adversaries, namely the Soviet Union and Communist China. The deemphasis on ideology also could have contributed to a pragmatic policy toward the emerging Marxist regimes in Africa in the mid 1970s. It was accompanied, however, by a treatment of the global balance of power which looked unfavorably upon the appearance of new Marxist governments anywhere. It was hardly surprising, then, when Kissinger actively opposed the Marxist Angolan Popular Liberation Movement (MPLA) as it rose to power in Angola in 1975.[3]

A second aspect of Kissinger's philosophy was his assertion that power had been dispersed in the world. There were now five principal centers of power. According to Kissinger and Nixon, they consisted of Japan, Western Europe, Communist China, the United States, and the Soviet Union.[4] This scheme also included a few regional states, such as Iran, in its power equation.

Critics have charged that the policy implemented by Kissinger and Nixon ignored this view and focused largely on global US-Soviet relations. This accusation possesses some validity. Certainly, a number of cases can be cited where the administration ignored European and Japanese sensitivities in its interaction with the Soviets and others. However, the power configuration delineated by the president and his national security advisor does provide an understanding of the administration's behavior in Africa. For the role of Europe in their world scheme did play a part in their reluctance to seriously question European policies in Africa. This was illustrated by the Nixon administration's friendly relationship with Portugal despite its atavistic behavior in its colonial holdings. Moreover, since Europe could be given primary responsibility for much of the Continent, there was little need for a large commitment of American resources. This precept was only breached twice. First, in 1975 when Kissinger sought congressional approval of military aid for the Angolan foes of the MPLA. It was also violated in 1976 when Kissinger requested aid for Rhodesia which would assist the independence process. Kissinger was correct in his assessment that power had been dispersed in the world. What he failed to formally incorporate into his policy was a realization that the dissemination of power extended to numerous state and nonstate actors, beyond those he identified. Therefore, the "big five," and smaller regional powers were constrained in their ability to produce desired policy outcomes in their respective spheres of influence.

We are now brought to the final aspect of Kissinger's philosophy to be dealt with. This was his belief that the US should be selective in its direct utilization of force abroad to preclude Communist geopolitical breakthroughs. It was reflected in the Nixon Doctrine enunciated by the president in July 1969. Other states were to carry the primary burden for their own defense.[5] A consequence of this position was that few resources would be transferred to sub-Saharan Africa, which was not of primary importance in Kissinger's scheme. In addition, the Western Europeans would be given a free reign on the Continent.

2. The Nature of the Policy

A closer assessment of Nixon and Ford administration policies on the Continent is called for.

Two phases in America's sub-Saharan African policy can be identified during the Nixon-Ford years. The first phase lasted through the April 1974 Portuguese coup, and in a diminished form for a number of months afterwards. This phase was monopolized by the assumptions which flowed from the policy option adopted in response to "National Security Study Memorandum 39" ("NSSM 39") of 1969.[6] The second phase began following the Portuguese coup and culminated with Secretary Kissinger's policy declarations at Lusaka, Zambia in April 1976. This phase was characterized by policy improvisation on the part of Kissinger as the configuration of power in the southern African area and the Horn of Africa was transformed drastically. Earlier policy postures were discarded at an accelerating rate.

Phase one was ushered in by "National Security Study Memorandum 39." In April 1969, a memorandum was issued to the secretary of state, the secretary of defense, and the director of the Central Intelligence Agency from National Security Adviser Kissinger on behalf of the president. This memorandum, "NSSM 39," ordered a review of US policy toward the southern Africa area. The review was to lead to an identification of policy options for this region.[7] The study directed by "NSSM 39" was conducted by an inter-agency group headed by David Newsom, the assistant secretary of state for African affairs.[8] The report of the group listed five options. Four were rejected by Dr. Kissinger and the president.

The first option, which was rejected, would have required a dramatic improvement in relations with the white regimes. This would be carried out without regard to the negative reaction in black ruled states. Economic and strategic ties with the white states would be enhanced.[9] This option may have been included to make the second option appear relatively moderate. Option three was also rejected. It would have maintained the policy of the Johnson administration. Limited sanctions against the Republic of South Africa and Rhodesia would be retained. However, the US would not go beyond these measures. Steps which would jeopardize scientific and military facilities in the area would be avoided.[10] Moreover, option four was discarded. This option entailed a tougher stance toward the white-led governments until they engaged in significant reforms. Force and new sanctions would not be implemented against Portugal and South Africa, but "defensive military equipment" would be sold to black states in the region.[11] Finally, option five was not accepted. It would have removed the US as an active actor from southern African issues. Ties would be diminished with the white controlled states, but the US would not endorse new measures directed against these states.[12]

The option which was approved by President Nixon in early 1970, following a January 1970 recommendation from Kissinger, was option two.[13] This option was constructed on the assumption that any movement toward more inclusive political systems in the southern Africa area would be a slow and deliberate process. Overt confrontation with the whites would be counterproductive, and preclude even limited improvements in racial relations. Therefore, an enhancement of US ties with the whites was suggested in order to usher in incremental changes.[14]

Contrary to the opinion of many critics of option two, it was not simply wishful thinking devoid of any support among analysts familiar with the situation in southern Africa. There was an academic school of thought which believed that it was predicated on sound assumptions.[15] Indeed, an assessment of data available on the strength of the guerilla movements in the southern African area in the 1970 period led to the conclusion that their short-term prospects were poor.[16] What Dr. Kissinger failed to take into account was the cumulative effect of the guerilla wars on the Portuguese political system. Hardly an arcane subject, the CIA had issued memoranda on the subject as early as the beginning of the 1960s.[17] Moreover, David Newsom, assistant secretary for African affairs and head of the inter-agency task force initiative to assess America's southern Africa policy had asked for studies on the topic.[18]

The policy recommendations of option two included the following: first, the maintenance of a public posture critical of the racial policies of the white regimes. This was to be accompanied, however, by an effort to establish a better rapport with the whites. Economic measures which inhibited this effort would be loosened up. Communication would be emphasized. The core concern of black states was actually internal development and, therefore, American economic aid would be increased. Most importantly, the US privately would not object to the development of political structures in southern Africa which would not lead to majority rule.[19]

David Newsom had argued that the acceptance of option two by President Nixon did not produce a major overhaul of our African policy. He asserts that "it is not the wording of option two which is important. It is what was done as a result of that wording. What was done as a result of that wording was very modest."[20] Deputy Assistant Secretary for African Affairs Clyde Ferguson, who served from 1972 to 1973, expressed a contrary opinion. He contended that option two did contribute to significant changes in our African policy.[21]

An overview of this policy reveals that Ferguson is correct. While option two did not revolutionize American policy, it did have a visible impact on American policies on the sub-Continent.

The overriding tenet of America's African policy for the Nixon administration continued to be a desire to maintain close ties between Africa and the West. Therefore, it could be kept out of the orbit of the Soviets and their allies. Yet, Kissinger treated containment as a doctrine in which choices would have to be made between core and noncore interests.[22] He felt even more strongly than most high level policymakers in the previous two administrations that containment in Africa should be practiced largely by America's European allies.

The integral part played by containment in America's Africa policy during Nixon's tenure was expressed by Assistant Secretary Newsom in an interview in 1981. When asked to identify the main components of this policy, he stressed the "general desire" of the United States "to minimize as far as possible the advances of adversaries in Africa . . . "[23] During the administration, official statements incorporated this concern. Frequent references were made to US support of the independence of African states.[24] These references were often accompanied by expressions of concern about the new imperialism emanating from the East. Moreover, calls for US assistance to the Continent were often couched in the language of the East-West conflict. In January 1972 Newsom, speaking in California, raised an alarm over the potential consequences of recent deals between African nations and the Communist powers. The Soviets and the Chinese, he asserted, have "extended more credits to three African countries in the last six months than we have provided through the Agency for International Development in two years."[25]

The Congo (which was renamed Zaire in 1969) was a buffer against the Soviets in central Africa. It followed that the central government of Joseph Mobutu (renamed Mobutu Sese Seko after 1970) had to be supported. Madeline Kalb, in her work *The Congo Cables,* observes that "President Nixon was delighted to work with the anti-Communist Mobutu."[26]

The policy of "communication" and a relaxation of pressures against the Republic of South Africa was influenced by the geopolitical judgment that it was a bulwark against Soviet inroads. As the dominant regional power in the southern Africa area, it possessed the will and the means to protect Western interests. A conscientious effort was made to upgrade US relations with the Republic. In 1970, insurance necessary to finance exports to South Africa was extended from five to ten years by the Export-Import Bank. Visits by South African military personnel to the US were expanded.[27] US aircraft sales to South Africa, ostensibly for commercial usage, rose four-fold between 1967 and 1972. In addition, communications equipment sales to the country tripled from 1967 to 1972.[28]

While the US criticized South Africa's occupation of South-West Africa and took measures to inhibit investment there, it "discouraged" stronger measures.[29]

Similarly, US policy on the Portuguese colonies during the Nixon years was a derivation of its global strategic priorities. Lip service was paid to the desirability of self-determination for the colonies. Newsom, in a September 21, 1971 address, stated that "the people inhabiting the colonies are entitled to . . . self-determination."[30] Nevertheless, the US government did nothing to bar commercial transactions with Portugal which enhanced its military capabilities. The "number of US aircraft and helicopters sold for use in Mozambique increased from a total of $150,000 in sales from 1963 to 1968, to over $14 million in sales for the period of 1969-1972."[31] In 1970, Boeing 707s worth $35 million were delivered to Portugal without limitations on their use as troop transports.[32] The message conveyed to the Portuguese by these transactions was clear. The continuation of Portuguese intransigence on the question of independence for its colonies would not adversely affect its interaction with the US. The administration was somewhat self conscious about its image on the issue of the Portuguese colonies. In June 1972, Newsom asserted that Export-Import Bank credits for American exporters interested in the Portuguese market did not help Portugal in its colonial wars.[33] However, Donald Easum, who served as assistant secretary for African affairs during the 1974-1975 period, reports that behind the scenes, Kissinger was an aggressive advocate of assisting the Portuguese. Just prior to the Portuguese coup in April 1974, he was on the verge of sending the Portuguese jets to suppress the colonial rebellions.[34]

In Rhodesia the internal situation worsened during the Nixon years. In 1969, Rhodesia declared itself a Republic.[35] Subsequently, it stepped up internal repression and showed few signs of accepting majority rule.[36] The US response was tepid. The lack of urgency with which high administration officials addressed the developments in Rhodesia indicated that they had few anxieties about the course of events. The inaction of the administration can be attributed in part to the feeling that Marxism was not an imminent threat in Rhodesia at the beginning of the administration. Why adopt stern measures here when energy should be channeled into the East-West conflict elsewhere? Consequently, the administration moved deliberately and was ambivalent on the Rhodesian issue. It was slow in closing down its consulate in Salisbury when Rhodesia emphatically rejected British authority and became a Republic.[37] Most significantly, its support of sanctions against Rhodesia was weak.[38] David Newsom publicly endorsed majority rule in 1969 and was an ardent supporter of sanctions publicly and privately.[39] Newsom and the African Bureau found themselves isolated within an administration which cared little about expediting movement toward majority rule.

Africa's low status in the hierarchy of US strategic concerns played a part in the Nixon administration's limited commitment of human and physical resources to the Continent. The continued prominence of this second premise of America's African policy was readily apparent shortly after the inception of the administration. Deputy Assistant Secretary Clyde Ferguson noted that Kissinger exhibited interest in Africa only briefly. He did so during the reassessment of America's southern African policy from 1969–1970, and around the time of his April 1976 Lusaka, Zambia speech.[40] *Africa Report* noted in 1974 that with a couple of minor exceptions Kissinger had not delivered "any policy statement" on Africa for almost a year.[41] Ferguson's observation is somewhat overstated. However, the Nixon administration devoted even less high-level attention to sub-Saharan Africa than the Kennedy and Johnson administrations. The Congo and Rhodesia commanded sporadic high level interest during these administrations. Moreover, some resources were forthcoming. This pattern did not survive Nixon's election.

Despite a trip to Africa as vice president and a subsequent speech on the subject which raised the consciousness of a few policy-makers, Nixon had little interest in the political and economic affairs of Africa. To his credit he had displayed humanitarian concern for the breakaway Nigerian state of Biafra during the presidential campaign of 1968.[42] After assuming the presidency, however, Nixon's attention in the foreign arena was directed toward relations between the superpowers, Southeast Asia and the Middle East. This was dictated not only by the urgency of these matters but by Nixon's personal preferences. Moreover, Nixon's alter ego, Henry Kissinger, had a fascination with big-power politics and an empirically weak belief in their ability to manipulate events in the Third World. This predilection did little to enhance the administration's concern with African events. Kennedy had an intellectual curiosity about events in Ghana, Guinea and the Congo. Johnson, under prodding from his advisers, delivered what was intended to be a major speech on Africa in 1966. Nixon did not possess intellectual curiosity about the Continent. Kissinger felt up until the latter half of 1974, at least, that the young black sub-Saharan states were not terribly important to the world power equation.

There were isolated instances of administration attention to the Continent. They included the 1969–1970 deliberations over how to treat southern African issues. Furthermore, in 1970, Secretary of State Rogers made a fifteen day trip to Africa.[43] It was perhaps fitting that the high level official who Kissinger scorned the most would be sent to the Continent. He was an outsider to the small inner council of the administration as displayed by the short-lived nature of the 1969-1970 Rogers plan for the Middle East. Africa's status was hardly better relative to other areas.

Continuing the trend of recent administrations, the Nixon foreign assistance program for sub-Saharan Africa was small. In the three fiscal years through 1975, US Food for Peace, and Agency for International Development help averaged around $250 million per year.[44] This figure was not consistent with the outlines of option two which had called for a somewhat larger increase of aid to the black states.[45]

A perusal of the Nixon administration's treatment of individual issues on the Continent does not change the judgment that it expended little time and few resources on Africa.

Zaire was experiencing a rare period of relative stability during the early years of the administration. Kissinger was a strong supporter theoretically of adjusting American policy to long-term historical trends. The ad hoc approach of policy bureaucrats and lawmakers with legal backgrounds was to be abandoned. In practice, this approach was difficult to implement, especially in the Third World where Kissinger's knowledge of historical patterns was limited. Consequently, improvisation characterized American behavior in the Congo as in much of the Third World. Its leader, Mobutu Sese Seko, was pro-American, and he did not appear to be threatened. Nixon and Kissinger had no inclination to construct imaginative policy approaches here when other crises beckoned.[46]

The Republic of South Africa was the chief beneficiary of the Nixon administration's rejection of confrontation as a mechanism for inducing change in southern Africa. It was hoped that this stance would contribute to the amelioration of the status of blacks in the Republic, and a stabilization of the area. After setting this policy in motion in 1970, however, the top echelon of the administration did not follow up on it to see if the desired policy outcomes were in fact realized. Inertia overtook the policy, and communication became an end into itself. US resources transferred to the Republic, in the absence of a policy framework, did little to facilitate desired change.[47]

On the Portuguese colonies, the administration conducted itself as if Portuguese control would not be jeopardized for the foreseeable future. Continuing the practice of the Johnson administration in its latter years, Nixon officials provided few incentives to the Portuguese to accelerate the self-determination process. The resources that were forthcoming bolstered Portuguese rule. From 1972 through 1973, US aircraft sales to Portugal for use in Mozambique were 75 percent assisted by Export-Import Bank guarantees.[48] This assistance could be interpreted, in part, as a reward for American use of the Azores and Portuguese collaboration with the North Atlantic Treaty Organization.

Finally, on the Rhodesian issue the Nixon administration's behavior was characterized by timidity and a lack of time investment by high officials on the crucial question of sanctions. In 1971, these officials did almost nothing to prevent the passage of the sanctions-busting Byrd Amendment. Similarly, in the 1972 through 1974 period they gave minimal help to congressmen who unsuccessfully sought to repeal it.[49] Anti-Byrd Amendment initiatives were left in the hands of two Assistant Secretaries for African Affairs: David Newsom, followed by Donald Easum, and their deputies. Newsom, Easum, and Deputy Assistant Secretary Clyde Ferguson would later express their disappointment at the indifference displayed by the White House toward the sanctions question.[50] It is possible that had the Watergate scandal not intervened, the Nixon administration, in the period following the April 1974 Portuguese coup, would have devoted more time to Africa and attempted to increase its assistance. This is in fact what occurred during the subsequent presidency of Gerald Ford.

The third premise of America's African policy acquired more prominence during the Nixon administration than it had during the Kennedy and Johnson years. This was the tendency to allow the European allies to set the tone for America's policy on the Continent. As one of Kissinger's world power centers with historical ties to Africa, it was appropriate that Europe assume primary responsibility for the Continent. In so doing, the US could concentrate on interests more vital to its security and economic needs. Specific American policies reflected this position.

On the Republic of South Africa, the US, during the Nixon years, did not endorse punitive measures which would open schisms with its allies, particularly Britain and France.[51] The Kennedy administration's willingness to move more rapidly on the question of sanctions than its major European partners was not repeated during the Nixon years. On the South-West African issue the US reaffirmed its position that South Africa's occupation of the territory was illegal. It did not believe that this state of affairs justified new sanctions.[52]

America was more conscious of Portuguese sensitivities during the Nixon presidency than it had been at any point since the beginning of the 1960s. Nothing resembling the Kennedy administration's censure of the Portuguese at the UN, and punitive reduction of aid in the early 1960s, occurred under Nixon. Arms sales to the Portuguese grew by leaps and bounds.[53]

On Rhodesia, the Nixon administration wavered somewhat from the previous administration's almost unequivocal support of British policy. This was particularly so with regard to sanctions. It granted exceptions to the sanctions in 1970, and exerted little high-level pressure against the Byrd Amendment. Yet, it would be an exaggeration to state that the Nixon administration embarked on a policy independent of the British. They did not challenge the United Kingdom's basic responsibility for Rhodesia.[54]

In October 1969, Assistant Secretary Newsom issued the following statement before the House of Representatives Foreign Affairs Subcommittee on African Affairs. "Primary responsibility for Rhodesia has rested and continues to rest with the United Kingdom, the legal sovereign."[55] In 1971, Newsom reiterated this stance. "The United States ... continues to regard Rhodesia as a dependent territory of the United Kingdom."[56] Moreover, the administration overcame its misgivings and closed down its consulate in Rhodesia in 1970 when the British pressed it to do so. In addition, it opposed efforts in the UN to condemn Britain for its refusal to use force in Rhodesia.[57]

Hence, from 1969 through the Portuguese coup of April 1974, US African policy was characterized by a reliance on European actors to prevent encroachments and assist the Continent economically. The Portuguese coup introduced new powers into the southern African area. A right wing government intent on maintaining direct control over its African colonies indefinitely was replaced by a government eager to end Portugal's massive military involvement on the Continent. Events were soon set in motion in one of Portugal's colonies, Angola, which culminated in independence, a civil war, and the introduction of Cuban troops. Portugal could no longer be relied upon to assume an active role in African affairs. This development was accompanied by an escalation of the guerilla war in Rhodesia and the overthrow of a pro-Western government in Ethiopia in the 1974 to 1975 period. The complacency which had marked the outlook of the upper echelon of the US government on most African questions since the early 1960s, was shattered. The emergence of a string of Marxist governments in sub-Saharan Africa, a scenario dismissed since the early 1960s, was becoming a reality.

The reaction of top US officials to this turn of events was slow, however. The Watergate scandal which led to the resignation of President Nixon in August 1974, and the emergence of Gerald Ford as chief executive sapped their energy. Moreover, Secretary of State Kissinger was not only hampered by the shadow of Watergate, but absorbed by developments in Southeast Asia, the Middle East, and Europe where Portugal itself faced the possibility of a Communist takeover. The centralization of the foreign policy apparatus in Kissinger's hands prevented other officials from initiating a comprehensive response to African events. Finally, America's African policy in the past, with a few notable exceptions, had consisted of passing the buck to the Europeans. When a key European actor abandoned its position on the Continent, a vacuum appeared. American officials were confused about how to fill it.

Yet, by the 1975 to 1976 period, an altered American African policy was taking shape. Under Kissinger's guidance, a policy distinguishable from that which prevailed during the Nixon years was being forged. Kissinger attempted to revise the chief premises of American policy as they had been delineated since 1969.

First, the anti-Soviet thrust of American policy was retained. However, Africa's peripheral status in the context of American global interests was to be changed.

Second, more time was to be spent on Africa by high level officials, and the flow of resources to the Continent was to be increased.

Third, the decline of European influence in Africa forced the US to adopt a higher profile on the Continent.

Fears that Eastern Bloc influence was on the rise in southern Africa and the Horn of Africa evoked a strong reaction on the part of the Ford administration.

The spirit of the times was captured by Kissinger in September 1975, in a toast at a dinner party given at the US Mission to the United Nations. Borrowing a phrase used by Assistant Secretary for African Affairs G. Mennen Williams during the Kennedy administration, Kissinger made the following observation: " 'Africa for the Africans' means Africa for the Africans and not Africa as a hunting ground for alien ambitions."[58] Williams' comment had been construed by many in the early 1960s as a critique of Western European colonialism. By 1975, traditional Western colonialism was no longer a factor in Africa. The activities of the Soviet Union and its proxies was a factor. It was these activities that drew Kissinger's wrath. The tactical policy changes implemented by Kissinger in 1976 can be attributed in part to this search for new means to preclude a growth in Soviet influence. These changes were highlighted in his speech in Lusaka, Zambia on April 25, 1976, in which he "endorsed self-determination, majority rule, and equal rights for the inhabitants of southern Africa."[59] Kissinger revealed his motives for these changes on the same trip where, in a veiled reference to the Soviets, he proclaimed that "external intervention could only diminish African self-determination."[60] In May 1976, before the Senate Committee on Foreign Relations, Kissinger bared his soul, blasting "massive extracontinental interference" in Africa.[61] This interference, from his standpoint, extended from southern Africa to the Horn.

Zaire, while not a focal point of the Ford administration's African interests, retained the ardent backing of its top officials. The brief interval in which it appeared to be on the road to stability had ended abruptly, however. In 1974, sharp increases in oil prices and a precipitous drop in copper prices sent the economy into a tailspin.[62] Moreover, corruption by Mobutu and other officials served to further delegitimize the government.[63] Its days in the shadow of conflicts in Angola and Rhodesia would be short-lived.

Nor were the internal racial policies of the Republic of South Africa a major African concern of Kissinger's. Notwithstanding his comments on behalf of majority rule throughout the region in 1976, there was no indication that he considered white rule in the Republic to be in imminent danger. Kissinger did see South Africa as an actor with the capability to assist the movement of Rhodesia and South-West Africa toward self-determination under governments free of Soviet tutelage. This, in conjunction with his perception of South Africa as a regional anti-Soviet power, prevented him from discarding the policy of communication with the Republic which dated from the acceptance of option two in 1970. Thus, in October 1974, the United States vetoed a resolution in the UN Security Council to expel South Africa.[64] Furthermore, in late 1976, it voted against a UN resolution which labeled South Africa a threat to international peace and security, and called for comprehensive sanctions.[65] Moreover, US commercial interaction with South Africa continued.[66]

There were limited exceptions to the policy of communication. In 1975, the US halted shipments of enriched uranium to South Africa until it accepted provisions of the Nuclear Nonproliferation Treaty.[67]

On another dimension, the US, during Ford's tenure in office, did express reservations about South Africa's policies in South-West Africa (Namibia). It went so far as to support a UN resolution in January 1976 which called on South Africa to accelerate the pace of Namibia's movement toward self-determination.[68] Three months later, the US requested that South Africa enunciate a specific timetable for South-West Africa's independence.[69] Yet, America under Ford energetically opposed undertakings in the United Nations and elsewhere to punish South Africa through economic and political means for its behavior in Namibia.[70]

Among African trouble spots, Kissinger felt Angola had the most serious ramifications for the world balance of power during Ford's presidency. It was here that he attempted to reverse the decline in America's willingness to exert its will abroad. Having just undergone a humiliating defeat in Vietnam, Angola was to be a new testing ground for American resolve. In the words of William Schaufele, who served as assistant secretary of state for African affairs between 1975 and 1977, Angola was seen by high level administration personnel as having "the greatest likelihood of Soviet interest penetration in Africa."[71] When speaking before the Senate Foreign Relations Subcommittee on Africa Affairs in February 1976, Schaufele had asserted that Angola was an example of Soviet sponsored aggression, initiated to change the global configuration of power.[72]

A brief chronology of events in Angola during the mid 1970s is called for. Following the overthrow of the Portuguese regime in April 1974, Angola's move toward independence was swift. In January 1975, a transitional government for the period prior to independence in November 1975 was started. It consisted of three rival guerilla groups. They were the MPLA (Popular Movement for the Liberation of Angola), the FNLA (National Front for the Liberation of Angola), and UNITA (National Union for the Total Independence of Angola).[73] Even at this early juncture, it was clear that a struggle would soon be waged between these antagonistic factions. Kissinger felt it imperative that the US influence the outcome of the struggle. In light of long-term ties between the US and the FNLA, and the Soviet leanings of the MPLA, an administration review board approved a $300,000 program of covert support to the former in January 1975.[74]

By March 1975 the coalition government was in shambles, and fighting raged between the FNLA and the MPLA.[75] The Central Intelligence Agency around this time posed the possibility of significantly stepped up aid to the FNLA and UNITA.[76] After an inter-bureaucratic battle which culminated in the resignation of Assistant Secretary Nathanial Davis, additional covert aid was authorized in July 1975.[77] Kissinger was a fervent backer of this decision. On the ground in Angola, the struggle between the contending factions was heating up. By July Cuban advisers for the MPLA began to trickle into the country. They were accompanied by supplies of Soviet weapons. In August and September 1975, Zairean military units were sent into Angola to assist the FNLA, and South African troops operating on behalf of UNITA made incursions into southern Angola. Simultaneously, Cuban troops arrived in growing numbers.[78]

In September 1975, Secretary Kissinger, at a news conference, called for a negotiated solution to the conflict.[79] His initiatives on behalf of aid to anti-MPLA elements indicated that he believed an MPLA victory could only be averted through military means. In October and November major advances by the South Africans in the south, and Zaire in the north triggered the direct entrance of Cuban troops into battle in large numbers.[80] It was at this point that American will, in Kissinger's estimation, failed once again. In December 1975 the US Senate passed the Tunney Amendment barring further covert aid to Angola.[81] The administration partially circumvented this ban.

Yet, by January 1976 the MPLA, assisted by 10,000 to 12,000 Cuban troops and Soviet weaponry, had gained the upper hand. The FNLA and Zairean troops were in flight, and South African troops left the south.[82]

Kissinger's policy of confronting what he perceived as Soviet proxy forces had failed. Pro-Western forces were beaten, though UNITA would continue to wage a guerilla war in the south. Moreover, MPLA dependence on the Soviet bloc had been enhanced.

Angola convinced Kissinger that in the post-Watergate and post-Vietnam era, any American consensus on behalf of even indirect military operations abroad to maintain the balance of power could not be sustained. The consummate tactician, Kissinger, in 1976 would embark on a new course of action. It had three components. First, he would proclaim America's support of majority rule and racial justice in the southern African area. Second, he would actively promote negotiations to facilitate the movement toward majority rule. Third, he would urge the South Africans to assist the independence process in Namibia and Rhodesia. Kissinger's goals were to discourage the emergence of pro-Soviet regimes on a regional level. Thereby, he could slow the momentum of Soviet successes globally.

Rhodesia was the chief object of Kissinger's new strategy. At Lusaka in 1976, we have seen how he advocated majority rule. He also urged that independence in Rhodesia be realized within two years of the end of negotiations, and asserted that the US would strengthen its sanctions policy to help this process.[83] In September 1976, Rhodesian minority leader Smith announced his support of majority rule, following the timetable of the Americans and the British.[84]

By 1975 it was evident that Kissinger recognized that more time and resources would have to be expended on Africa if further Soviet inroads were to be prevented. Hence, in 1975, both the Forty Committee, a high level group which passed judgment on covert operations overseas, and a task force headed by Assistant Secretary Davis examined America's Angolan policy.[85] This demonstrated greater high level interest in Africa than had occurred during the previous administration. Most importantly, Kissinger participated in deliberations on Angola. His attention to African affairs reached its height in 1976 when he traveled to the Continent to announce a new phase in America's policy.[86]

Though Kissinger's discovery of African issues was criticized by the presidential candidate Jimmy Carter in 1976 as an attempt to influence American black voters, his motives were more complex. He saw Angola, and to a somewhat lesser extent Ethiopia, as efforts by the Soviet Union to exploit Third World trouble spots during a period of American paralysis abroad. A refusal to meet this challenge would encourage Soviet adventurism throughout the world.

Kissinger's interest in the outcome of the conflict in Rhodesia and Namibia represented a maturation of his treatment of African issues. Though his actions on these issues were cut short by Ford's election defeat in 1976, he skillfully manipulated bilateral and third party channels including the Republic of South Africa and Britain in dealing with them. Kissinger, the student of power politics, had finally applied his considerable abilities to the African sub-Continent.

The Ford administration also attempted to increase the flow of physical resources to Africa. American commercial cooperation with South Africa continued.[87]

In 1976, the administration sent aid to anti-MPLA forces, and unsuccessfully sought to increase the aid.[88] It is significant that American involvement in Angola did not entail the introduction of American military personnel in even a secondary capacity. Kissinger felt an American consensus could not be formed around even a highly constrained use of American military personnel. He asked for covert aid.

Finally, promises of economic assistance were included as part of the American-British package for assisting the independence process in Rhodesia. As articulated by William Rogers (then serving as undersecretary for economic affairs) in September 1976, it was to include help to upgrade industrial, mineral, and agricultural production.[89] Moreover, Kissinger asserted at a news conference in September 1976 that US aid would be extended to white settlers who wanted to depart or remain in Rhodesia.[90] Following independence, financial assistance was also to be given to Mozambique and other states adversely affected by the war in Rhodesia.[91]

America did acquire a higher profile in Africa during the Ford years. It no longer held itself hostage to European whims on the Continent. On many issues, however, cooperation with the Western allies continued.

On the question of South Africa, the US joined with the British and French to rebuff overtly punitive measures. Among them were efforts to expel it from the world body.[92]

Portugal's internal turmoil following the 1974 coup influenced Kissinger's decision to seek greater American involvement in Angola. It was accompanied, however, by the introduction of Zaire and South Africa into the conflict.

American policy in Rhodesia under Ford was coordinated with that of the British, though the British became increasingly outspoken on the question of independence. Kissinger mentioned during his Lusaka speech that the US supported the British proposals for Rhodesia.[93] In addition, his promises of financial help, both at Lusaka and on his return to the US, were publicized as joint ventures with Britain and other parties.[94]

The onset of the Carter administration in January 1977 signaled the end of eight years of Republican dominance of the White House. During this period, the chief tenets of American foreign policy toward sub-Saharan Africa had been modified. This policy had evolved from detachment, if not indifference toward African affairs, to relatively active involvement.

3. Factors Behind the Policy

The forces behind the development of this policy must now be addressed. Our assessment will begin with bureaucratic forces. A few salient features of the foreign policy bureaucracy of the Nixon and Ford administrations deserve delineation.

First, the bureaucracy was highly centralized. In effect, the two presidents of this era, and Kissinger made the crucial foreign policy decisions. Centralization reached its height during the Nixon administration.

Second, deliberations on foreign policy matters for eight years were influenced by Kissinger's globalist philosophy. The oversights as well as the chief components of this philosophy helped to determine the contours of America's African policy.

Third, there was resistance to Kissinger within the bureaucracy. There is little evidence that it significantly affected foreign policy outcomes.

During Nixon's presidency, Kissinger sought to implement a selective approach to containment in which regional actors would adopt greater responsibility. In sub-Saharan Africa, the Western Europeans and the South Africans were to play the role of policemen. Bureaucratic challenges to this philosophy were easily suppressed.

The first challenge came during the 1969–1970 review of America's southern African policy. Members of the State Department African Bureau largely opposed a major change in the current policy. They had few allies. Among their most vigorous adversaries was the Defense Department.[95] It favored a stance which would strengthen US strategic ties with the Portuguese and South Africans. This view coincided with Kissinger's. In early 1970, Nixon accepted his recommendation that the US adopt a policy (option two) of relaxing pressures against the white regimes.[96]

Attempts were made to inhibit the application of option two to individual issues. These attempts were spearheaded by second-level officials in the African Bureau including Deputy Assistant Secretary Clyde Ferguson and members of the International Organization Bureau.[97] They failed to slow the shipment of equipment to the Portuguese which could be used militarily in the territories. By early 1974, approval of the shipment of jet fighters appeared imminent.[98] Moreover, African Bureau officials mounted a campaign to repeal the Byrd Amendment. They received little assistance from the White House.[99] Chief of Staff Bob Haldeman and staff member Patrick Buchanan stonewalled requests for help on the sanctions question.[100]

A third challenge to Kissinger's African position came from Assistant Secretary for African Affairs Donald Easum, who assumed his post in early 1974. He wrote a report which warned of the negative consequences for America's relations with black Africa if it sold jet fighters to the Portuguese. He sought repeal of the Byrd Amendment and suggested that funds go to the new left wing government in Mozambique. Finally, Easum publicly asserted that there were circumstances in which the US would support the expulsion of South Africa from the UN. His display of independence earned Kissinger's wrath, and he was dismissed in late 1974.[101]

Kissinger's power in foreign affairs did not dissipate when Ford became president in August 1974. Ford, inexperienced in foreign policy, relied on Kissinger's expertise. Kissinger did begin to modify his tactics. He moved toward an endorsement of a more assertive role in containing the Eastern Bloc and its allies. Kissinger successively supported covert and open mechanisms for realizing this role. It was the covert approach which led to a new test of his control of the foreign policy apparatus. In early 1975, the new Assistant Secretary for African Affairs, Nathaniel Davis, was given the responsibility of heading a task force to examine options in Angola. It was clear that Kissinger favored large-scale assistance to anti-MPLA factions. Davis's judgment conflicted with Kissinger's. In May 1975, Davis sent a memorandum to Kissinger which argued that US support for UNITA would be risky because of its ties to South Africa. Davis's subsequent task force report expressed a preference for diplomatic and political initiatives in Angola as opposed to covert military aid. The anxiety was expounded that additional military aid would trigger a reciprocal response from the Soviets. The Central Intelligence Agency opposed Davis's stance. Kissinger also found his position unacceptable. Covert military aid was approved, and by Labor Day 1975 Davis's intended resignation was public knowledge.[102]

Davis later observed that Kissinger's "intellect and will dominated the Department of State."[103] This observation could be extended to the entire executive foreign policy hierarchy, and applied to the period which encompassed the terms of two presidents. Kissinger's mastery over the foreign policy machinery of the executive branch played a major part in determining America's African policy.

Kissinger could not implement his philosophy in a vacuum. His initiatives were affected by domestic and geopolitical forces.

Domestically, lobbyists, Congress and public opinion interacted to help define the policy which emerged.

The efficacy of conservative lobbyists relative to liberal lobbyists remained a reality. The liberal American Committee on Africa (ACOA) displayed its frailties by failing to take note of the presence of the Byrd Amendment on the floor of the Senate in September 1971. Liberal church groups and other organizations which depended on the ACOA for information were not alerted to this development.[104]

The major lobby groups from the non-conservative side of the spectrum in the 1969 to 1976 period were the Biafran lobby and Trans-Africa.

The Biafran lobby was composed of a wide array of groups concerned about starvation in the breakaway Nigerian state of Biafra. For a few months in late 1968 and early 1969, it managed to achieve a high profile. Yet many of its constituent groups possessed neither the will nor the political savvy to strive effectively for systemic changes in America's African policy. Nor did the Biafran lobby have a strong financial base. Satisfied with humanitarian gestures by the Nixon administration, it faded away as a political force in 1969.[105]

In September 1976, the Congressional Black Caucus sponsored a conference on Africa.[106] The first modern black lobby group devoted exclusively to African affairs, Trans-Africa, emerged from the conference. It was not incorporated until July 1977, however, and was not a variable in the domestic political scene during Ford's presidency.[107]

The weakness of the ACOA, the ephemeral nature of the Biafran lobby, and Trans-Africa's late arrival meant that conservative lobby groups once again monopolized the realm of pressure group politics. Foote Mineral, Union Carbide, and Anglo-American Trust, among others, financed lobbyists promoting conservative viewpoints on southern African issues.[108]

The asymmetry of the influence of liberal and conservative lobbyists meant that Kissinger's benign approach to the continuance of Western European and white hegemony in parts of the sub-Continent between 1969 and 1974 could proceed without hindrance from organized pressure groups.

Nor did Congress and the public at large pose impediments to the Nixon administration's African policy.

In Congress, liberals were preoccupied with non-African questions. On the few occasions when African issues arose, they proved themselves to be disorganized compared to their conservative foes. One of these occasions was in 1971 when the Byrd Amendment passed the Senate. Conservative Senator Harry Byrd of Virginia outmaneuvered Senate liberals.[109] Playing on sensitivities about US dependence on Soviet chrome, and adeptly using his encyclopedic knowledge of parliamentary procedures, Byrd steered his amendment to passage in the Senate in October 1971.[110] Four liberal presidential candidates did not even vote when the amendment passed.[111] With the exception of Charles Diggs of Michigan, members of the Congressional Black Caucus exerted little energy on the Byrd Amendment issue. An aide to one black congressman stated: "The issue came up pretty rapidly and sort of caught us by surprise. And it was not a terribly important issue."[112] In November 1971 Nixon signed the Byrd Amendment into law.[113] The Watergate scandal of 1974, combined with external events, did lead to a resurgence of liberals in Congress. This was reflected in the December 1975 passage of the Tunney Amendment followed by the Clark Amendment in 1976. These amendments prohibited additional covert assistance to Angola.[114]

Public opinion on Africa was even more inchoate than that of Congress. African issues, with the exception of Biafra, neither mobilized the public in sizable numbers nor contributed to the legitimacy or illegitimacy of national figures.

It can be concluded that Congress and public opinion over the duration of the 1960–1977 period had little impact on the philosophical thrust of America's African policy. They did set parameters on the initiatives the executive branch could take on the Continent. The transfer of resources was never a popular notion and military intervention, direct or indirect, even less so.

Geopolitical factors shed relatively more light on the evolution of America's African policy from 1969 to 1977. Four salient geopolitical factors stand out for the 1969–1974 period.

First, Africa's minimal strategic importance for the US in a global context, and the limited nature of Soviet and Chinese encroachments on the Continent. In 1969–1970, the interagency group reviewing southern African policy reaffirmed an observation which had not been revised since the Kennedy presidency. It asserted in its report that "although the US has various interests in the area, it has none which could be classified as vital security interests."[115] Some concern was expressed about access to South African airfields, seaports, and the Cape Route. The consensus of the review group, however, was that these were not central interests of the US.[116] Nor was Africa a major concern of the Soviets and Communist Chinese at this time. Soviet political analysts had long since revised their belief of the early 1960s that parts of Africa were ripe for revolution.[117] Members of the Politburo felt likewise, for Soviet activity on the Continent was highly circumscribed. It included arms supplies to Egypt, and later to Uganda's Idi Amin and Libya's Colonel Qaddafi.[118] Guinea and Congo-Brazzaville were also recipients of Soviet assistance. None of these states possessed anything resembling the vanguard party of the Soviet Union. The Communist Chinese had enhanced their ties with the Tanzanians and Zaire, but had little leverage over the policies of these states.[119]

A second geopolitical characteristic of the 1969–1974 span was the continuing military role played by Western Europeans on the Continent. The French intervened when their interests were assaulted, and the Portuguese were immersed in ongoing conflicts. A National Security Council study growing out of "NSSM 39" did not foresee any major successes for the anti-Portuguese guerillas over the short-term.[120]

Finally, the administration was preoccupied with Southeast Asia and the Middle East between 1969 and 1974.

Kissinger's African policy was attuned to these factors. Thus, little time and aid was expended on the Continent, and containment was to be left in the hands of the Europeans and South Africa. In the short span of 1974–1975, the geopolitical picture underwent drastic change. The Portuguese and Ethiopian governments fell, and the Ian Smith regime in Rhodesia appeared increasingly tenuous. From southern Africa to the Horn, indigenous Marxists, in some cases backed by Cuban troops, were emerging as the new power brokers. These events coincided with the fall of pro-Western governments in Southeast Asia, and what appeared to be a rising tide of popularity for Western Europe's Communist parties.

Kissinger felt that the emerging international environment made it imperative for America to take an active part in African affairs, both in resource allocation and in the diplomatic arena. He indicated at a news conference in September 1976 that the consequences of radicalization in Africa would be serious for Europe and the Middle East.[121]

Kissinger's perception of the international configuration of power was influenced by his cultural values. Though initially an outsider to the establishment which had dominated US foreign policy in the post-World War II era, he shared its disdain for totalitarianism. As a refugee from Nazi Germany, he was well aware of the human suffering engendered by highly centralized regimes with messianic pretensions, regardless of their ideological coloration. Yet, as a student of nineteenth century power politics, he was less grounded in moral absolutism than some of his predecessors. This endowed him with the flexibility and willingness to revamp his policies, which they had not possessed. Hence, the changes we have described in 1970, 1975 and 1976. There were inconsistencies in Kissinger's pragmatism, however. His aversion to the new revolutionary charismatic leaders of the Third World prevented him from reaching accomodations with leaders in Africa which would have complemented his goals in the realm of power politics. The foremost of these goals was limiting the growth of Soviet influence.

A few words about economic factors and their effect on the African policy of the Nixon-Ford era deserve mention. Three patterns can be discerned.

First, spurred by a precipitous rise in oil prices, trade with black Africa grew faster than trade with South Africa during this period.[122] This was offset in part, however, by a sharper rise in US investment in South Africa than in black Africa. In 1968, US investment in South Africa was 25.8 percent of all investment on the Continent. By 1973 it had risen to 30.4 percent.[123] The percentage rose again in 1974 as the Nigerian government increased its management of oil resources.[124]

Second, in a global context, Africa remained unimportant as a recipient of US investment and as a trading partner.[125]

Third, it is possible to identify members of the White House staff during the 1969–1977 period with long standing links to companies with interests in South Africa and the Portuguese colonies.[126] Yet, this observation does not apply to the pivotal policy makers of this period, namely, Nixon, Ford and Kissinger.

What we learn from these patterns is that an examination of gross economic figures or personalistic economic ties does not lead to any simple conclusions about why our African policy developed the way it did.

Therefore, our bureaucratic and geopolitical models emerge as the best explanatory frameworks for understanding the evolution of America's African policy during the Nixon-Ford years. While the policies were an outgrowth of bureaucratic interaction, they were a response to geopolitical variables. Domestic, cultural, and economic factors placed parameters on the policies which could be undertaken.

4. The Effectiveness of the Policy

Judgment can now be passed on the degree to which the African policies of the Nixon and Ford administrations fulfilled America's security needs globally and regionally. The two criteria we have cited in earlier chapters for an effective policy pose no conflict with Kissinger's own criteria. First, a policy which lowers the probability of regimes hostile to the US, particularly pro-Soviet regimes, from appearing. Second, the maintenance of an orderly international system which does not jeopardize US political and economic values.

An overview of the 1969–1977 period reveals that the two administrations failed dramatically to meet these criteria. When the White House awoke in 1976 to institute policy changes, serious damage had already been rendered to US interests.

Inertia characterized US policy toward Zaire as unquestioning support of Mobutu continued. Even when financial problems and corruption reached a new peak in 1974, few new wrinkles were introduced into this policy. Moreover, the groundwork was laid for the invasions of Shaba province in 1977 and 1978, as the US encouraged Mobutu's support of the militarily and politically inept FNLA.

In the southern African area the policies which emanated from "NSSM-39" were an almost unmitigated disaster.

On the Republic of South Africa, the policy of communication with the government reaped limited dividends. It did exert pressure on Rhodesia in the latter part of the Ford administration to negotiate more seriously on the issue of majority rule. Moreover, progress was made in 1976 on nudging South Africa toward discussions on South-West Africa's status.[127] However, the question remained whether this policy contributed to Afrikaner illusions about their own longevity, therefore increasing the possibility of a racial Armageddon on the sub-Continent. The study which emerged from "NSSM-39," however, exaggerated the quiescent nature of the South Africa black population. This view was not changed after other premises of option two were rendered obsolete by the events of 1974. Violence with hundreds of casualties did erupt in 1976 in South Africa, perhaps a harbinger of the future. More ominously, just a few years after the end of the Ford administration, sabotage operations acquired a new momentum within the nation.

On Rhodesia, the indifference of the top echelon of the administration to the Byrd Amendment had negative repercussions. Regionally, it prolonged the war between the Smith government and its adversaries, giving Smith the impression that the US, if not fully supportive of his actions, was certainly not hostile. Globally, it had an adverse impact on US credibility as a partner in international agreements.[128] It was not until 1976 that Kissinger placed his support firmly behind the principle of majority rule in Rhodesia.

We are now brought to the Portuguese colonies. The errors of the administration were threefold here.

First, a failure to adequately monitor the situation in the colonies and Portugal from 1969 through early 1974. A former CIA operative reports that the US did not even have its own intelligence agents in Angola from the late 1960s until 1975.[129] Moreover, intelligence data on the weakness of the Portuguese government itself which had been coming in since the early 1960s, was ignored in the policy calculations of the Nixon administration.[130] Thus, the administration constructed a policy for the Portuguese colonies based on faulty premises which neglected field data. When the Portuguese government fell in 1974, the Nixon administration was taken by surprise. It had no policy alternatives, and only limited outdated contacts with the factions contending for control in Angola.

95

A second error was Kissinger's ultimate decision to give military assistance to the FNLA and UNITA. As Nathanial Davis pointed out, Kissinger should have known that such an initiative would trigger a reciprocal response on the part of the Soviets.[131] In the post-Watergate era and waning days of Vietnam, Kissinger should have known that the US could not match Soviet military assistance in the country. Kissinger ignored these facts and compounded the error by encouraging the South Africans to enter the country. In so doing, the anti-MPLA forces were further delegitimized.

The final mistake was to refuse to recognize the MPLA government. This was the only viable mechanism available to Kissinger in 1976 which could have somewhat diminished the MPLA dependence on the Soviet bloc.

As the Ford administration left office in January 1977, this was the strategic picture in Africa. The Congolese faced an impending invasion from Angola; an invasion which only European intervention would help to stem. The Republic of South Africa was no closer to recognizing the need for systemic internal changes. In fact, the machinery of repression had been stepped up with the uprisings in the black township of Soweto and elsewhere. Despite earlier hopes that the Rhodesian war would soon be over, it continued. In Angola, thousands of Cuban troops introduced a new source of instability into the southern African area. New Marxist governments were emplaced in Angola, Mozambique, Guinea-Bissau, and Ethiopia. While even a major change in US policy could not have averted some of these developments, their negative impact on US security interests could have been mitigated.

The tragedy of the Nixon-Ford years is that policies could have been forged which would have more effectively met US security needs and not have been incompatible with the flexible balance of power philosophy of Henry Kissinger. The very centralization of power which characterized the Nixon and Ford White Houses, and the relative insulation of African issues from major domestic constraints, gave Kissinger the leeway to formulate a better African policy. As it was, Africa was neglected for five years before he turned his attention to the Continent. By this time, US security interests had already been seriously compromised.

NOTES TO CHAPTER FOUR

1. Gaddis, *Strategies of Containment*, pp. 302–3.
2. Ibid., p. 287.
3. Ibid.
4. Ibid., p. 280.
5. Ibid., pp. 298–99, 304–6.
6. Henry Kissinger, National Security Study Memorandum 39, "Southern Africa," 10 April 1969, John F. Kennedy Presidential Library, Boston.
7. Ibid., p. 1.
8. Lake, *Tar Baby Option*, pp. 126–27.
9. Mohammed A. El-Khawas and Barry Cohen, eds., *The Kissinger Study of Southern Africa, National Security Study Memorandum 39* (Westport, Connecticut: Lawrence Hill and Co., 1976), pp. 103–4.
10. Ibid., pp. 109–10.
11. Ibid., p. 112.
12. Ibid., p. 114.
13. Lake, *Tar Baby Option*, p. 130.
14. El-Khawas and Cohen, *Kissinger Study of Southern Africa*, p. 105.
15. In the late 1960s and early 1970s political science literature appeared which incorporated some of the assumptions held by the advocates of option two. These assumptions included the observation that any erosion of white control in the southern African area would probably be a slow process. See John Marcum, "The Exile Condition and Revolutionary Effectiveness: Southern African Liberation Movements," in *Southern Africa in Perspective: Essays in Regional Politics*, eds. Christian Potholm and Richard Dale (New York City: Free Press, 1972), p. 275; and Charles W. Peterson, "The Military Balance in Southern Africa," in *Southern Africa in Perspective: Essays in Regional Politics*, eds. Christian Potholm and Richard Dale (New York City: Free Press, 1972), pp. 311–17.
16. El-Khawas and Cohen, *Kissinger Study of Southern Africa*, pp. 152–56.
17. Central Intelligence Agency, "Portuguese Outlook and its Political Implications," pp. 1–7.
18. Personal Interview, David Newsom, Georgetown University School of Foreign Service, Washington, DC, 8 December 1981.
19. El-Khawas and Cohen, *Kissinger Study of Southern Africa*, pp. 106–7.
20. Interview, Newsom.
21. Personal Interview, Clyde Ferguson, Harvard Law School, Cambridge, 14 January 1983.
22. Gaddis, *Strategies of Containment*, pp. 277–78, 283, 298–99.
23. Interview, Newsom.
24. An expression of US support for the independence of African states can be found in the following source: US, Department of State, Bureau of Public Affairs, Arrival Statement by William Rogers in Addis Ababa, Ethiopia, "Secretary Rogers Visits Africa," 11 February 1970, *Department of State Bulletin* 62 (23 March 1970): 370.
25. US, Department of State, Bureau of Public Affairs, Address by David Newsom, "Aid to Africa—A Moral and Economic Necessity," 22 January 1972, *Department of State Bulletin* 66 (14 February 1972): 201.
26. Kalb, *Congo Cables*, p. 379.
27. Edgar Lockwood, "National Security Study Memorandum 39 and the Future of US

Policy Toward Southern Africa," *Issue: A Quarterly Journal of Africanist Opinion* 4 (Fall 1974): 67.

28. Ibid., p. 65.

29. US, Department of State, Bureau of Public Affairs, Address by John Stevenson, Legal Adviser, "US Oral Statement on Continued Presence of South Africa in Namibia," 9 March 1971, *Department of State Bulletin* 64 (26 April 1971): 547; On executive branch discouragement of strong measures against South Africa see Lockwood, "National Security Study Memorandum 39 and the Future of US Policy," pp. 65–66.

30. US, Department of State, Bureau of Public Affairs, Address by David Newsom, "A Look at African Issues at the United Nations," 21 September 1971, *Department of State Bulletin* 65 (11 October 1971): 377.

31. Lockwood, "National Security Study Memorandum 39 and the Future of US Policy," p. 67.

32. Ibid.

33. US, Department of State, Bureau of Public Affairs, Address by David Newsom, "Southern Africa: Constant Themes in US Policy," 28 June 1972, *Department of State Bulletin* 67 (24 July 1972): 122.

34. Personal Interview, Donald Easum, African-American Institute, New York City, 23 March 1982.

35. Lake, *Tar Baby Option,* p. 135.

36. For an overview of events in Rhodesia during this period see Lake, *Tar Baby Option,* pp. 20–27.

37. Ibid., p. 135.

38. Interview, Newsom; Interview, Easum; and Interview, Ferguson.

39. In an interview with the author in 1981 Newsom stressed that he was a strong supporter of retaining sanctions against Rhodesia during his tenure as assistant secretary. Interview, Newsom. Moreover, testifying before the Subcommittee on Africa of the House Committee on Foreign Affairs in late 1969 he endorsed majority rule and sanctions. See the following source: US, Department of State, Bureau of Public Affairs, Statement by David Newsom, "Department Presents Views on Southern Rhodesia," 17 October 1969, *Department of State Bulletin* 61 (17 November 1969): 422–23.

40. Interview, Ferguson.

41. Goler Teal Butcher, "US-Africa Relations: America's New Opportunity," *Africa Report* 20 (September–October 1974): 17.

42. Herbert Howe, "Event, Issue, Reconsideration: The United States and the Nigerian Civil War" (Ph.D Dissertation, Harvard University, 1978), p. 186.

43. In January 1970 Rogers visited Africa. See Rogers, "Secretary Rogers Visits Africa," pp. 365–80.

44. US, Department of State, Bureau of Public Affairs, Address by William Schaufele, "United States Economic Relations with Africa," 18 February 1975, *Department of State Bulletin* 74 (8 March 1975): 297.

45. References to option two's endorsement of increased aid to the black African states can be found in El-Khawas and Cohen, *Kissinger Study of Southern Africa,* pp. 106, 108.

46. On the Nixon administration's attitude toward Mobutu see Kalb, *Congo Cables,* p. 379. On Joseph Mobutu's decision to change his name to Mobutu Sese Seko in 1977 following an African authenticity campaign see Kalb, *Congo Cables,* p. 380.

47. On the Republic of South Africa's intensification of components of apartheid during the 1969–1974 period see the *New York Times;* and *Issue: A Quarterly Journal of*

Africanist Opinion (Waltham, Massachusetts: Brandeis University African Studies Association).

48. Lockwood, "National Security Study Memorandum 39 and the Future of US Policy," p. 67.
49. Interview, Newsom.
50. Interview, Newsom; Interview, Easum; and Interview, Ferguson.
51. An illustration of the US refusal to support firm punitive measures directed against South Africa can be found in the following source: US, Department of State, Bureau of Public Affairs, Statement by Stephen Hess, US Representative to UN, "US Reaffirms Commitment to Self Determination and Independence for Namibia," 10 December 1977, *Department of State Bulletin* 76 (17 January 1977): 44.
52. Newsom, "Southern Africa: Constant Themes in US Policy," p. 121.
53. Interview, Easum; and Lockwood, "National Security Study Memorandum 39 and the Future of United States Policy," p. 67.
54. US, Department of State, Bureau of Public Affairs, Statement by David Newsom, "Department Presents Views on Southern Rhodesia," 17 October 1969, *Department of State Bulletin* 61 (17 November 1969): 422.
55. Ibid.
56. US, Department of State, Bureau of Public Affairs, Statement by David Newsom, "Department Reviews US Position on Southern Rhodesia," 7 July 1971, *Department of State Bulletin* 65 (26 July 1971): 114.
57. US, Department of State, Bureau of Public Affairs, Statement by US Representative to United Nations Charles Yost, "US Deplores Minority Rule in Southern Rhodesia," 24 June 1969, *Department of State Bulletin* 61 (21 July 1969): 58.
58. US, Department of State, Bureau of Public Affairs, Toast by Henry Kissinger, "The United States and Africa: Strengthening the Relationship," 23 September 1975, *Department of State Bulletin* 73 (13 October 1975): 572.
59. M. Crawford Young, "Multilateralizing United States African Policy," *Harvard University Conference on United States Policy Toward Africa* (Cambridge: Harvard University Committee on African Studies, 1981), p. 359.
60. US, Department of State, Bureau of Public Affairs, Address by Henry Kissinger, "America and Africa," 30 April 1976, *Department of State Bulletin* 74 (31 May 1976): 684.
61. US, Department of State, Bureau of Public Affairs, Statement by Henry Kissinger, "The United States and Africa," 13 May 1976, *Department of State Bulletin* 74 (7 June 1976): 715.
62. Kalb, *Congo Cables*, p. 380.
63. Ibid., p. 387.
64. Donald Easum, "United States Policy Toward South Africa," *Issue: A Quarterly Journal of Africanist Opinion* 5 (Fall 1975): 69.
65. Hess, "US Reaffirms Commitment to Independence for Namibia," p. 44.
66. Easum, "United States Policy Toward South Africa," p. 68.
67. Robert Rotberg, *Suffer the Future: Policy Choices in Southern Africa* (Cambridge: Harvard University Press, 1982), p. 148.
68. US, Department of State, Bureau of Public Affairs, Address by Henry Kissinger, "United States Policy on Southern Africa," 27 April 1976, *Department of State Bulletin* 74 (31 May 1976): 676.
69. Ibid.
70. US reluctance to punish South Africa was reflected in its opposition to initiatives within the United Nations to declare the Namibian situation a threat to the peace,

and grant observer status to the South West African Peoples Organization. See the following source: Hess, "US Reaffirms Commitment to Independence for Namibia," pp. 44–45.

71. Personal Interview, William Schaufele, Harvard University, Cambridge, 27 October 1981.
72. US, Department of State, Bureau of Public Affairs, Statement by William Schaufele, "The African Dimension of the Angolan Conflict," 6 February 1976, *Department of State Bulletin* 74 (1 March 1976): 281.
73. Stockwell, *A CIA Story*, pp. 47–48.
74. Ibid., p. 110.
75. Ibid., p. 48.
76. Nathaniel Davis, "The Angola Decision of 1975: A Personal Memoir," *Foreign Affairs* 57 (Fall 1978): 110–11.
77. Ibid., p. 121.
78. Ibid.
79. Kissinger, "The United States and Africa: Strengthening the Relationship," p. 574.
80. Davis, "The Angola Decision," p. 122.
81. Ibid., p. 119.
82. Ibid., p. 122.
83. Kissinger, "United States Policy on Southern Africa," pp. 674–75.
84. US, Department of State, Bureau of Public Affairs, Statement by William Rogers, "The Search for Peace in Southern Africa," 30 September 1976, *Department of State Bulletin* 75 (25 October 1976): 533.
85. Davis, "*The Angola Decision,*" pp. 110–11.
86. Kissinger, "American Policy on Southern Africa," p. 674.
87. See *Issue: A Quarterly Journal of Africanist Opinion* (Waltham, Massachusetts: Brandeis University African Studies Association, 1974–1975).
88. Davis, "The Angola Decision," p. 110.
89. Rogers, "The Search for Peace in Southern Africa," p. 534.
90. US, Department of State, Bureau of Public Affairs, Henry Kissinger, "Secretary Kissinger's News Conference of September 11," 11 September 1976, *Department of State Bulletin* 75 (4 October 1976): 409.
91. Kissinger, "American Policy on Southern Africa," p. 675.
92. Easum, "United States Policy Toward South Africa," p. 69.
93. Kissinger, "US Policy on Southern Africa," p. 674.
94. Ibid., p. 675; Kissinger, "Kissinger's News Conference of September 11," p. 410; and Rogers, "The Search for Peace in Southern Africa," p. 534.
95. Lake, *Tar Baby Option*, pp. 125–26.
96. Ibid., p. 130.
97. Interview, Ferguson.
98. Interview, Easum.
99. Interview, Newsom.
100. Lake, *Tar Baby Option*, p. 255.
101. Interview, Easum; and Bruce Oudes, "The Sacking of the Secretary," *Africa Report* 20 (January–February 1975): 17–19.
102. Davis, *The Angola Decision*, pp. 110–14.
103. Ibid., p. 123.
104. Lake, *Tar Baby Option*, p. 233.
105. Howe, "The United States and the Nigerian Civil War," pp. 79–186.
106. William Trautman, "Trans-Africa: A Case Study of the Politics of a Black Foreign

Policy Lobby in Light of the Development of Black Consciousness and Black Politicization in the US," (Thesis, Harvard University, 1979), p. 71.

107. Trautman, "Trans-Africa: A Case Study," p. 2.
108. Lake, *Tar Baby Option,* pp. 230-31; and Interview, Ferguson.
109. Ibid., pp. 199-213.
110. Ibid., p. 211.
111. Ibid.
112. Ibid., pp. 231-32.
113. Ibid., p. 213.
114. Davis, "The Angola Decision," p. 119; and Steven Roberts, "Senate Votes to End Ban on Aid to Angolan Rebels," *New York Times,* 1 October 1981, p. A-9.
115. El-Khawas and Cohen, *The Kissinger Study of Southern Africa,* p. 89.
116. Ibid., pp. 122-23.
117. For an overview of the changing assessments by Soviet analysts of Africa's prospects for revolution see Charles, *The Soviet Union and Africa.*
118. Colin Legum, "The Soviet Union, China and the West in Southern Africa," *Foreign Affairs* 54 (July 1976): 749.
119. Ibid., p. 749.
120. El-Khawas and Cohen, *The Kissinger Study of Southern Africa,* pp. 152-56.
121. Kissinger, "Kissinger's News Conference of September 11," p. 411.
122. Lockwood, "National Security Study Memorandum 39 and the Future of US Policy," p. 67.
123. Ibid., p. 66.
124. Schaufele, "United States Economic Relations with Africa," p. 296.
125. US, Department of State, Bureau of Public Affairs, Address by Donald Easum "African-American Commerce: Potential for Mutual Benefit," 17 May 1974, *Department of State Bulletin* 70 (17 June 1974): 658.
126. Interview, Ferguson.
127. Interview, Schaufele.
128. An elaboration of this point can be found in Lake, *Tar Baby Option,* pp. 239-64.
129. Stockwell, *A CIA Story,* p. 52.
130. Central Intelligence Agency, "Portuguese Outlook and its Political Implications," p. 3.
131. Davis, "The Angola Decision," pp. 112-14.

CHAPTER FIVE

The Carter Administration:
THE RHETORIC OF CHANGE ACCOMPANIES MODERATE POLICIES:
January 20, 1977
Through
January 20, 1981

1. Opening Observations
and the Nature of the Policy

With Jimmy Carter's emergence as the first president from the deep South since the nineteenth century in early 1977, the belief was expressed in many circles that America's African policy would undergo fundamental changes. This belief did not arise from any definitive sense of Carter's position on the American ideological spectrum. He had not run as a relatively radical third force in American politics as Henry Wallace had done in 1948. Nor did he represent the left-wing of the Democratic party as George McGovern had in 1972. Expectations of a major foreign policy overhaul emanated from three sources.

First, Carter brought a new freshness and vigor to the White House. He had run as an outsider contending that he would end the secrecy and Machiavellian machinations that had characterized the foreign policy apparatus since the beginning of the Kissinger era in 1969. Many felt that change was in the air. Jimmy Carter would take small town American idealism and apply it to the international arena. If the administration was not the dawning of a new Camelot, perhaps it marked the onset of a less cynical era.

Second, the rhetoric of the Carter administration in its virginal days conveyed the impression that significant policy revisions were probable. In a global context "candidate Carter" had stated "we must replace balance of power politics with world order politics . . . " He had "called for a 5 to 7 percent cut in Pentagon spending and for vast arms reductions around the world."[1] This rhetoric persisted during the administration's first days. On a regional level, in May 1977 Carter asserted at Notre Dame that "Americans were committed to majority rule in all of southern Africa."[2] Around this time, Vice President Walter Mondale, following a meeting with the South African Prime Minister stated: "Every citizen in South Africa should have the right to vote and every vote should be equally weighted."[3] Moreover, United Nations Ambassador Andrew Young pointed out in May 1977 that the administration was devoted to "justice in southern Africa."[4]

Third, some of the personnel appointed to key foreign policy positions seemed to be advocates of liberal initiatives abroad. Andrew Young and Patricia Derian, civil rights activists in the United States, were appointed to the posts of ambassador to the United Nations and human rights director, respectively.[5] Cyrus Vance and Anthony Lake, who had become disillusioned with the Vietnam War, were placed in the positions of secretary of state and head of the State Department Policy Planning Staff.[6]

However, American foreign policy was not revised drastically under Carter.

Two stages in the administration's global and African policy can be delineated. In the first stage, which extended roughly through the first two years of Carter's tenure, one tenet of America's African policy was retained, but there was a subtle movement away from two of the other tenets. This movement was interrupted and then largely reversed by the reaction of American officials to the introduction of Cuban troops into Ethiopia, and the twin shocks of Western setbacks in Iran and Afghanistan.

During the second stage, which spanned its last two years in office, a policy which followed the traditional precepts of America's African policy emerged. It would be incorrect to exaggerate the distinctions between these two stages. Few of the administration's initiatives broke new ground. Those that did were largely part of the reintroduction of super-power military influence into the Continent which accelerated in the mid 1970s.

The first stage was marked by a deemphasis of the premise that all US actions abroad should be adjusted in accordance with the global dictates of the East-West conflict. Yet, Carter did not significantly alter the tactics employed by Kissinger in the latter part of the Ford administration. The selective approach to containment of the Kissinger years was continued though there was more of an effort to interpret African events in regional terms than had been the case under Kissinger.[7] When Carter proclaimed in his Notre Dame speech of May 1977 that the "Nixon-Ford years had been tainted by an inordinate fear of communism . . . ", many commentators predicted that foreign policy abroad under the administration would not simply be business as usual.[8] It is true that Carter and his chief advisors, including National Security Adviser Zbigniew Brzezinski, believed that relations between the super powers should not wholly eclipse the issues of enhancing economic ties between the developed and developing nations, and among the industrialized democracies.[9] Hence, in Africa, the administration placed its stress not on overtly confronting perceived Soviet encroachments, but on economic aid and the promotion of majority rule in southern Africa. The goal of the administration according to Secretary of State Vance, was to examine African issues on their own merits.[10] Former Carter administration officials William Schaufele (assistant secretary for African affairs from 1975–1977), and Donald McHenry (United Nations ambassador from 1979–1981), when interviewed after leaving office, concurred with the view that the beginning of Carter's presidency was distinguished by a tendency to not see the world strictly through East-West eyes.[11] However, this stance did not constitute an abandonment of containment. Economic aid and majority rule were not promoted simply as ends into themselves. Comments of administration members provide evidence that they were intended to create conditions less conducive to revolutionary upheavals by pro-Soviet elements. In so doing, Carter officials were adopting an approach to containment closer to its creator George Kennan's original intentions than that of most of their predecessors in the post-World War II period.[12] The non-military dimension of containment assumed increasing importance during Carter's early days. An appraisal of how the administration handled specific issues validates this observation.

In Zaire, administration officials, appalled by the pervasiveness of corruption, initially tried to detach the US from the Mobutu led government. This step was both a derivation of Carter's human rights policy and an effort to avoid poor relations with a successor government if Mobutu were to be overthrown.[13] Containment to high officials was not enhanced by identifying the US with governments devoid of a popular base. By 1978 the policy toward Zaire had undergone a change. Invasions of Zaire's Shaba Province in 1977 and 1978 by exiles based in neighboring Angola convinced the administration that the military dimension of containment could not be wholly discarded.[14] Mobutu's continuance in office did not negate this judgment. Thereafter, the administration's Zaire policy would incorporate a mix of military, political and economic measures closer to those of previous presidencies.

The evolution of the administration's treatment of containment can also be discerned by examining its southern African area policy. It endowed the need for majority rule in the area with a high profile. Majority rule was deemed a practical as well as a moral necessity. It would diminish the chances for effective Soviet meddling, in addition to bringing a better life to many of the region's inhabitants. Observers have dwelled on the disparity between the rhetoric of Carter officials on majority rule and their reluctance to implement concrete strategies which would facilitate this goal. In reality, the rhetoric directed at South Africa grew more conciliatory as time wore on.

Many liberals assigned the administration high marks for its early South African policy. Carter and Mondale's pledges in May 1977 on behalf of majority rule throughout the southern African area evoked praise from liberals.[15] Vance followed suit in an address the following month when he expressed the government's advocacy of a transformation of South African society . . . toward full participation."[16] Within a few months of the administration's inception, its officials, operating on the assumption that pressuring South Africa could yield policy dividends, threatened to suspend intelligence links and terminate the tax credits of US corporations in the country. There were also threats to bring the US military attaché home, and cut back on Export-Import Bank loan guarantees.[17] By late 1978, a few measures had been carried out including an intensification of the embargo on arms to South Africa and a limitation of Export-Import Bank assistance.[18] Yet, by this point it was increasingly clear that the measures directed against the Republic would be moderate in nature.

The administration ceased to castigate South Africa as ardently as it had in the past. Its officials began to openly articulate their belief that

US influence over the Republic had been exaggerated. Anthony Lake expressed this sentiment in October 1978 when addressing a gathering in San Francisco. "Recognizing our influence" in South Africa "is limited, it is . . . in our interest to do what we can to . . . promote peaceful change."[19] Moreover, the crucial role played by South Africa in Western plans for the movement of South-West Africa (Namibia) and Rhodesia toward independence convinced most officials that attempts to punish the Republic would be counterproductive. Therefore, they were largely bypassed during the Carter administration's second phase. Officials reasoned that containment could best be fostered through a policy which enlisted South Africa in the movement toward pragmatic change in the southern African area.

On another front, the Ford administration's decision to stop the passage of uranium to South Africa unless it honored the Nuclear Nonproliferation Treaty was reaffirmed.[20] A 1978 law reinforced this action.[21] Earlier the administration had reprimanded South Africa for a possible explosion of a nuclear device.[22]

The Carter administration's Namibian policy followed the contours of the pattern of conduct just presented. A confidence in the potential efficacy of pressure tactics gave way to a less confrontational approach.

An effort was initiated in April 1972 by the US in collaboration with Canada, France, the Federal Republic of Germany, and the United Kingdom (the Western Contact Group) to resolve the Namibian issue.[23] Discussions were to be based on finding a mechanism for free elections in Namibia under United Nations supervision leading to independence for the territory.[24] According to Donald McHenry, a key negotiator on Namibia and later UN ambassador, in the beginning of the administration a note was sent to the South Africans. It stated that unless they started talking on the Namibian problem, the US would not block sanctions.[25] They did start talking, but raised objections to Contact Group proposals. Sanctions did not ensue. For the administration's policy on Namibia mellowed as it refused to go beyond feasibility studies on sanctions. In McHenry's words: "I don't believe there was much of a way of advocacy of economic sanctions . . . "[26] Thus when South Africa repudiated Contact Group plans offered in April 1978 and subsequent years, the possibility of turning to coercive measures was not entertained by most high echelon US officials.[27] Nor did the breakdown of an agreement on Namibia in August 1978, and South Africa's decision to unilaterally hold elections in December 1978 without UN supervision change the administration's posture on sanctions.[28] The Carter administration, for all of its initial rhetorical thunder, had privately begun to settle into a policy of dialogue with South Africa to assist Namibia's move toward independence and preclude Soviet gains in the region. This trend would be reinforced during the next stage.

The Carter administration's security concerns played a salient role in its treatment of Angola and Mozambique. These concerns did not contribute to a resurrection of the covert military activities of the Ford administration. Instead, diplomatic means and economic mechanisms were used to encourage ties between Angola and Mozambique, and the West.

Mozambique was the easier case. Soviet Bloc troops were not a major factor here. Therefore, diplomatic relations were maintained and economic assistance continued.[29] The prevailing assumption was that these steps would enhance President Samora Machel's pragmatic outlook on international affairs.

Carter's Angolan policy was complicated by the presence of large numbers of Cuban troops.[30] The policy which emerged during the first phase was one of non-recognition. Diplomatic recognition was to be contingent on the withdrawal of these troops who were considered Soviet proxies.[31] Yet, officials openly acknowledged that Angola had been an asset in negotiations on African disputes. These disputes included Namibia.[32] Angola was not written off as a Soviet client. There was no attempt to isolate it comparable to the effort directed at Cuba starting in the 1960s. The hope was entertained that Angola could perhaps be wooed away from the Soviets in the future.

The calls of Carter administration officials for majority rule were not limited to South Africa and Namibia. This theme reappears in connection with Rhodesia. There was little new about the theme, which Secretary of State Kissinger in a metamorphosis had endorsed in 1976. What was novel was the fervor with which the administration pursued it. This pursuit was given high priority by Anthony Lake, who was an advocate of majority rule.[33]

The ardor with which this pursuit took place can be attributed to the evangelistic zeal, particularly in the verbal realm, of Andrew Young and Carter on human rights issues. Behind these postures loomed the belief of officials that the realization of majority rule would strengthen containment. How did the administration promote majority rule in Rhodesia? Among its important steps was active advocacy of the repeal of the Byrd Amendment. President Carter cast his lot for repeal at the beginning of his administration.[34] Then in February 1977, Julius Katz, assistant secretary for economic and business affairs, and Secretary Vance offered testimony before Congress against the Amendment. They contended that its repeal would bring the United States back to compliance with the UN Charter, and that US industry did not rely on Rhodesian

108

chrome. Moreover, it was asserted that repeal would contribute to an improvement of human rights by accelerating the movement toward racial justice in Rhodesia.[35] Another challenge to the eventual emergence of majority rule came in April 1977. During this month, the Rhodesian leader Ian Smith proposed an internal settlement which would have prevented the participation of nationalist forces who were battling the government. The Carter administration was emphatic in rejecting this endeavor. William Schaufele conveyed the administration stance when he stated in April 1977 that an "internal solution cannot last . . . to attempt it would . . . lead to increased bloodshed . . ."[36]

By mid 1977, the administration's devotion to majority rule was firmly established. When the British offered formal proposals leading to this result in the second half of the year, the US endorsed them enthusiastically.[37] In subsequent months an Anglo-American peace plan for Rhodesia surfaced. It included a call for free elections in which the entire population could participate.[38] In this manner a program developed to resolve the Rhodesian problem and diminish the possibility that Soviet opportunism would bear fruit.

An understanding of how the Carter administration initially dealt with the first premise of American policy is incomplete without a few comments about the Horn of Africa.

We have seen how following the downfall of Ethiopia's pro-Western government in the 1974–1975 period, Kissinger expressed concern over the potential for Soviet mischief. This concern continued among portions of the Carter administration. In mid-1977, however, when Somalia invaded Ethiopia and terminated its ties with the Soviet Union, the United States refused to get involved militarily.[39] It felt that a shipment of arms to Somalia would exacerbate the conflict and perhaps increase the probability of a clash between the superpowers. In March 1978, the Ethiopians assisted by thousands of Cuban troops repulsed the Somali invasion.[40] To many centrist-to-conservative policy analysts, including Brzezinski, commenting a few years later, Carter's inaction in the 1977–1978 period as Soviet proxies established themselves in the Horn of Africa was a retreat from responsibility. The US foreign policy pendulum from the standpoint of many of these observers had swung excessively in the direction of isolationism on national security questions. To many liberals, on the other hand, the administration's African policy as embodied by its behavior in the Horn was historically sound in avoiding unwanted conflicts. They also argued that the Carter African policy was more attuned to local circumstances than that of previous administrations.[41]

Thus, there was an attempt during the first stage to formulate an approach to containment which was subtle and cognizant of regional realities. The competitive nature of US–USSR relations was not neglected. On the contrary, it was felt that the promotion of governments with solid bases, and the amelioration of local conflicts would serve Western interests.

We move to the Carter administration's attitude toward the second tenet of America's African policy.

The latter part of the Kissinger era had experienced an enlarged devotion of time and resources to Africa, a departure from the standard pattern of previous years. This trend picked up momentum when Carter entered office. It manifested itself in two ways.

First, the energy devoted to African issues reached a level which had been surpassed only briefly since 1960. The Congo had intermittently acquired the attention of high level policy makers as had Rhodesia during the 1960s. The Nixon years, with the exception of the reassessment of southern Africa policy at the inception of the administration, had been marked by a neglect of sub-Saharan African affairs. Ford had witnessed a reawakening of interest in Africa in his final year as a consequence of geopolitical shifts on the sub-Continent.

What was distinctive about the outset of the Carter administration was the scope of concern about African issues among top officials. The head of the State Department Policy Planning Staff, Anthony Lake, had written a book about Rhodesian policy and the UN Ambassador, Andrew Young, gravitated toward African issues.[42] Moreover, concerns about human rights, Soviet activities, and the emergence of a regional power, Nigeria, played roles in the involvement of the vice president, UN ambassador and president with African questions. In May 1977, Vice President Mondale discussed southern Africa with the South African prime minister.[43] The same month, Andrew Young attended a conference in Mozambique focusing on Rhodesian and Namibian self-determination.[44] In March and April 1978, President Carter visited Nigeria and Liberia. Prior to Carter, the only US president to visit the Continent had been Franklin Roosevelt, who stopped in Liberia in 1943.[45] The issues which drew the most high level attention during this stage were Zaire, Namibia, Rhodesia and Ethiopia. They were subordinate to security concerns in the Middle East and Europe. Nonetheless, energy was expended to elevate their importance.

Second, the administration tried to channel new resources to the Continent. Limited increases occurred. It requested $450 million in aid for the fiscal year 1978.[46] Congress accepted $329.7 million versus $219 million in fiscal year 1977.[47] Military assistance was $54 million for fiscal year 1977, and $110.7 million for fiscal year 1978.[48] Major recipients of military aid included Zaire, Kenya, the Sudan and Chad.[49] In 1977, Carter officials, picking up on an idea of the Ford presidency, promised help for Rhodesian development projects in collaboration with Britain. Assistance of $520 million was mentioned as an incentive for the white minority government to speed up the independence process.[50]

The third tenet deserves analysis. An examination of the extent to which the administration's African initiatives strayed from those of its European allies leads to the following observations.

The foundation was laid for a more independent policy. Andrew Young talked about the dawning of a new African policy. Yet, other areas of the world beckoned. The US had to rely on European actors with long-term ties to the Continent to fill the vacuum. An overview of individual issues validates this judgment.

In Zaire, Carter officials distanced the US from Mobutu. In so doing, they broke ranks with some European parties who found the human rights posturing of the administration objectionable. Yet, when Zaire was invaded in 1977 and 1978, France, and to a lesser extent Belgium and Morocco, fulfilled the security function America was unwilling to undertake. They defeated the invaders.[51] In mid-1978, Vance told the Senate subcommittee on Africa that in Zaire it was US policy to work with European states in meeting local military requirements.[52]

On Namibia the US departed from the position of the more conservative members of the Western Contact Group, particularly Great Britain. This pertains most graphically to the administration's early threat that it might not impede sanctions. However, American positions on Namibia were largely formulated in collaboration with the Contact Group.[53] This strategy strengthened the ability of Western democratic regimes to influence policy outcomes on Namibia.

The state where Carter officials adhered most closely to the third tenet of America's external policy was Rhodesia. This was the case for both the first and second phases of the administration. Policy here was openly coordinated with the British. Vance and Young met with British Foreign Secretary Owen on Rhodesia in August and September 1977, respectively.[54] State Department personnel in April, July, and August 1977 emphasized at a series of gatherings that the US supported the United Kingdom on the Rhodesian issue and would work in conjunction with it.[55] This process continued over the next few years as Rhodesia moved hesitantly toward independence with majority rule.

Having depicted stage one, the question arises, when did it end? When did the administration recognize that the global policies of some of its post-World War II predecessors could not be discarded? According to conventional analysis this took place following the seizure of

American hostages in Iran in November 1979, and the December 1979 Soviet invasion of Afghanistan. These events convinced Carter that he should place more stress on the military dimension of US power, and that his containment policy should move closer to the concept of universalism.[56]

A more comprehensive assessment yields a number of observations.

First, Carter's foreign policy in general and African policy in particular were not major departures from the policies of previous administrations. As established earlier, the initial policies of the Carter administration were similar to those of the Ford administration in its waning months.

Second, there were members of the administration, most prominently Zbigniew Brzezinski, whose global vision was close to that of the mainstream of post-World War II policy makers.

Third, the policy shifts of the administration began in a limited fashion much sooner than late 1979. Among the geopolitical catalysts in Africa were the continued presence of Cubans in Angola, the invasion of Zaire by insurgents from Angolan territory in 1977 and 1978, and the utilization of Cuban troops by the Ethiopian government starting in 1977.[57] Outside contributing factors included new revelations about the Soviet military presence in Cuba, the 1978 Soviet backed Vietnam invasion of Cambodia, and the early 1979 incursions into North Yemen by Marxist South Yemen.[58]

By 1979, it was evident that many of the tenets which had dictated American African policy during the post-colonial period had reasserted themselves. An analysis of these tenets during the second stage is called for.

First, Carter largely revived the universal approach to containment of the latter part of the Truman, Kennedy, and Johnson administrations.[59] He also began to place more emphasis on military means for exercising US power. This meant that reestablishing the capability for military responses when US global interests were jeopardized was to receive additional attention. This capability was to accompany such components of containment as encouraging majority rule and resolving local conflicts. The change in President Carter's perception of the world was captured vividly in his January 1980 State of the Union Address. Two revisions in his treatment of world politics can be extracted from this speech.

On one level he adopted a more encompassing view of containment. He designated the Persian Gulf and the Middle East as vital US interests.[60] This commitment was dubbed the "Carter Doctrine." The speech left the impression that the US would no longer countenance direct or indirect exploitation of third-world trouble spots by the Soviet Union.

Secondly, the president made references to the salience of military strength in discouraging Soviet expansionism. He called for military superiority. The US was to "remain the strongest of all nations."[61] The president listed the areas where military power should be enhanced. They included plans for a rapid deployment force, registration for a possible military draft, and the construction of military facilities within reach of the Persian Gulf. Moreover, he requested that Pakistan, confronted by the Soviets in Afghanistan, should receive a large military aid package.[62] In his State of the Union message, the president also mentioned non-military mechanisms for punishing Soviet misconduct. He recommended a decrease in the sale of high technology and grain to the USSR, and a boycott of the Olympics to be held there.[63]

Following the speech, its military focus was embodied in an administration request for the sale of military equipment to Communist China as a counterbalance to the Soviets.[64] In addition, Carter requested a 5.7 percent increase in defense spending including the development of the MX missile.[65]

The ideas expressed in Carter's 1980 State of the Union Address were not a transitory response to the Soviet invasion of Afghanistan. They can be found in the second stage handling of Zaire, the Horn of Africa, and Liberia. A relatively more conservative policy with implications for containment was directed at South Africa. Only on Rhodesia, and to a lesser extent on the Angolan and Mozambique issues did the assumptions of the beginning of Carter's tenure remain the dominant mode of thought and basis for action.

In Zaire, the administration's advocacy of reform was not terminated. In March 1979, Richard Moose asserted that US policy in Zaire took "into account . . . reforms since all else hinged on it."[66] He proceeded to draw a distinction between political, economic, and security reforms. Political reforms included elections. Economic reforms were to incorporate a diminishment of Zairian sovereignty on financial questions. Operating on the premise that Zairian personnel had proven themselves neither competent enough nor honest enough to run the economic apparatus of a modern nation-state, an outsider was to be designated as head of the Zairian central bank. Moreover, foreigners were to be placed in the Finance Ministry. Security reforms were to incorporate an alleviation of hostilities with Angola.[67] This reform package was reiterated by Deputy Assistant Secretary for African Affairs Lannon Walker in March 1980.[68] However, what was significant about the administration's behavior toward Zaire as time evolved was its decision to stick with Mobutu through thick and thin. A leader considered earlier as dispensable was to be actively backed. Thus, military concerns rose to the surface. The US endorsed French, Belgian, and Moroccan decisions to provide direct military assistance to Zaire in 1977 and 1978. This stance was accompanied by a rise in US military requests for Zaire.[69] Reform was acceptable, but systemic change was not. A new primacy was placed on protecting the county from external enemies.

The dominant approach to South Africa during phase two was a moratorium on new forms of pressure and limited cooperation. The US sought deliberate change in the southern African area which would discourage the escalation of conflicts conducive to Soviet penetration.[70] The activist role of the first few months of the Carter administration was not revived, and there were attempts to work with South Africa.[71] To administration members, these tactics were successful, as reflected in South Africa's modest internal reform program, and its willingness to accept a regime change in Zimbabwe.[72] Assistant Secretary Moose sounded a moderately optimistic note, in the latter part of Carter's tenure, when he asserted that opposition to apartheid had taken root among some members of the Afrikaner community and the South African military.[73] It would be inaccurate to claim that all pressure tactics aimed at South Africa were abandoned during the administration's second stage. The arms embargo was extended to include a prohibition on all exports to the police and armed forces.[74] In October 1979, Vance warned that South Africa's failure to assure equality could have a deleterious impact on its relationship with the US.[75] In June 1980, the US supported a UN Security Council resolution which informed South Africa that it should release all political prisoners.[76] These stances were exceptions to the administration's adoption of a spirit of conciliation in its interaction with the Republic.

Repeated frustrations on Namibia did not shake the administration from its newfound faith in negotiating with South Africa in a non-cantankerous fashion. Sanctions were not seriously contemplated by the administration at this stage, according to a retrospective by Donald McHenry in 1982.[77] In February 1979, South African demanded that South West Africa People's Organization (SWAPO) bases outside Namibia be monitored. They also asserted that these bases should not be placed in areas where SWAPO did not have a preponderance of military power.[78] When these objections were met, South Africa raised new ones. It accused the UN of bias, contending that its acceptance of SWAPO as the representative of the Namibian people raised questions as to its ability to conduct elections "impartially."[79] This position was not altered for the remainder of the administration culminating in the apparent collapse of the Namibian negotiations in January 1981.[80] The administration had succeeded in locking the Soviets out of a direct role in resolving the

Namibian problem for a few years. However, its efforts to create a stable independent government in Namibia, which could institutionalize conditions favorable to containment on a long-term basis had failed.

The Carter administration's second stage attempts to subtly nudge Angola and Mozambique closer to the West were only partially successful. Overtly hostile approaches to these governments were avoided while tentative overtures were made. Diplomatic contacts with Mozambique were not ended. Mozambique, faced only by nascent anti-government guerila forces, exercised more independence from the Soviets than its self-proclaimed Marxist cousins in Angola and Ethiopia. Economic self-interest encouraged capital-starved Mozambique to cultivate ties with the Western Europeans. In Angola, the US firms of Texaco, Gulf, and Boeing were allowed to expand their commercial interests. Moreover, Export-Import Bank loans to the country were not impeded.[81] The retention of Cuban troops in Angola served as a rationalization for the US to refuse to extend full recognition to it. Nonetheless, Angola played a constructive role in resolving regional disputes by striving for a less contentious relationship with Zaire, and supporting a Namibian settlement.[82] The impact of the US position of maintaining economic and political links with Angola and Mozambique on the decisions of these states to conduct reasonably independent foreign policies was marginal at best. They did so because it served governmental interests. Carter administration behavior toward Angola and Mozambique increased the probability that the US could improve relations with them in the future, lessening their dependence on the Soviet Bloc.

Few African issues during the Carter years were characterized by the continuity in treatment which distinguished its Rhodesian policy. The administration did not depart from its advocacy of majority rule, and opposition to an internal settlement. In March 1979, Moose and Vance made statements on behalf of sanctions.[83] In April of 1979 elections were held in Rhodesia limited to the white minority government and its black allies. Despite aggressive lobbying by conservative groups and congressmen on behalf of lifting sanctions, the administration held its ground.[84] On June 7, 1979, the president observed that "the April elections . . . preserve extraordinary powers for the four percent white minority . . . I can not conclude the . . . elections were . . . fair." It is not in the "best interests of the US to lift sanctions."[85] Less than a week later, Secretary Vance explained the administration's reasoning. According to Vance, lifting sanctions would adversely affect Great Britain's legal status in Rhodesia and diminish the prospects for peace. Furthermore, it would harm US relations with black Africa.[86] In December 1979, the Rhodesian negotiations were successfully concluded.[87] The administration played a minor role in these negotiations, but its willingness to maintain sanctions contributed to this result. It helped convince Rhodesian officials that they were largely isolated in the international arena.[88] In early 1980, Robert Mugabe, a radical, won the election for the Prime Minister's post.[89] In April 1980, Rhodesia became the independent state of Zimbabwe.[90] The Carter administration, which continued to draw distinctions between pro-Soviet and anti-Soviet radicals, did not disavow Mugabe. It made a concerted effort to cultivate ties with the new government.[91] In the administration's Rhodesian policy, we find the most sophisticated expression of its containment policy in Africa, in addition to a principled advocacy of government by consent. This policy was not disrupted when the administration adopted a more orthodox approach in other parts of the Continent.

A full understanding of how the military component of containment assumed increasing importance is acquired through a brief analysis of the administration's Horn of Africa and Liberian policies.

As late as February 1979, Richard Moose articulated the desire to minimize arms shipments to the Horn.[92] Steps that could exacerbate regional tension were deemphasized. By early 1980, changes in the administration's Horn policy were evident. Following setbacks to Western interests in Iran and Afghanistan, officials concluded that a revamping of America's global policy was necessary. Containment was broadened, and the ability to project military forces abroad was focused on. This translated into efforts to get access to overseas bases in exchange for military aid. Details of bilateral agreements between the US and Somalia, Kenya, and Oman began to reach the public in February 1980. US military forces were to be given the privilege of using military facilities in these states. The quid pro quo was military and financial assistance. The Somali pact signed in August 1980 had three components.[93] First, the US was given the right to use Somali military facilities. Second, economic and security assistance was to be rendered. Finally, Somalia was to be responsible for its "own defense."[94] It was told to not use American arms for its irredentist goals in Ethiopia and Kenya.[95]

In Liberia a bloody coup in mid 1980 brought a low ranking military officer to power. The aftermath of the coup witnessed blood letting against the deposed Americo-Liberian elite.[96] The Carter administration issued statements of regret about the lives lost, and ultimately attempted to increase its military and economic aid to the country.[97] It did so as a function of its global containment policy. Liberia was to be dissuaded from turning to the Soviet Bloc.

In assessing the administration's conception of containment shortly before it left office, many conservatives observed that it had finally discovered that the old time religion wasn't so bad after all. However, it had not rebuilt America's military presence abroad at a fast enough pace. Nor had it shown the will to intervene militarily abroad when American interests were threatened. The abortive Carter plan to rescue the Iranian hostages in 1980 was branded too little to late. Some liberals felt betrayed by the president's emergent Soviet policy. It overemphasized sticks at the expense of carrots, they cried. In actuality Carter's containment policy was more assertive than those on the right recognized, and less bellicose than those on the left acknowledged. Carter's ambivalence reflected the national mood. Reluctant to repeat the Vietnam experience, but angered by affronts to American honor and Soviet impudence, the American public searched for answers. There were few in a rapidly changing international environment.

The second premise of America's African policy reestablished its primacy as the Carter administration's concern for African issues declined during its latter years. The acquisition of a universal view of containment did not mean equal high level attention to all regions. It meant that regional events were often interpreted in the context of the US-Soviet conflict. This affected both the salience attached to these events, and the strategy for dealing with them.

As the high politics of security became an increasing preoccupation of upper echelons of the bureaucracy, Africa found itself drifting to the periphery of administration interests. Early attention to Africa had, in part, been a derivation of the administration's desire to elevate the status of human rights and North-South economic matters. Ties had been drawn between these issues and the East-West contest for global hegemony. It was acknowledged that constructing these ties required conceptual depth and patience. These were not characteristic of the pragmatic American character nor the American bureaucracy with its ad hoc treatment of problems. The Carter administration could not escape these realities. After a flurry of African related activities and a presidential trip to the Continent in 1978, it found its status slipping.[98] US–Soviet relations and the Middle East consumed the administration's energy. Some African issues which received attention were related to these issues. They included North Africa and the Horn. The middle levels of the bureaucracy handled most African issues. Inertia overtook the administration's policies in Zaire, Angola and Mozambique, and South Africa. During the 1980 presidential campaign, Carter would be accused of hiding behind the walls of the White House Rose Garden to escape his opponents' criticisms. By late 1978, a wall had been erected between African issues and influential policy makers. Even those who tried to scale this wall, as the soon-to-be-deposed Andrew Young, were no longer actors of great consequence within the administration.[99]

America's African aid during stage two was modest. In fiscal year 1979, $317.2 million in economic aid was designated. It included $54 million in security assistance. The total aid for fiscal year 1980 was $455.7 million.[100] In 1980, there were new aid pledges. Zimbabwe was to receive $20 million in aid.[101] Somalia was to be the recipient of $20 million in foreign military sales credits, and $53 million in development support.[102] Almost $12 million was to go to Liberia, of which over half was military help.[103]

In its waning years, the administration allowed Europe to set the pace for its African policy. It did so in accordance with the third premise of this policy.

A quote by Richard Moose in 1979 on Zaire illustrates the low priority the administration assigned to an independent African policy. Moose observed: "Our program for Zaire will complement those of our Belgian and French allies whose commitment far exceeds our own."[104] For other African issues the principle remained the same, though the actors on which the US relied differed. On Namibia it was the Contact Group of Great Britain, France, West Germany and Canada. In all fairness, the US took an active role in the Namibian negotiations. For Angola and Mozambique it was an assortment of Western and Northern European states, and on Zimbabwe it was Great Britain. There were exceptions, for independent policies were formulated for Somalia, Liberia, and Morocco. Somalia was a part of the administration's strategy for the Middle East and the Indian Ocean. The US had long-term historical ties with Liberia. US support of Morocco was seen as a test of its resolve in supporting friends following the Shah of Iran's overthrow.[105]

Buffeted by domestic constraints and pressing geopolitical interests, the US, in the latter days of the administration conceded that Africa would most likely remain a European domain.

Jimmy Carter was defeated in his bid for reelection in 1980. His African policy had been heralded by its most enthusiastic proponents in the administration's early days as a bold experiment. If so it was an experiment in repackaging established policy themes. There were more threads of continuity than discontinuity between the Carter administrations's African initiatives and those of previous presidencies. It sought to recapture some of the precepts of the early Kissinger and pre-Kissinger era while not discarding certain liberal goals. Hence the eclectic policy of the administration's second stage. A commitment to majority rule in the southern tier of the Continent was accompanied by a support of enhanced European influence in parts of Africa, and remilitarization. In select areas, remilitarization would be the chief responsibility of the US.

2. Factors Behind the Policy

What were the principal contributing factors to the evolution of the Carter administration's African policy? More specifically, why were the changes introduced by the Carter administration into America's African policy so modest?

The bureaucratic model has been widely employed by analysts to explain Carter's foreign policy. It is acceptable provided it is utilized in conjunction with other models. However, it has been used poorly by a number of observers. Three analytical errors can be identified.

First, the terms globalist and regionalist have been used loosely in reference to contending factions within the administration. The least sophisticated assessments have placed Vance and Young in the regionalist camp, and Brzezinski in the globalist.

A second error has been to trace the ascendancy of the globalists to the latter stages of 1979. The years prior to this date are designated as a period of regionalist paramountcy or policy incoherence. Hence, David Ottoway, writing in *Foreign Affairs* in 1980, noted that the main question as 1979 ended was whether the architects of the Carter African policy were losing out to the globalists.[106]

A third mistake has been the tendency of analysts to limit their assessments to the upper levels of the bureaucracy.

Careful study reveals that at the beginning of the Carter years, globalist precepts were held by many of the top ranking officials. Leslie Gelb, director of the State Department's Bureau of Politico-Military Affairs during the administration, points out that its chief policymakers were pragmatic and political centrists. He identifies the chief cleavage during the first six months of Carter's tenure as that between the president and most of "his senior foreign policy advisors" including "Vance and Brzezinski."[107] These advisors were less inclined than Carter to subordinate global balance of power politics to the "world order" goals of encouraging human rights and limiting arms sales.[108] They felt these goals should not be pursued in a dogmatic fashion which compromised American security interests. This mild globalist orientation helps explain the administration's treatment of Africa. There was never a consensus on behalf of abandoning containment or channeling resources to the Continent when they were needed elsewhere. Such sharp breaks from past American practice as wholly repudiating Mobutu, and leveling comprehensive sanctions against South Africa were never entertained by many top officials.[109] It would be misleading to assert that there were not differing degrees of dedication to globalist principles among policy makers. On one end of the continuum was Brzezinski who, in an inter-

119

view with the *New York Times* stressed the importance of improving the US strategic position relative to that of the Soviets. In the same interview, Brzezinski spoke of the need to make the US "historically more relevant" in a "world of change."[110] Nonetheless, he was one of the administration's most outspoken advocates of forging policies which were cognizant of the relationship between regional events and the global American-Soviet rivalry. At the other end of the continuum was Andrew Young who spoke of the dangers of ignoring regional factors. The primacy of the globalist perspective was reinforced by Young's resignation in November 1979.[111] He was replaced at the UN by Donald McHenry who shared his aversion to traditional globalist thinking, but lacked his domestic political base and accompanying policy clout with the president.[112]

Another factor which played a role in the movement toward globalist precepts was the ideological transformation of administration members who came to accept the salience of the military dimension of the US-Soviet contest. For the president, this metamorphosis came about under the prodding of top advisers.[113] His views became somewhat more conservative, and, by 1979, according to a Washington insider, he began to lose his enthusiasm for the Rhodesian sanctions before independence negotiations were completed.[114] The president's journey to the political center was accelerated by Afghanistan and Iran in 1979. For others, such as Anthony Lake, who came into office with a less sanguine view of the world, the US-Soviet conflict was never far from their consciousness, but the events of 1979 hardened their opinions.[115] Subsequently, the administration's African initiatives would be closely integrated into its international policy for dealing with the Soviets. Bases would be established in Kenya and Somalia, and arms would go to these states, Morocco, and Liberia among others. The reservations of State Department Africanists about the US partnership with Somalia and Morocco could not stem the wave of globalist sentiment in other sectors of the bureaucracy.[116]

In Africa, European actors were relied upon by the US when possible, and the nonmilitary and military components of containment implemented when necessary.

A final comment on bureaucratic factors will be helpful. An appraisal of these factors which relegates itself to high level policy battles is inadequate. This is particularly applicable to African issues, which only sporadically reached that level. The Carter administration was no exception to this rule. The fact that few of its programs fell outside the parameters of previously established policy can partially be attributed to the fact that the innately conservative middle level of the bureaucracy handled them. This form of conservatism must be distinguished from ideological conservatism. On many occasions major segments of the African Bureau in the State Department found themselves at the liberal end of the administration's ideological spectrum. However, the bureaucratic instinct for self-preservation discouraged major policy revisions in a number of instances. Angola, Mozambique, and South Africa come to mind. In other instances the prevailing sentiment was that a realist approach would be most efficacious for realizing the administration's security goals. Hence, in Zaire, most State Department professionals felt the president's propensity to keep Mobutu at a distance was naive. They asserted that there were no viable alternatives to Mobutu, and that US credibility in assisting allies was at stake in Zaire.[117] Thereafter, the administration was more supportive of him.

Our second model encompasses domestic nonbureaucratic forces. There was some domestic support for a more liberal African policy. Yet, it was poorly organized, could not attract sustained attention in Congress and from the standpoint of liberals had a disappointingly shallow base with the American public.

Liberal church groups and the American Committee on Africa continued to strive during the Carter years for major revisions in American policy, particularly in the southern African region. They were joined by the ethnically based lobby group, Trans-Africa.[118] These groups championed sanctions against Rhodesia and a major curtailment of US investments in South Africa. They had a marginal if discernible effect on the administration's behavior on the former issue and almost none on the latter. Single issue and conservative lobbies financed in part by foreign governments remained the powers within the small community of African issue pressure groups. The South African, Zaire and Moroccan lobbies were active on Capitol Hill and elsewhere. The South African lobby with its ties to former congressmen and high-powered law firms, retained its status as the financial superpower of the group.[119]

Congressional liberals were assertive on African issues during Carter's tenure relative to their behavior during the Kissinger years. However, this assertiveness was intermittent and sometimes ineffective. It did bear fruit on the Rhodesian and to a lesser extent, on the Zaire issue.

On Rhodesia, Congress repealed the Byrd Amendment, and beat back conservative efforts to drop sanctions.[120] Stephen Weissman, then staff associate for the House of Representatives Foreign Affairs Subcommittee on Africa, challenges the conventional wisdom and claims that congressional liberals were more enthusiastic about maintaining sanctions than President Carter. He asserts that the "House as a whole managed to preserve the Carter" sanctions policy in spite of "the president whose devotion was less strong . . . "[121]

On Zaire, liberals in collaboration with some fiscal conservatives trimmed the administration military aid requests. They continued to do so after key members of the executive branch overcame their reservations about assisting Zaire following the 1977 and 1978 Shaba invasions. Skepticism over internal repression in the country and apprehension over Mobutu's fragile popular base contributed to this outcome.[122]

Most African issues including the Republic of South Africa and Namibia received little congressional attention.[123] Others, as Somalia and Morocco, were caught up in the post 1979 resurgence of centrist to conservative thinking. Liberals were not successful in placing major constraints on growing American military links with Somalia and Morocco in 1980. In both states they found central governments with weak human rights records involved in disputes which could widen into conflagrations drawing in the United States.[124] Despite the hue and cry of some liberals, progress continued toward the establishment of a US base in Somalia, and enlarged military aid packages for Somalia and Morocco.[125] In short, Congressional liberals did not have the will, the time, or the strength to come up with alternatives to the Carter administration's policy in Africa.

Our last domestic variable is public opinion. Comments may be rendered on the views of members of the general public and the attentive public (the minority which pays close attention to foreign affairs).

Surveys directed toward the general public were carried out by Harris Associates (June and December 1977; and July 1978), and the Chicago Council on Foreign Relations (November and December 1978). Surveys were also conducted by the Public Agenda Foundation (1978), and the Carnegie Endowment for International Peace (1979).[126] These surveys generated four observations.

First, that there was little knowledge of Africa, or interest in the Continent among members of the general public.[127]

Second, a majority of those surveyed opposed racial injustice in South Africa.[128]

Third, there was little desire to use firm economic or military means to influence events in South Africa, or elsewhere on the sub-Continent.[129] It was clear that the post-Vietnam syndrome of opposition to sustained direct intervention abroad was still a force.[130]

The fourth observation was that blacks in the latter half of the 1970s were more interested in Africa than other segments of the populace. However, they were also reluctant to accept drastic economic or military actions to usher in racial justice in South Africa.[131] Moreover, among blacks, any residual sense of African consciousness from the black power movement of the late 1960s and early 1970s found little direct political expression on African questions. A preoccupation with domestic concerns and an amorphous sense of identity with Africa precluded active engagement in African issues by many members of the black bourgeoisie.[132]

There are a few polls of members of the public actively interested in foreign affairs during Carter's tenure. One was conducted by the Council on Foreign Relations of "members of the Council and affiliated committees (approximately 2,300 people)."[133] Sixty percent of those polled among committee members believed that the president's African policy was poorly conceived. A majority felt the USSR had been more successful than the US on the Continent, and that there should not be vigorous sanctions against South Africa.[134] Such elite attitudes, in conjunction with those of the public at large, may have had a limited effect on Carter's decision to move gingerly on the question of sanctions against South Africa.

Thus, domestic forces helped define the outlines of the emergent African policy, but give us little insight into why specific policy courses were undertaken.

In contrast, geopolitical variables are more informative. Throughout this chapter, references have been made to the influence exerted on US African policy by displays of Western impotence in the face of perceived acts of aggression in Africa and elsewhere. Consequently, this policy moved toward post-colonial orthodoxy. Premises of the late Eisenhower era reappeared. Prevailing regimes were to be the recipients of support with fewer accompanying human rights conditions. Moreover, military links were pursued. This was clear following Iran and Afghanistan. Additional factors strengthened the policy pattern outlined on an issue-by-issue basis. Among them were access to minerals in South Africa and Zaire.[135] Elsewhere Somalia was to play a part in America's Indian Ocean and Persian Gulf military strategy, and Morocco was termed a vital North African and Arab ally.[136] Liberia was the home of an American telecommunications station. Furthermore, it was feared that Liberia might distance itself from the West.[137]

The question emerges, why, from a geopolitical standpoint, did the administration not adopt a more conservative policy than it did.

First, it assumed that progressive positions, as embodied in the advocacy of majority rule in Rhodesia, would hinder Soviet plans for the Continent.

Second, black Africa's voting strength in international forums was a variable in US calculations.

Third, strategically important black actors as Nigeria with definitive views, especially on racial issues, could no longer be ignored without incurring costs. By the late 1970s, 25 percent of imported US petroleum came from sub-Saharan Africa, and Nigeria was the second largest supplier of crude oil to the US.[138] The post-1973 changes in the international hierarchy of power, manifested in the Organization of Petroleum Exporting Countries' increasing prominence, had elevated Nigeria's status as a regional power broker.

Cultural theory provides insights into Carter's vacillations on global and African issues. In Carter we find a statesman torn between the absolutist dictums of evangelical Christianity, and the cautiousness of the engineer. Hence, his declarations on human rights and intermittent use of pragmatic power politics. This internal contradiction was exacerbated by the nature of his foreign policy advisers. Andrew Young reflected his evangelical impulses, and Vance his more pragmatic and deliberate propensities. Brzezinski combined both the fervor of the true believer (ardent anti-communism), and the careful calculation of the practitioner of realpolitik. Little wonder that Carter's policies were sometimes inconsistent.

Our last model examines the extent to which economics played a deterministic role in US policy. Fundamental trends were not altered radically from the last part of the Ford years. It is hard to discern how they affected policy outcomes.

South Africa found its share of sub-Saharan trade with the US declining when Carter entered office. The main contributing factor to this pattern was oil. Seventy-five percent of the funds devoted by the US to African imports went to oil.[139] More than two-thirds of US imports from sub-Saharan Africa were from oil rich Nigeria alone, whereas 12 percent came from South Africa.[140]

Nigeria's economy was increasing at over 10.3 percent annually versus South Africa's 1.4 percent, improving the former state's potential as a future market.[141] However, over one-third of US direct investment in all of Africa remained in South Africa. This was a higher figure than had been the case a few years earlier.[142] Over 50 percent of Fortune's top one hundred US companies were in South Africa.[143] Investment in black sub-Saharan Africa was smaller. South Africa was also deeply indebted to US banks during Carter's tenure, a factor which gave them a stake in the preservation of the current government.[144]

Second, sub-Saharan Africa's economic importance for the US on a global level was negligible. By 1977, US exports to sub-Saharan Africa, and investments in this region hovered at around 3 percent of worldwide totals.[145] This percentage had not increased significantly since the dawn of independent post-colonial Africa in the 1950s.

Finally, only limited correlations can be drawn between the US government's treatment of states, and the level of US investment in these states. For instance there were $380 million in US investments in closely aligned Liberia in the latter part of the Carter administration.[146] In Angola, with whom the US did not even have diplomatic relations, Texaco alone signed a $350 million agreement for oil exploration in 1979.[147]

Thus, the bureaucratic and geopolitical models emerge as the most salient in comprehending Carter's African initiatives. Their explanatory powers are enhanced if they are supplemented by a use of the domestic non-bureaucratic, cultural, and economic models.

3. The Effectiveness of the Policy

We can conclude this chapter with an appraisal of the efficacy of Carter's policies in advancing US strategic goals.

It is the mid 1980s and only a short time has passed since the end of Carter's presidency. Scholarly literature on the administration is scarce, and it will be a number of years before its documents are declassified. A few tentative observations may be made.

In Zaire, the Carter administration was confronted by three options. It could abandon Mobutu completely or detach itself from the government while retaining ties with its opponents. It could provide assistance and remain silent on the subjects of internal corruption and abuse of human rights. Finally, it could support the government and promote reforms. The administration toyed with the first option but, ultimately adopted the last one. It did so by supplementing the direct assistance of other actors with economic and military aid. Simultaneously, it encouraged reforms. It is probable that the administration contributed to a minor reduction in the most blatant violations of human rights in Zaire.[148] Yet, its influence in other areas was limited. It could not root out the corruption which could be traced to Mobutu. Nor could it construct a popular base for a government which was indifferent to the mass misery which surrounded it. Officials were not oblivious to the potential long-term consequences of identifying the US even peripherally with Mobutu. There was always the possibility of a regime change unfavorable to Western interests. They could discern few viables alternatives.

On South Africa, the Carter administration eventually came to the conclusion that the Republic's regional military predominance made its cooperation on regional matters necessary. Its nonconfrontation policy led to breakthroughs only on Rhodesia where South Africa accepted the principle of a black run government. It did so on the erroneous assumption that the white minority and its black allies would retain significant power. The inability of the administration to realize desired policy outcomes in South Africa, and Namibia cannot be attributed to the inherent analytical flaws of its policy. It can be correlated to the limited leverage of the US in the area. Moreover, some assert that America's long-term interests in the South African area were not served by the administration's reluctance to adopt stronger sanctions against South Africa. It was the position of the administration in its latter years that this stance would have a questionable long-term impact and would severely damage the immediate goals of independence for Rhodesia and Namibia.

We can now proceed to Angola and Mozambique. The administration did not foster or exploit cleavages between the Soviet Union and Angola. Its non-recognition policy reinforced Angolan political dependence on the East. When the Angolan government suppressed an uprising by a pro-Soviet faction in May 1977 the US took no action.[149] If the administration can be faulted for its conceptual shortcomings in its interaction with Angola and Mozambique, its policy was not an unmitigated disaster. Through private sector commercial channels for Angola, and diplomatic and economic assistance channels for Mozambique, it preserved contact with these states.

Carter's Rhodesian policy, with its focus on sanctions, exhibited resolve and pragmatism. The administration sought to work with nationalistic forces to create a government which would resist the Soviets. In so doing it avoided the pre-occupation with ideological pronouncements which had adversely affected US foreign policy elsewhere. Therefore, the Marxist rhetoric of guerilla forces was not to be allowed to skew its initiatives. There was a recognition that ideology had limited salience in Africa.[150] The emergent Zimbabwe government, despite its movement toward an authoritarian internal model would remain outside the Soviet bloc.

The administration's skillful Rhodesian policy stands in stark contrast with its behavior in the Horn of Africa. Lured by facilities of questionable strategic value, it established close ties with the irredentist Somali government. In the process it foreclosed any short-term possibility of reestablishing a beneficial relationship with the most strategically valuable regional actor, Ethiopia. It also increased the possibility of a confrontation with the Soviets who were backing the Ethiopians. It is challengeable whether these costs were worth incurring in light of the limited advantages accruing to the US from access to the Somali port and airstrip at Berbera. The principal advantage was that they were closer to the Persian Gulf than those in Kenya and Diego Garcia.[151]

The Carter administration must be given mixed reviews for its African measures. As a component of its global policy they were also plagued by inconsistency, and the president's inability to resolve policy divisions within his inner circle. More specifically, little could have been done to enhance a policy in Zaire which was hampered by geopolitical constraints. On South Africa there was no consensus within the administration for drastic action. A subtle Rhodesian policy was accompanied by missed opportunities in Angola and a myopic strategy in Somalia. In spite of its shortcomings the Carter administration's global and African policies made limited contributions to an orderly international system compatible with US security needs. This contribution could have been enlarged had pragmatic diplomacy been substituted for dogmatism in Angola, and the Horn of Africa. International and domestic constraints would not have precluded the initiation of diplomatic relations with Angola, and a decision to not take the bait of military facilities at Berbera.

NOTES TO CHAPTER FIVE

1. Leslie Gelb, "Beyond the Carter Doctrine," *New York Times*, 10 February 1980, sec. 6, p. 26.
2. Edgar Lockwood, "The Future of the Carter Policy Toward Southern Africa," *Issue: A Quarterly Journal of Africanist Opinion* 7 (Winter 1977): 13.
3. Kenneth Adelman, "The Black Man's Burden," *Foreign Policy* no. 28 (Fall 1977), p. 86.
4. US, Department of State, Bureau of Public Affairs, Statement by Andrew Young, "US Reiterates Support for Independence of Namibia and Zimbabwe," 19 May 1977, *Department of State Bulletin* 77 (8 August 1977): 56.
5. "Nine Who Helped Shape Carter's Policy," *US News and World Report* 88 (28 January 1980): 24-25.
6. Ibid.
7. Gaddis, *Strategies of Containment*, pp. 345-52.
8. "Carter's U Turn," pp. 23-24.
9. Gelb, "Beyond Carter Doctrine," p. 26.
10. US, Department of State, Bureau of Public Affairs, Statement by Cyrus Vance, "Issues Facing the US in Africa," 12 May 1978, *Department of State Bulletin* 78 (July 1978): 29; and US, Department of State, Bureau of Public Affairs, Address by Cyrus Vance, "US Relations With Africa," 20 June 1978, *Department of State Bulletin* 78 (August 1978): 10-12.
11. Interview, Schaufele; and Personal Interview, Donald McHenry, Georgetown University, Washington, DC, 26 April 1982.
12. An assessment of Kennedy's interpretation of containment can be found in Gaddis, *Strategies of Containment*, pp. 25-53.
13. Kalb, *Congo Cables*, pp. 383-84.
14. US, Department of State, Bureau of Public Affairs, Statement by Richard Moose,

"Africa: US Policy Toward Zaire," 5 March 1979, *Department of State Bulletin* 79 (May 1979): 43.

15. References to Carter and Mondale's endorsements of majority rule in southern Africa can be found in the following sources: Lockwood, "Future of Carter Policy," p. 13; and Young, "US Reiterates Support for Independence of Namibia and Zimbabwe," p. 56.

16. US, Department of State, Bureau of Public Affairs, Address by Cyrus Vance, "The United States and Africa: Building Positive Relations," 1 July 1977, *Department of State Bulletin* 77 (11 July 1977): 169.

17. Adelman, "Black Burden," p. 104.

18. US, Department of State, Bureau of Public Affairs, Address by Anthony Lake, "Africa: US Policy Toward South Africa," 31 October 1978, *Department of State Bulletin* 79 (January 1979): 19.

19. Ibid.

20. Joseph Lelyveld, "South Africa Struggles to Build a Nuclear Industry," *New York Times,* 24 June 1981, p. A-2.

21. Judith Miller, "US Easing Policy on Nuclear Sales to South Africa," *New York Times,* 19 May 1982, p. A-7.

22. Foreign Policy Study Foundation, *South Africa: Time Running Out,* p. 358.

23. US, Congress, House, Subcommittee on Africa of Committee on Foreign Affairs, "The Current Situation in Namibia," 96th Cong. 1st Sess., 1979, p. 4.

24. Young, "US Reiterates Support for Independence of Namibia and Zimbabwe," p. 57.

25. Interview, McHenry.

26. Ibid.

27. House, Subcommittee on Africa, "Current Situation in Namibia," p. 7.

28. Ibid., pp. 7–8; and US, Department of State, Bureau of Public Affairs, Address by Warren Christopher, deputy secretary of state, "Africa: Peaceful Solutions to Conflicts in Namibia and Southern Rhodesia," 9 August 1978, *Department of State Bulletin* 78 (October 1978): 15.

29. US, Department of State, Bureau of Public Affairs, Statement by Richard Moose, "Africa: FY 1980 Assistance Proposals," 14 February 1979, *Department of State Bulletin* 79 (April 1979): 10.

30. US, Department of State, Bureau of Public Affairs, Statement by Richard Moose, "The United States and Angola," 30 September 1980, *Department of State Bulletin* 80 (December 1980): 28–29.

31. Ibid., p. 29.

32. Ibid., pp. 28–29.

33. For insights into Anthony Lake's views on the concept of majority rule for Rhodesia see Lake, *Tar Baby Option.*

34. Young, "US Reiterates Support for Independence of Namibia and Zimbabwe", p. 58.

35. US, Department of State, Bureau of Public Affairs, Statement by Julius Katz, assistant secretary for economic and business affairs, "Department Urges Passage of Bill to Halt Importation of Rhodesian Chrome," 10 February 1977, *Department of State Bulletin* 76 (28 February 1977): 173–74; and US, Department of State, Bureau of Public Affairs, Statement by Cyrus Vance, "Department Urges Passage of Bill to Halt Importation of Rhodesian Chrome," 10 February 1977, *Department of State Bulletin* 76 (28 February 1977): 170.

36. US, Department of State, Bureau of Public Affairs, Statement by William Schaufele, "United States Relations in Southern Africa," 16 April 1977, *Department of State Bulletin* 76 (9 May 1977): 466.

37. US, Department of State, Bureau of Public Affairs, Joint News Conference by British Foreign Secretary David Owen and Ambassador Andrew Young, "Rhodesia-Proposals for a Settlement," 2 September 1977, *Department of State Bulletin* 77 (3 October 1977): 418.
38. US, Department of State, Bureau of Public Affairs, Joint US-UK Statement, "Africa: Southern Rhodesia Executive Council Members Visit US," 9 October 1978, *Department of State Bulletin* 78 (November 1978): 13.
39. US, Department of State, Bureau of Public Affairs, Statement by Richard Moose, "Horn of Africa," 28 February 1979, *Department of State Bulletin* 79 (April 1979): 12; and David Ottaway, "Africa: US Policy Eclipse," *Foreign Affairs: America and the World 1979* 58 (1980): 657.
40. Graham Hovey, "US and Somalia Sign Arms Accord," *New York Times,* 23 August 1980, p. A-3.
41. Interview, McHenry.
42. Lake, *Tar Baby Option.*
43. Adelman, "Black Burden," p. 86.
44. Young, "US Reiterates Support for Independence of Namibia and Zimbabwe," p. 55.
45. US, Department of State, Bureau of Public Affairs, Remarks by President Carter during March 28–April 3, 1978 trip to Latin America and Africa, "The President: Visit to Latin America and Africa," *Department of State Bulletin* 78 (May 1978): 1; and Jean Herskovits, "Dateline Nigeria: A Black Power," *Foreign Policy* no. 29 (Winter 1977-1978), p. 167.
46. Vance, "The United States and Africa: Building Relations," p. 166.
47. US, Department of State, Bureau of Public Affairs, Statement by Goler Butcher, assistant administrator for Africa of Agency for International Development, "787 Million Request for Economic and Security Assistance," 7 February 1980, *Department of State Bulletin* 80 (April 1980): 17.
48. Ibid.
49. Vance, "Issues Facing US," p. 29.
50. Owen and Young, "Rhodesia—Proposals for a Settlement," pp. 424, 439.
51. Galen Hull, "Internationalizing the Shaba Conflict," *Africa Report* 22 (July–August 1977): 7-8.
52. Vance, "Issues Facing US," p. 29.
53. House, Subcommittee on Africa, "Current Situation in Namibia," p. 4.
54. Young, "US Reiterates Support for Independence of Namibia and Zimbabwe," p. 57.
55. Schaufele, "United States Relations in Southern Africa," p. 465; and Christopher, "Peaceful Solutions to Conflicts," p. 16.
56. "Carter's U Turn," pp. 25-26; and Ottaway, "Africa: US Policy Eclipse," pp. 656–58.
57. Gelb, "Beyond Carter Doctrine," p. 26.
58. "Carter's U Turn," p. 5.
59. Gaddis, *Strategies of Containment,* pp. 345-57.
60. Gelb., "Beyond Carter Doctrine," p. 40.
61. Ibid.
62. Ibid., p. 19.
63. Ibid.
64. Ibid.
65. "Carter's U Turn," p. 5.
66. Moose, "US Policy Toward Zaire," p. 42.
67. Ibid., p. 43.
68. US, Department of State, Bureau of Public Affairs, Statement by Lannon Walker,

"US Policy Toward Zaire," 5 March 1980, *Department of State Bulletin* 80 (August 1980): 46–47.

69. US, Department of State, Bureau of Public Affairs, Statement by Richard Moose, "Africa: Security Assistance to the Sub-Sahara," 2 March 1978, *Department of State Bulletin* 78 (April 1978): 30.

70. Lake, "US Policy Toward South Africa," p. 19.

71. Ottaway, "Africa: US Policy Eclipse," p. 637.

72. Ibid., p. 645.

73. US, Department of State, Bureau of Public Affairs, Statement by Richard Moose, "Southern Africa: Four Years Later," 13 October 1980, *Department of State Bulletin* 81 (January 1981): 9.

74. US, Department of State, Bureau of Public Affairs, Statement by William Dunfey, US alternative representative to UN General Assembly, "US Policy on Apartheid," 8 November 1979, *Department of State Bulletin* 80 (April 1980): 66.

75. Ibid.

76. US, Department of State, Bureau of Public Affairs, Text of United Nations Security Council Resolution 473 on South Africa, 13 June 1980, *Department of State Bulletin* 80 (September 1980): 64.

77. Interview, McHenry.

78. House, Subcommittee on Africa, "Current Situation in Namibia," p. 10.

79. US, Congress, House, Subcommittee on Africa of Committee on Foreign Affairs, "Namibia Update," 96th Cong. 2nd sess., 1980, pp. 4–6.

80. Ottaway, "Africa: US Policy Eclipse," pp. 644–645; and Joseph Lelyveld, "Namibia Parley Fails to Achieve Accord on Truce: South Africa Says West's Plan is Premature Now," p. A-1.

81. Moose, "The United States and Angola," p. 29.

82. Ibid., pp. 28–29.

83. US, Department of State, Bureau of Public Affairs, Statement by Richard Moose, "Promoting Peace in Southern Rhodesia," 7 March 1979, *Department of State Bulletin* 79 (May 1979): 47; and US, Department of State, Bureau of Public Affairs, Statement by Cyrus Vance, "Southern Rhodesia," 17 March 1979, *Department of State Bulletin* 79 (June 1979): 22.

84. Ottaway, "Africa: US Policy Eclipse," pp. 640–41.

85. US, Department of State, Bureau of Public Affairs, Remarks by President Carter, "Africa: Decision on Southern Rhodesia Sanctions," 7 June 1979, *Department of State Bulletin* 79 (August 1979): 25.

86. US, Department of State, Bureau of Public Affairs, Statement by Cyrus Vance, "Africa: Decision on Southern Rhodesia Sanctions," 12 June 1979, *Department of State Bulletin* 79 (August 1979): 29; and Vance, "Southern Rhodesia," p. 22.

87. US, Department of State, Bureau of Public Affairs, White House Statement, "Southern Rhodesia Settlement," 17 December 1979, *Department of State Bulletin* 80 (February 1980): 12.

88. Ottaway, "Africa: US Policy Eclipse," pp. 638–42.

89. US, Department of State, Bureau of Public Affairs, Statement by Cyrus Vance, "Southern Rhodesia Holds Elections," 2 March 1980, *Department of State Bulletin* 80 (April 1980): 31; and US, Department of State, Bureau of Public Affairs, Statement by Richard Moose, "Southern Rhodesia: Eve of Independence," 27 March 1980, *Department of State Bulletin* 80 (June 1980): 19.

90. US, Department of State, Bureau of Public Affairs, Department Statement, "Zimbabwe Becomes Independent," 18 April 1980, *Department of State Bulletin* 80 (June 1980): 20.

91. Moose, "Southern Rhodesia: Eve of Independence," p. 19.
92. Moose, "Horn of Africa," p. 12.
93. US, Department of State, Bureau of Public Affairs, Statement by Richard Moose, "Access Agreement with Somalia," 26 August 1980, *Department of State Bulletin* 80 (October 1980): 19.
94. US, Department of State, Bureau of Public Affairs, Statement by Matthew Nimitz, under-secretary for security assistance, science and technology, "Somalia and the US Security Framework," 16 September 1980, *Department of State Bulletin* 80 (December 1980): 24.
95. Moose, "Access Agreement with Somalia," p. 19.
96. US, Department of State, Bureau of Public Affairs, Statement by William Harrop, deputy assistant secretary for African affairs, "Coup d'Etat in Liberia," 29 April 1980, *Department of State Bulletin* 80 (July 1980): 18; and US, Department of State, Bureau of Public Affairs, Statement by Richard Moose, "US Policy Toward Liberia," *Department of State Bulletin* 80 (December 1980): 26.
97. Moose, "US Policy Toward Liberia," pp. 27–28.
98. Interview, Schaufele.
99. The *New York Times* provides excellent coverage of the Carter presidency.
100. Butcher, "787 Million Request for Assistance," p. 17.
101. US, Department of State, Bureau of Public Affairs, Department Statement, "US Aid to Zimbabwe," 14 April 1980, *Department of State Bulletin* 80 (June 1980): 19.
102. Nimitz, "Somalia and US Security Framework," p. 24.
103. Moose, "US Policy Toward Liberia," p. 27.
104. Moose, "FY 1980 Assistance," p. 11.
105. US, Congress, House, Subcommittee on International Security Affairs and Subcommittee on Africa of Committee on Foreign Affairs, "Proposed Arms Sale to Morocco," 96th Cong., 2nd Sess., 1980, p. 8.
106. Ottaway, "Africa: US Policy Eclipse," p. 637.
107. Gelb, "Beyond Carter Doctrine," p. 26.
108. Ibid.
109. Interview, McHenry.
110. "Brzezinski on Aggression and How to Cope With It," *New York Times,* 30 March 1980, p. E-4.
111. Ottaway, "Africa: US Policy Eclipse," p. 639.
112. Ibid., p. 639.
113. Gelb, "Beyond Carter Doctrine," p. 26.
114. Personal Interview, Stephen Weissman, staff associate, House Foreign Affairs Subcommittee on Africa, House Office Building Annex One, Washington, DC, 26 April 1982.
115. "Carter's U Turn," p. 5.
116. Ottaway, "Africa: US Policy Eclipse," p. 656.
117. Kalb, *Congo Cables,* pp. 384–85.
118. An overview of Trans-Africa's early activities can be found in the following source: Trautman, "Trans-Africa: A Case Study," pp. 76–85.
119. Interview, Weissman.
120. US, Department of State, Bureau of Public Affairs, Department Statement, "Rhodesian Sanctions," 26 July 1978, *Department of State Bulletin* 78 (September 1978): 18; and Interview, Weissman.
121. Interview, Weissman.
122. On Congressional opposition to assistance to Zaire in the early stages of the Carter

administration see Kalb, *Congo Cables*, p. 385. On Congressional opposition on this same issue later in the administration see the following source: US, Congress, House, Subcommittee on Africa of Committee on Foreign Affairs, "Political and Economic Situation in Zaire," 97th Cong., 1st Sess., 1981, p. 2.

123. Ottaway, "Africa: US Policy Eclipse," p. 340.

124. On Congressional opposition to military ties with Somalia see the following sources: "US–Somalia Pact Drawing Opposition: House Panel Asserts Military Aid Increases Danger of Involving Americans in Fighting," *New York Times,* 29 August 1980, p. A-6; and US, Congress, House, Subcommittee on Africa of the Committee on Foreign Affairs, "Reprogramming of Military Aid to Somalia," 96th Cong., 2nd Sess., 1980. On Congressional critiques of US military ties with Morocco see the following source: House, Subcommittee on Africa, "Proposed Arms Sale to Morocco," p. 8.

125. For information on enhanced US military ties with Somalia, see the following source: "US Somalia Pact Drawing Opposition," p. A-6. On enhanced military ties with Morocco see the following source: House, Subcommittee on Africa, "Proposed Arms Sale to Morocco," p. 8.

126. Mildred Fierce, "Black and White American Opinions Toward South Africa," *Journal of Modern African Studies* 20 (December 1982): 671; and Ottaway, "Africa: US Policy Eclipse," p. 648.

127. Ibid., pp. 674, 677, 678.

128. Ibid., p. 671.

129. Ibid., pp. 671–72, 675.

130. Ibid., p. 674.

131. Ibid., p. 682.

132. Trautman, "Trans-Africa: A Case Study," pp. 63–65.

133. Ottaway, "Africa: US Policy Eclipse," p. 648.

134. Ibid.

135. For information on South African minerals, see the following source: Karen Mingst, "South African Commodity Trade With the United States: The Impact of Political Change," *Africa Today* 24 (April–June 1977): 18. For information on minerals in Zaire see the following source: Walker, "US Policy Toward Zaire," p. 46.

136. House, Subcommittee on Africa, "Reprogramming Military Aid to Somalia," p. 11; and House, Subcommittee on Africa, "Proposed Arms Sale to Morocco," p. 1.

137. Moose, "US Policy Toward Liberia," p. 27.

138. US, Department of State, Bureau of Public Affairs, Address by Douglas Bennet, administrator of the Agency for International Development, "Political and Economic Interests in Africa," 13 December 1979, *Department of State Bulletin* 80 (April 1980): 27; and Herskovits, "Nigeria," p. 167.

139. Wellington Nyangoni, *United States Foreign Policy and South Africa* (New York City: SCI Press, 1981), p. 220.

140. Adelman, "Black Burden," p. 91.

141. Herskovits, "Nigeria," p. 167.

142. Harvard University Advisory Committee on Shareholder Responsibility, "The Report of the Advisory Committee on Shareholder Responsibility with Respect to South Africa Shareholder Responsibility," *Harvard University Gazette,* 7 April 1978, p. 5.

143. Ibid.

144. *Report of a Study Mission to South Africa: July 3–11, 1980* (Washington, DC: Government Printing Office, 1981), p. 26.

145. Adelman, "Black Burden," p. 91.

146. Moose, "US Policy Toward Liberia," p. 27.
147. Ottaway, "Africa: US Policy Eclipse," p. 650.
148. Kalb, *Congo Cables,* p. 385.
149. Hull, "Internationalizing Shaba Conflict," p. 9.
150. On the limited salience of ideology in sub-Saharan Africa see Martin Kilson, "The African Revolution: The Fading of Dreams," *Harvard International Review* 5 (April 1983): 7–8.
151. The strategic value of US access to facilities in Somalia is addressed in the following source: "Reprogramming Military Aid to Somalia," p. 29.

CHAPTER SIX

The First Three and One Half Years of the Reagan Administration:
WATERED DOWN CONSERVATISM:
January 20, 1981
Through
August 31, 1984

1. Opening Observations and the Nature of the Policy

Ronald Reagan assumed the presidency in January 1981. A former governor of California and consummate master of the media, he rode to office on the crest of an American yearning for a bygone era of economic prosperity and global military primacy. If the fine brush of a southern engineer could not resolve America's problems, perhaps some

135

bold strokes by a man with a single-minded devotion to conservative principles could do so. The new administration moved aggressively to place a conservative stamp on domestic policy. Its actions in the foreign arena were more deliberate. Within a few months, however, two events occurred which seemingly marked a watershed in U.S.-African relations.

On March 3, 1981, Reagan declared on television that the United States could not abandon South Africa because it had "stood behind us in every war we've ever fought."[1]

Less than two weeks later, five South African military officers arrived in Washington. There was contact with high US officials, violating a policy that such exchanges could not take place. The White House contended initially that the officers had obtained their visas surreptitiously, hiding their identities from US officials. The suspicion surfaced that this was the harbinger of vastly improved ties between the two states.[2] The events of March 1981 confirmed the worst fears of many liberals. They believed that the administration was embarking on a retrograde policy of aligning itself with South Africa. It was ressurecting the most rigid post World War II view of East-West relations to direct its behavior on the sub-Continent. Far right conservatives were heartened, though they decried its refusal to meet openly with the South African military. America had an administration with backbone that would shed itself of sentiment about racial justice in southern Africa, and stand up to the Russians on the Continent. Neither the fears of the liberals nor the conservatives would be fully realized. Like the Kennedy and Carter administrations before it, the Reagan adminis-tration in its first three and a half years would not sharply overturn the African policy of its predecessor. Caution and inertia as opposed to revolu-tion and bureaucratic innovation would be the trademarks of this policy. It was a policy which possessed both ideological and pragmatic features.

Let us outline the principal features of the Reagan administration's African policy.

First, it was explicitly committed to the tenet that Russian influence must be limited. The trend toward universal containment of the previ-ous administration's latter years picked up momentum. This develop-ment was manifested in theory and practice alike.

During the 1980 presidential campaign and the preinaugural period, there were signs that the one-dimensional containment strategy of the early Eisenhower years would become Reagan's foreign policy blueprint. Independent radical states would not be differentiated from those in the Soviet orbit. Containment's non-military component would be neglected. Less than a month prior to the election, the *New York Times* noted that Reagan intended to forestall the growth of both "Soviet power" and radical movements.[3] It was a theme of the campaign that this could be facilitated through a reversal of the decline of US military power and a willingness to assist allies when they were in peril. Following Reagan's election, his transition team asserted that the US had divorced itself from the super-power contest in Africa, adversely affecting American security. The Carter administration from their standpoint had viewed Africa excessively in regional terms. By adopting a more active continental role, the US could discourage further Soviet inroads.[4]

After the Inauguration, voices of conservative purity initially appeared to be ascendant. Aspects of the administration's foreign policy included the following. Its chief focus was to be global security defined in military terms. Little attention was to be given to "human rights," nuclear proliferation, arms sales and "economic relations between the developed and developing states."[5] Arms control was to follow a military buildup. Regional instability was placed in the lap of the Soviet Union. Secretary of State Haig rebuked the USSR for its Central American activities.[6] Assistant Secretary of State for African Affairs Chester Crocker proclaimed in June 1981 that the US would be a credible ally to its African friends.[7]

Within a short time, however, the Reagan administration was drawn back from the right wing of the American political continuum. The administration moved toward arms control talks with the Soviets and the tough confrontational tone of its early days on Latin America, Eastern Europe, and elsewhere was tempered.[8] A perusal of administration speeches and actions on Africa after the first few months also discloses a moderation of its policies.[9] Through word and deed, it suggested that radical African states and those which received Soviet aid were not invariably in bed with the Soviets.[10] This belief was expounded by Haig prior to a mission by subordinates to Africa in 1981. It was reiterated by Alan Keyes, an African specialist for the State Department Policy Planning staff, in early 1982. Both observed that pragmatic considerations made it imperative to maintain ties with ostensibly radical governments.[11] As time elapsed, the administration rid itself of an exclusive preoccupation with military mechanisms in its search for means to preclude Soviet advances. Both Crocker and the deputy assistant secretary for African affairs in Harvard addresses delineated a variety of objectives for America's African policy. They ran the gamut from promoting economic development to breaking diplomatic impasses.[12]

In mid-1983, Secretary of State George Shultz would declare that the administration pursued neither containment as it was conceived in the era of Harry Truman, or detente as it emerged in the early 1970s.[13] In fact, its Soviet strategy consisted of an amalgam of measures borrowed from both administrations it admired and vilified. This strategy cannot escape the broad label of containment. In Africa this made for a policy with uneven results. An appraisal of it awaits us.

In Zaire, reservations about the honesty of Mobutu's government were set aside. Administration support was firm. Hence, Mobutu was greeted warmly on a 1981 Washington visit.[14] Aid requests for fiscal year 1982 were 50 percent higher than they had been at the end of Carter's term.[15] Vice President Bush visited Zaire in 1982, assuring Mobutu of US backing.[16] Administration members encouraged Zairian reform. However, they considered Zaire an ally whose abandonment would damage the credibility of global containment. They adopted a position taken for granted by Kennedy, Johnson, and Nixon and accepted reluctantly by Carter. Arguments that Mobutu's demise would be accompanied by chaos prevailed.[17]

Our exploration of containment moves to southern Africa. Here a policy entitled constructive engagement was implemented. Its theoretical genesis was in Chester Crocker's writings prior to his emergence as assistant secretary.[18] Constructive engagement was interpreted by many critics and supporters as a major departure from America's historical relationship to South Africa. Such an interpretation is a misreading of history. It shared some of the assumptions of both the policies of the Nixon administration and the Carter administration in its latter phase.

Among the assumptions was that US regional goals would best be fostered through the active cooperation of the most potent regional actor, South Africa. Moreover, coercive measures would be counterproductive in dealing with it. Containment was to be one outcome of this approach. Crocker spoke about constructive engagement in August 1981. "The US seeks to build a more constructive relationship with South Africa, one based on shared interests, persuasion and improved communication."[19] In pursuit of this relationship, Reagan officials eased restrictions on the entry of South African military officers to the US, and often refrained from singling out the Republic for criticism in the United Nations.[20] In addition, they backed an International Monetary Fund loan to South Africa.[21] These steps went beyond those advocated by Carter.

A further comparison of the South African policies of Carter and Reagan can be made through an assessment of how they treated the internal reform, nuclear and Namibian questions.

In both administrations, internal reform was viewed as a long-term problem relative to other regional issues. Nonetheless, both favored an open South African political system. The Carter administration endorsed the concept of one man, one vote, a stance given less prominence as time wore on. Reagan administration officials were more equivocal on the racial justice issue. In the early days, Crocker argued that it was not the nation's "task to choose between black and white."[22] Apartheid was rejected, however. In Crocker's words, "neither will we align ourselves with apartheid policies that are abhorrent to our own multiracial democracy."[23]

In June 1983, Lawrence Eagleburger, under secretary of state for political affairs, expressed the same sentiment: "The political system in South Africa is morally wrong . . . we must reject the legal and political premises and consequences of apartheid."[24] Incremental moves away from the most rigid mode of apartheid were welcomed during Carter's and Reagan's tenure. Hence, Assistant Secretary Richard Moose's optimistic appraisal of the pattern of change in South Africa in the waning period of Carter's presidency.[25] Crocker, Eagleburger and other Reagan administration figures sounded a similar note. They praised the loosening of restrictions on black unions, and plans for giving members of the colored and Indian communities an input into national affairs.[26] They did likewise in regard to attempts to give black migrant workers the right to live in urban areas permanently.[27] In the spring of 1983, Crocker asserted that "anyone who would say there is no positive change going on in South Africa has . . . missed the boat . . ."[28] This comment would not have been out of character for Moose. Nor did the Carter administration show itself, particularly in its latter stages, any more willing than the Reagan administration to support sanctions over the internal reform question.[29] What distinguished the Reagan administration from the Carter administration on the racial justice issue was the inability of the former to dispel the impression that it did not have a sincere interest in the principle. Eagleburger attempted to do so in a mid-1983 address. Yet, the administration's behavior could not obliterate the memory of Reagan's expression of friendship for South Africa, and Crocker's 1981 statement that the US could not abandon the Republic if reform did not occur.[30]

On the issue of nuclear exchanges between the US and South Africa, we find a gap between the two administrations. Carter had continued the prohibition on the supply of enriched uranium to South Africa initiated by Ford.[31] Under Carter's leadership US nuclear cooperation with it reached a new low. The Reagan administration stated its opposition to nuclear collaboration unless the Republic endorsed the Nonproliferation Treaty or agreed to international inspection of its nuclear facilities.[32] Yet, the Reagan administration broke the precedent of its immediate predecessor by approving the export to South Africa of "dual use" materials which had non-military nuclear related functions. They also permitted US companies to "broker nuclear fuel" shipments to South Africa.[33] In practice, the Reagan administration deemphasized the nuclear proliferation issue, a salient concern of Carter's. Nuclear exchanges were integrated into its constructive engagement policy. It was hoped they would contribute to a climate of trust conducive to progress on Namibia.[34]

The chief object of constructive engagement was Namibia. It was here that the threat of heightened Soviet penetration cast a shadow over Western interests on the sub-Continent. It could come through an intensified imbroglio over the South African controlled territory, and an expansion of the Cuban troop presence in neighboring Angola. Therefore, after a brief appraisal of whether a Namibian effort was feasible, it resurrected the Namibian negotiations. Its actions were based on the belief articulated by the State Department's Alan Keyes that the Namibian issue could be resolved only if South African security needs were realized.[35] Hence, the policy of constructive engagement. The ingredients of Reagan's Namibian policy were fourfold. The first three ingredients were not major aberrations from those of the Carter administration in its final stages. The fourth might have become a formal position of that administration had it survived.

First, pressure tactics against South Africa would harm US regional goals. They would produce a domestic counterreaction precluding a Namibian compromise. Thus, a few months after Reagan took office the US Ambassador to the UN, Jeane Kirkpatrick, vetoed a resolution calling for South African sanctions over its Namibian conduct.[36] Carter administration behavior, in addition to comments in a post-administration interview by UN Ambassador Donald McHenry, provide evidence that it would have acted similarly.[37] Moreover, Reagan administration officials were more apprehensive than their predecessors about singling out South Africa for verbal castigation over Namibia. There were exceptions, as illustrated by US support in late May 1983 of a Security Council Resolution criticizing South Africa for its "occupation of Namibia" and urging a "speedy independence" process.[38]

A second trait was US flexibility on constitutional and electoral provisions for Namibia. In conformity with constructive engagement, Reagan administration members attempted to assuage South African concerns over these provisions. Initially, these concerns revolved around a constitution to protect the territory's non-Ovambo minority.[39] Though this idea was not compatible with earlier UN plans for Namibia, the US did not treat it as illegitimate.[40] When South Africa raised questions about whether the electoral system should be by proportional representation or from geographical districts, the US expressed sympathy.[41] The previous administration had displayed sensitivity toward other South African electoral anxieties.

Third, Reagan officials continued a policy of consulting parties involved directly or indirectly with the Namibian issue. They included South Africa, the South-West-African Peoples organization, Angola, members of the Western Contact Group, black African states, and the USSR.

Finally, the concept of linkage became an integral part of the Reagan administration's Namibian negotiating package. Though assigned a variety of euphemisms in deference to Angolan sensitivities and those of other black African states, its outline was evident by mid 1981. Namibian independence was contingent on a withdrawal of Cuban troops from contiguous Angola.[42] Linkage was a logical outcome of constructive engagement. Keyes pointed out that Namibian independence was improbable unless South Africa received a quid pro quo related to its security requirements.[43] The Cuban troop issue provided such a concession.

A *New York Times* columnist contended in a 1982 article that the concept of linkage could be traced to a June 1981 South African trip by then Deputy Secretary of State William Clark. Pessimistic about prospects for reviving the Namibian negotiations, Clark informed the South Africans that the US would work on behalf of a Cuban troop withdrawal in exchange for a settlement.[44] In contrast, the Reagan administration claimed that the Cuban troops had been a latent concern of the South Africans since the mid 1970s, and an impediment to a successful conclusion of the Namibian talks.[45] From late 1981 through mid 1984, the Cuban troop issue increasingly monopolized Namibian discussions.[46]

In the winter/spring 1983 issue of the *SAIS REVIEW,* Crocker observed that "a commitment on the Cuban troop issue from the Angolan government . . . will enable us to make parallel progress while the UN plan for Namibia is being implemented . . . "[47] While displeased with the Cuban troops in Angola, Carter officials had not included linkage formally in their Namibian package. It is questionable whether it could have been avoided had they retained power.

Short-term containment absorbed much of the energy of the Reagan administration in the foreign sphere. It skewed its interest toward the Namibian and Cuban troop question at the expense of the nuclear and internal reform problems. Under Carter, the Namibian issue gained ascendancy but never wholly eclipsed the issues of nuclear proliferation and internal change.

US governmental interaction with Angola and Mozambique during Reagan's tenure was dictated by its policies of containment and constructive engagement with South Africa. It was less doctrinaire than some had anticipated.

American Angolan policy during Reagan's first two and a half years was directed toward two principal concerns: first, the removal of Cuban troops; second that nothing be done to jeopardize US relations with

South Africa and prospects for a Namibian settlement. Angola was informed that its security could be achieved if its neighbor, South Africa, did not feel threatened.[48] These concerns helped spawn linkage, and efforts to end congressional restrictions on aid to Angolan guerilla groups. They also played a role in the largely uncritical manner with which the US greeted South African raids into Angola.

Linkage remained the driving engine for US-Angolan relations well into the Reagan presidency. During Lawrence Eagleburger's June 1983 address on southern Africa he made the following observation: "The departure of Cuban forces" from Angola will open "the way to peace in Namibia, and Angola . . . "[49] The Cuban troops were viewed as part of a global Soviet strategy accelerating in the mid 1970s to exploit areas of Western vulnerability.

Furthermore, the administration sought to repeal the 1976 Clark Amendment which banned military assistance to Angolan guerillas. The Amendment was perceived as an unjustifiable constraint on the president's exercise of authority in foreign affairs.[50] Concretely, repeal would allow Reagan officials to exert leverage on the Cuban troop question. There were suspicions denied by these officials that the transfer of funds to the southern Angolan guerilla leader Jonas Savimbi would follow repeal. These suspicions were fueled by his December 1981 talks in Washington with administration members.[51]

Attempts to rescind the Amendment flourished in late 1981, and were rendered moot following Congressional victories by Democrats in November 1982.[52]

During Reagan's presidency, South Africa invaded Angola in pursuit of members of the South-West African Peoples Organization.

Among the most extensive incursions were those of August 1981, March 1982, August 1982 and December 1983.[53] The US reaction to each episode was mild. Following the August 1981 invasion, a State Department spokesman said the US opposed the invasion. However, it was to be understood in its full context. He cited guerilla attacks on Namibia and the Cuban troops in Angola.[54] In late August 1981 the US cast the lone veto at the UN of a resolution censuring South Africa for its Angolan raid.[55] After the March 1982 episode, an administration member pointed out that the lives lost gave credibility to the need for a resolution of the Namibian question.[56] Nor did punitive US measures follow a South African operation about five months later.[57] US caution in criticizing South Africa stemmed from its belief that alienating the Republic would deliver a fatal blow to the Namibian talks.

Reagan administration deference to South Africa security interests in Angola and Namibia was balanced off somewhat by its support of an

Export-Import Bank loan to Angola, and willingness to hold talks with the Angolans. Moreover, it promoted a February 1984 troop disengagement accord between Angola and South Africa.[58] There were hints that the administration would extend full diplomatic relations to Angola if Cuban troops were withdrawn.[59]

US policy toward Mozambique, like that toward Angola, was largely a function of its desire to enhance ties with South Africa. The goal of displaying toughness internationally was also a factor.

The administration did not firmly rebuff South Africa for attacks into Mozambique in late January 1981, May 1983, and October 1983.[60] These attacks, directed against the anti-apartheid guerillas of the African National Congress, were seen as one component of multifaceted regional violence. Responsibility lay in the hands of a number of parties.[61]

Mozambique was also the object of US retaliation for the expulsion of four American diplomats in March 1981. The US suspended food aid. Moreover, diplomatic relations were downgraded. Contending that Cuban agents were behind the expulsion, members of the National Security Council were forceful in calling for US assertiveness.[62]

The tension generated by South African raids, and the recriminations which followed the March 1981 events did not preclude an improvement in US relations with Mozambique. This pattern accelerated in 1983 and 1984 as Mozambique sought US economic help and assistance in discouraging South African raids.[63] Chester Crocker observed in February 1983 that the outlook for US ties with Mozambique was good.[64] Six months later a new US ambassador to Mozambique was named. Subsequently, Mozambique signed a nonaggression treaty with South Africa and the US took steps to resume direct economic aid.[65]

To the consternation of some right-wing Americans, and surprise of many liberals the Reagan administration initially did little to alter the Zimbabwe policy of the Carter administration. The Reagan foreign policy apparatus did not include in its ranks a scholar comparable to Anthony Lake, who had written about the country, or a fiery advocate of black political rights like Andrew Young. Its Zimbabwe policy was largely an outgrowth of the political assessments of Crocker and others. Zimbabwe's Robert Mugabe was prone to radical rhetoric but independent of Moscow. Zimbabwe bordered South Africa. It was in the geopolitical interest of the US to maintain good relations with Zimbabwe, discouraging any drift away from the West.[66] Consequently, in 1981 the administration pledged $225 million over a three year period.[67] This figure compared favorably with that of Britain's which was estimated at a little over $300 million during the first three years of independence.[68] In addition American officials encouraged private investment in Zimbabwe.

Chester Crocker participated in conferences devoted to this initiative, including one in New York City in March 1982.[69]

Despite Zimbabwe's movement toward a one party state intolerant of dissent, the period from 1982 to early 1983 witnessed affirmations of the US commitment to Zimbabwe from Assistant Secretary Crocker and other members of the State Department's African Bureau.[70] In the second half of 1983, administration attitudes toward Zimbabwe cooled as it adopted a critical stance toward the US in the UN. Nonetheless, the administration's fiscal year 1984 economic aid request for Zimbabwe was still the fifth largest for sub-Saharan African states.[71]

Pragmatism in the East-West contest had prevailed over ideological purity.

In the African Horn the administration continued the policy it had inherited.[72] Regional and global containment of a largely military nature was the dominant theme. The ports of Berbera in Somalia, and Mombasa in Kenya, components of the regional network for the American rapid deployment force, were improved.[73] Positive relations with Somalia were preserved, and military aid offered after attacks by Somali dissidents and Ethiopians in July 1982 and July 1983.[74] The administration's advocacy of military mechanisms in the Horn was reinforced by the Ethiopian offensive and displays of anti-American sentiment in the upper levels of the Ethiopian government.[75] In an interview, the State Department's East African regional director identified Libyan assistance to anti-government Somali guerillas as another factor influencing US policy.[76] Looming in the background were US fears of Soviet gains. Among the non-military US initiatives in the Horn were diplomatic attempts to heal the rift between Somalia and Kenya.[77]

In Liberia, Chad and Morocco, the administration sought to display its willingness to actively back pro-Western elements. The timidity and ambivalence of the post-Vietnam era were to be exorcised from US policy. Its policy adhered to the first tenet of America's African policy, and resembled that of the latter part of Carter's presidency. Administration anxieties about Chad, and to a lesser extent Morocco, swirled around expansionism by the perceived Soviet surrogate, Libya.[78]

President Reagan met with the Liberian head of state, and Chester Crocker spoke of the need to help Liberia rebuff Soviet overtures. US military and economic aid was stepped up.[79]

In Chad there was a fourfold policy.

First, the administration stated its opposition to Libyan designs on Chad. It rejected a Libyan/Chad merger plan and called for the preservation of Chad's territorial integrity.[80]

Second, it backed the Organization of African Unity (OAU), and

French initiatives to reconcile internal factions and discourage further Libyan encroachments.[81]

Third, the administration gave assistance to the OAU peacekeeping force.[82]

Finally, it backed pro-Western forces in Chad under Hissen Habre before and following his ascension to power.[83] Support rendered to Mr. Habre prior to his takeover was covert.

Initially, the outcome of this policy, which was largely dependent on OAU and French opposition to the Libyans, appeared to be a clear Western victory. Libyan troops were withdrawn in November 1981.[84] OAU forces began to arrive the same month, and Hissen Habre took over the reins of government in June 1982.[85] It was perhaps a Pyrrhic victory, however. For in mid-1983 a Libyan backed force began a major invasion of Chad. It was successful in the early stages of the invasion, before encountering a stalemate with French supported governmental troops.[86]

Moreover, officials made new overtures to Morocco. Arms sales were increased. They were no longer considered contingent on progress in the Spanish Sahara conflict, of which Morocco was a party.[87] A joint military commission was established and US military transit rights negotiated.[88] Morocco was considered a strategic partner of the US, sharing its aversion to Eastern Bloc influence in North Africa and the Middle East.[89]

Therefore, globally and in Africa, the Reagan administration's treatment of the Soviets and their Eastern bloc allies mellowed with time. It was an administration which entered office with few foreign policy goals beyond those of building up the military, and meeting threats to US interests head on. It discovered this formula was inadequate. Arms control, cooperation with international organizations, and collaboration with governments of a variety of ideological hues could be avoided only at a peril to the national interest. In Africa, it took part in protracted negotiations, as well as increasing arms shipments to friends. It joined hands on matters of mutual interest with governments formerly categorized as ideologically unpalatable by many of the president's domestic supporters. An administration portrayed by many as the most rigidly ideological in the post World War II period had begun to swing back toward the center of the US political spectrum. Its treatment of containment had more in common with that of the late stages of Carter's presidency, and the Kennedy administration, than the one-dimensional containment policy of the early Eisenhower presidency.

An inquiry into the second premise of America's African policy beckons. To what extent did high level officials devote energy to African questions and what was the level of resource transfer to the Continent? The degree of commitment relative to that of other regions was limited. It was comparable to most of the administration's precursors. This outcome must be seen in the context of the press of other issues, and the national climate of fiscal conservatism during the Reagan presidency. The administration's behavior was in keeping with our second premise.

Unlike the Carter administration, one had to move down to the level of the assistant secretary to find an individual with a large reservoir of knowledge and deep-seated interest in sub-Saharan Africa. Reagan had neither the intellectual curiosity that Kennedy had about this region, nor the moral concern of Carter. This did not prevent high level attention. Reagan held White House discussions with African heads of state.[90] Secretary of State Alexander Haig and his successor, George Shultz, also hosted Africans in Washington.[91] July 1982 witnessed a trip to Africa by UN Ambassador Jeane Kirkpatrick. Central Intelligence Agency Director Casey did likewise three months later.[92] In late 1982 Vice President George Bush visited seven African states including Zaire and Zimbabwe.[93]

High-level dealings with Africa were not always episodic. One issue which received frequent attention was Namibia. Haig and the South African foreign minister had a discourse on this topic in May 1981.[94] Deputy Secretary of State William Clark met Prime Minister P. W. Botha of South Africa. Namibia headed the agenda.[95] In subsequent months, the Namibian negotiations experienced fits and starts. Nonetheless, special US envoy Vernon Walters traveled to Angola in July 1982 in search of a resolution of the Namibian conflict.[96] After George Shultz's accession to the secretary of state post in mid-1982, he "intermittently" tackled the Namibian question. In early October 1982, he talked with Angola's foreign minister on this question.[97] In April 1983, the number two man in the Angolan hierarchy, the interior minister, met Shultz.[98] A year and a half later administration efforts to resolve the Namibian question continued.[99] Other sub-Saharan issues invited the occasional attention of high echelon officials, as illustrated by Under-Secretary of State Lawrence Eagleburger's June 1983 speech on the southern African region.[100]

It was largely the East-West contest which drew the administration to the southern African area. However, its energy in the foreign arena was directed primarily toward Western and Eastern Europe, Latin America, and the Middle East. These areas seethed with ramifications for East-West relations, and had previously commanded US attention. Predictions that southern Africa could become the Middle East of the 1990s could not alter this pattern, for the US foreign policy apparatus remained geared toward crisis management as opposed to the resolution of long-term problems.

Just prior to assuming office, President-elect Reagan sent a message to an African-American conference. He stated that his administration would increase American investment, trade and economic assistance, and security-related support for the Continent.[101] It could hardly be argued that Africa discovered a pot of gold with the emergence of the Reagan administration. Yet, it must be kept in mind that this pot of gold had not been forthcoming during previous administrations. If sub-Saharan Africa remained a back alley in terms of US aid under Reagan this was not a new development.

The administration requested $390.5 million in development assistance for the sub-Continent for fiscal year 1982. This was not far removed from that of Carter's final year.[102] Early in the administration the head staff person for the Senate Subcommittee on Africa, Phil Christianson, and policy planner Alan Keyes commented on the aid program. They observed that the Reagan administration was more successful in getting its foreign aid requests through Congress than the previous administration. A foreign aid bill was passed for the first time in years.[103] This was facilitated in part by citing national security needs on behalf of assistance.[104]

Who were the winners in terms of aid? First, as previously indicated, aid to Zimbabwe despite a reduction in 1984 was not insubstantial. During the initial stages of Reagan's tenure Somalia received $20 million in military sales credits, and a similar amount in economic assistance was requested.[105] US aid to Liberia was $22 million in 1982 and by 1984 had reached $74 million.[106] During the crisis in Chad in 1982 the US channeled $12 million to an OAU force. It later promised $2.8 million in economic help.[107] The Libyan invasion of Chad in mid-1983 served as the backdrop for a promised military aid package of $25 million for Chad.[108] The Sudan and Kenya also received major aid packages, most prominently in the military sphere.[109]

An added wrinkle to the Reagan administration's assistance effort was the promotion of private investment in black Africa. This theme was stressed by Crocker in a November 1981 address, and in an interview published in early 1983.[110] Results were not very promising, though there were isolated successes.[111]

There were losers in the Reagan aid program. They were drawn primarily from countries designated as strategically peripheral or unfriendly. They included Tanzania, Mali, Sierra Leone, Togo, and Upper Volta.[112] Congress reduced aid requests for other states. Thus, in 1982 the Senate Foreign Relations Committee cut the amount programmed for Zaire to less than one-third of the administration proposal. The committee advocated a package of $11.3 million. The House of Representatives bill was $4 million.[113] Morocco also earned the wrath of the House. A committee halved the administration's military aid recommendation of $100 million for fiscal 1983.[114]

The Reagan administration aid effort must be put into perspective. The principle dispensers of aid remained the former colonial powers, especially France and multilateral banks.[115] By 1981, US bilateral African aid was still 14 percent of global US bilateral assistance.[116]

Our final tenet is that US African policy was often adjusted in accordance with that of the former colonial powers. This was generally the case under Reagan. There were exceptions.

On Namibia, periodic US consultation with Western Contact Group members continued.[117] On Chad, the US and France sent aid to rebuff the Libyan backed rebels.[118] The US expressed its concern about events.[119]

Two US stances contributed to divisions with its European allies. The first was US insistence on linkage as a requirement for a Namibian settlement. France and Portugal expressed their reservations about the concept publicly.[120] Britain, Canada and West Germany voiced their doubts privately. The Western European consensus was that linkage was a departure from the UN independence terms for Namibia arrived at during the 1970s.[121]

Moreover, the Cubans' role as a barrier against South African incursions was cited. The US also diverged from the allies when it vetoed a UN resolution in 1981 which condemned South Africa for a raid into Angola. The allies supported the resolution, or in the case of Britain, abstained.[122] Constructive engagement appeared to have taken precedence over allied harmony on certain southern African questions. The administration asserted that privately the Europeans supported linkage.[123]

In assessing the third premise it must be stressed that US boldness in southern Africa and the Horn of Africa was accompanied by a sensitivity to European concerns in large parts of western, central, and northern Africa. US African policy as a whole remained deeply bound to that of the Western Europeans.

The question arises, why an administration headed by a man whose views were largely forged on the anvil of right wing American political thought conducted a reasonably moderate African policy during its first three and a half years.

The administration did not initiate an overt strategic alliance with South Africa in pursuit of a south Atlantic equivalent of the North Atlantic Treaty Organization as some recommended. Furthermore, in early July 1983 after a speech which castigated apartheid by Lawrence

Eagleburger, the South African Prime Minister expressed anxieties about "Washington's intentions."[124] The Reagan administration's African policy was less conservative than that of Richard Nixon, an administration which operated on the flawed premise that major change in southern Africa was unlikely. The African initiatives of Reagan officials were somewhat more conservative than those of the latter part of the Carter presidency. Yet, the chief disparities between these administrations were in the realm of style rather than substance. Both accepted a major role for Western Europeans on the Continent in the areas of containment, and economic and military assistance. They endorsed a remilitarization of North Africa and the Horn, and a continuation of relations with Zimbabwe. The Reagan dialogue with South Africa involved more concessions to the Republic than the Carter White House agreed to. But it was also based on the belief that communication would reap more dividends on Namibia and other issues than confrontation. How can one explain the contours of the Reagan administration's African policy?

2. Factors Behind the Policy

Utilizing the bureaucratic model, three traits of the Reagan administration are evident.

First, there was near unanimity over fundamental globalist precepts.[125] The merits of universal containment were taken for granted. Aid was to be predicated largely on geographical criteria. This affected parts of Africa adversely. Administration policy cleavages were tactical in nature. Pragmatic globalists within the administration were more inclined than their ideological adversaries to explore containment's non-military dimensions. They also drew greater distinctions between pro-Soviet and independent radical states. Finally, the pragmatists were multilateralists, asserting that US foreign initiatives should be coordinated with US allies. The bureaucratic divisions were seldom neat and consistent, and the chief divisions were between individuals as opposed to units.[126] An identification of pragmatic and non-pragmatic globalists can take place. The pragmatists included Bush, Haig, Shultz, Crocker and segments of the African Bureau. It also incorporated some members of the State Department Policy Planning Staff. They were joined occasionally by Treasury Secretary Donald Regan and Commerce Secretary Malcolm Baldridge.[127] Non-pragmatic globalists included Secretary of Defense Caspar Weinberger, National Security Advisers Richard Allen and William Clark, and White House Counselor Edwin Meese. Other members of this camp were Jeane Kirkpatrick and William Casey.[128]

On some issues nonpragmatic globalists watched their views prevail initially, and then lose force. This pattern applied to their skeptical view of arms control, and advocacy of sanctions over the decision of the Western Europeans to finance a pipeline to the Soviet Union. On other issues as Latin America, the bureaucratic configuration of power fluctuated. The influence of the nonpragmatic globalists on African questions was reduced by two features of the foreign policy apparatus.

One feature was the disinterest of President Reagan in many foreign policy questions. This was particularly the case in the beginning of his presidency as he channeled his energies toward the domestic economic agenda.[129] This pattern was broken only sporadically thereafter. The consequences were twofold. A largely non-pragmatic globalist voice which could have dominated foreign policy proceedings was often silent. In addition, devoid of firm direction from the top, the administration was wracked by internal foreign policy battles.[130] This condition would dissipate with time, but it discouraged major policy revisions.

A third trait, and a contributor to pragmatic globalist predominance on African questions, was the administration's tendency to delegate them to the middle echelons of the bureaucracy.[131] Inertia prevailed on this governmental level. Moreover, the head of the State Department's African Bureau was the pragmatic globalist, Chester Crocker. Maligned in the administration's early days by right wing Senator Jesse Helms and South African Prime Minister P. W. Botha, he played an integral role in its African policy. As author of its constructive engagement policy, he received a frosty reception in South Africa in April 1981.[132] He opposed a full strategic relationship with the Republic. The administration's early decision to promote ties with Zimbabwe was actively backed by Crocker. When the administration acted impulsively on African questions or adopted ultra-conservative policies, it was often due to the infrequent intervention of the non-pragmatic globalists from upper bureaucratic levels. This occurred when the administration attempted to repeal the Clark Amendment and suspended food shipments to Mozambique. Neither posture had Crocker's enthusiastic support.[133]

Hence, the fact that African policy battles were often fought in the trenches of the middle levels of the bureaucracy contributed to its moderate nature.

The domestic non-bureaucratic model reveals only pockets of advocates of a liberal African policy. They could be found among lobby groups and a few congressmen. Though better coordinated than during previous administrations, they were handicapped by the continued absence of a widescale base among members of the American public.

Liberal lobby groups began to reach maturity during the first two and a half years of the Reagan administration. Among the groups with the highest profile was Trans-Africa. An embryo of an organization a few years earlier, its movement toward adulthood accelerated during the Reagan presidency. In November 1982, it organized a protest against the US stance on an International Monetary Fund loan to South Africa.[134] In April 1983, Trans-Africa displayed a newfound proficiency in coalition formation. In collaboration with groups which included the Americans for Democratic Action, labor unions, and the United Church of Christ it published a report criticizing the administration's southern African linkage policy.[135] Having moved beyond its ethnic base, Trans-Africa began a process which could increase its impact in the future.

Liberal pressure groups found strange bedfellows among corporations on certain issues. One of these issues was Angola. Gulf and other corporations with lucrative Angolan investments articulated their antagonism toward linkage. They also expressed concern about signs that the administration might funnel aid to anti-government guerillas.[136]

Angola was an exception to the rule. The increasing sophistication of left-of-center pressure groups was still offset in many cases by the relatively large financial resources of conservative lobbyists. In 1982, it was reported that the legal firm of Smathers, Symington and Herlong received $300,000 annually from the South African government to promote its views.[137]

Liberal lobbyists did score successes on the local level. By early 1984 three states and over twenty cities had halted the investment of public money in companies which dealt with South Africa.[138] But they were weakened nationally by two other domestic variables.

An important variable was Congress's limited responsiveness to liberal proposals on Africa. Aid was cut to Zaire and Morocco because of liberal objections.[139] The Clark Amendment was not repealed.[140] Liberal successes of this magnitude were infrequent, however, for following the 1980 election there was an upsurge in conservative representation in Congress. A bloc of ultra-right wing senators emerged from the election led by Senator Jesse Helms of North Carolina. This group was not successful in obtaining significant influence over the composition of the State Department's African Bureau. Nor were they able to discourage US ties with Zimbabwe.[141] Yet their presence placed limitations on the prospects for liberal proposals.

Liberal proposals were also harmed by congressional disinterest in Africa. African postures did not garner votes. In late 1981, the head staff person for the Senate Foreign Relations Subcommittee on Africa volunteered that many senators did not consider African issues a proper concern of Congress.[142] While Congress asserted its authority on matters related to other regions, African questions were often left to the discretion of the executive branch. The chief African adviser to the ranking Democratic member of the Senate Foreign Relations Subcommittee on Africa stated in December 1981 that the senator was willing to wait and see if constructive engagement would bring a Namibian settlement.[143] In so doing, he exhibited a spirit of bipartisanship which provoked memories of an earlier era in executive-congressional relations.

Hence, liberal African legislation fared poorly through mid-1984. Legislation was filed on behalf of tightening restrictions on nuclear exports to South Africa, and requiring fair employment practices by US corporations in the country.[144] Congressional liberals also endeavored to prevent the US from formally backing an International Monetary Fund loan to South Africa.[145]

A final domestic factor is public opinion. There was little evidence during Reagan's tenure that the public position on African issues had changed much since surveys were conducted during the late 1970s. On most African issues it remained a nonfactor. The attitudes which affected America's African policy most profoundly were the seemingly contradictory sentiments that the US should be less reticent abroad but shun deep seated involvement in foreign conflicts. This was also reflected by the public's aversion to direct involvement in Central America.

Thus, African issues more so than those of other regions remained the esoteric concern of a few during the Reagan presidency. They were considered by a select group, debated by even fewer, and dealt with in the political realm by tiny groups. By default, African questions remained the domain of the middle levels of the executive branch. The long range impact of political activist Jesse Jackson's efforts to alter this state of affairs as exhibited during his 1984 race for the Democratic presidential nomination was unclear.

We can now turn to geopolitical factors. Those which had contributed to the transformation of the Carter administration's African policy and its adoption of post-independence conventionality retained their salience. Globally and regionally, assertive behavior by the Soviet Union and its allies spurred a resurgence of universal containment. It also endowed military modes of containment with respectability. The Soviets remained mired in Afghanistan and encouraged a crackdown on internal dissent in Poland. Radical insurgencies blamed on the Soviet Union by administration spokesmen expanded in Central America. Cuban troops had not departed from Angola and Ethiopia.[146] Libya exploited instability throughout the sub-Continent.[147] Finally, mineral access and the defense of sea lanes were even more of a concern than they had been previously.[148]

In response to these developments, the US consolidated its military ties with African states. Military aid increased, and military facilities were upgraded.[149] Those states with geopolitical importance were dealt with less critically than they had been earlier.

There were also new geopolitical patterns which fueled the administration's ideological proclivities. They reduced the salience of power factors which had liberalized Carter's African policy. Cleavages within the Organization of African Unity over the Western Sahara and Chad weakened its status as a regional power broker.[150] These issues heralded the emergence of deep seated divisions among black African states which surpassed those of the Monrovia and Casablanca groupings of the early 1960s. The revolutions of the 1970s, and the tendency of these states to align themselves with the Eastern and Western blocs had rendered the concept of a truly unified continental grouping illusory. In addition, an oil glut reduced Nigeria's leverage on southern African questions.[151]

The question must be posed: what prevented the Reagan administration from adopting an even more activist African role in terms of aid and an American presence? The geopolitical model offers a few answers.

First, threats to US interests were more serious elsewhere.[152]

Second, France, despite the transition to a socialist government, remained a potent pro-Western regional actor, relieving the US responsibility.[153]

Finally, the Reagan administration had moved beyond the geopolitical rigidities of the early Eisenhower and Nixon periods. It recognized that displays of diplomatic flexibility could sometimes foster US interests at a low cost. Hence, the initial relationship with Zimbabwe and move toward reestablishment of full diplomatic ties with Mozambique.[154]

What do we learn from cultural theory? The principal lesson is that the administration's rejection of a one-dimensional approach to containment in sub-Saharan Africa had cultural roots. The policy makers who handled African issues, particularly in the African Bureau, were drawn from the mainstream of the American foreign policy establishment. They included career diplomats, and in Crocker's case a somewhat conservative academic from a reputable center for foreign policy studies. Averse to the dogma of the Republican Party's far right wing, they endorsed non-military mechanisms for exerting US influence in the East-West contest. A rightward swing was unlikely as long as these officials retained policy responsibility.

A use of economic data to understand policy under Reagan yields two conclusions.

First, the paucity of US economic interests in Africa may have contributed to its reliance on European and regional actors. Shortly before

Reagan's presidency, US exports to Africa were around 2 percent of the global total. Imports were about 6.5 percent.[155] Thus, US trade with Africa was less than 5 percent of its worldwide trade. US sub-Continental investment was proportionately smaller.[156]

Second, the administration's constructive engagement policy was not a derivation of the asymmetry in US economic stakes between the Republic of South Africa and black Africa. At the administration's inception, US imports from Nigeria, 90 percent of which consisted of oil, were around three times the value of those from the Republic of South Africa.[157]

It's worth noting that figures provided in 1983 indicated that US investment in South Africa was $2.6 billion. Investments for other foreign powers was $19 billion.[158] These figures do not sustain the argument that the US could exert much leverage on the Republic through economic mechanisms.

Therefore, domestic non-bureaucratic, cultural and economic variables established the boundaries beyond which Reagan administration African initiatives could not stray. Bureaucratic and geopolitical factors had a more direct impact on the form African policy assumed. For the future, there were grounds for limited optimism. There were few systemic constraints on a more novel African policy course.

3. The Effectiveness of the Policy

The Reagan administration marched into office determined to confront American security needs with a new realism. Did it meet these needs? What were its shortcomings and achievements during its first two and a half years?

One flaw of the administration was its failure to integrate its regional actions into a definitive global policy. The Defense Department drew up a five year defense plan in 1982.[159] However, this effort and others did not adequately incorporate African policy into a global framework. An administration which accused its predecessor of regionalities suffered from the same ailment.

A second weakness of the administration was its occasional proclivity for unilateralism in the international arena.[160] From the European pipeline controversy to Central America its record for sustained cooperation with allies was poor. In Africa, this trait can be seen in the administration's linkage policy.

Third, the administration sometimes displayed an inability to examine the impact of bilateral policies on the stability of the international environment.[161] In Africa this was reflected by its loosening of restrictions on the passage of nuclear materials to South Africa. In so doing, it placed another nail in the coffin of international nuclear nonproliferation.

Nor did Reagan officials demonstrate an understanding of the internal dynamics of developing societies. They handled the questions of regime succession incompetently. From East Asia to South America, they did little to prepare the US for regime change where formal institutions were fragile or the government lacked legitimacy. On the African sub-Continent, this applied to Zaire and the Republic of South Africa among other states.[162] Furthermore, the administration did not respond with dispatch or imagination to change within third world governments aligned with the USSR. Tensions between the Ethiopian government and the Soviets in late 1981 and early 1984, and between nationalist and pro-Soviet elements within the Angolan government in mid 1982 were not followed by adequate overtures.[163]

Reagan administration foreign policy achievements can be identified. Efforts during the latter part of Carter's presidency to strengthen the US conventional and nuclear capacity were accelerated. Moreover, ideological differences were not allowed to upset cold power calculations in its interaction with Zimbabwe, and by early 1983, with Mozambique. Mid-1984 was too early to judge the efficacy of constructive engagement in bringing Namibia to independence.

If the policy formulation process was not transferred from the African Bureau pragmatists to administration ideologues, the potential for regional policy successes would not evaporate.

Yet, globally it was questionable whether the administration contributed to an orderly international system, or diminished the chances of regimes emerging which were hostile to the US.

NOTES TO CHAPTER SIX

1. US, Department of State, Bureau of Public Affairs, Interview of President Reagan by Walter Cronkite, 3 March 1981, *Department of State Bulletin* 81 (April 1981): 10-11.
2. Bernard Gwertzman, "US Challenges Visit by Top Military Men from South Africa," *New York Times,* 15 March 1981, p. A-1.; "US Says Mrs. Kirkpatrick Met with South Africa's Top Military Intelligence," *New York Times,* 24 March 1981, p. A-14; and Francis Cline, "White House Says Mrs. Kirkpatrick Didn't Know South Africa's Role," *New York Times,* 25 March 1981, p. A-5.
3. Richard Burt, "Presidential Candidates Stake out Divergent Ground on Foreign Policy," *New York Times,* 19 October 1980, p. A-1.
4. Richard Burt, "Reagan Aides Diagnose Regionalitis in African Policy," *New York Times,* 6 December 1980, p. A-16.

5. Hedrick Smith, "Reagan Forced by Events Abroad to Temper His Hardline Policies," *New York Times,* 22 January 1982, p. A-1.

6. Alexander Haig, "Excerpts from Haig's Speech on Relations between US and Soviet Union," *New York Times,* 12 August 1981, p. A-1.

7. US, Department of State, Bureau of Public Affairs, Address by Chester Crocker, "Strengthening US-African Relations: What US Objectives in Africa Should Be," 30 June 1981, *Department of State Bulletin* 81 (August 1981): 57.

8. Smith, "Reagan Forced to Temper Policies," p. A-1.

9. Lecture by Chester Crocker, assistant secretary of state for African affairs, Harvard University, Cambridge, 15 April 1982; and Lecture by James Bishop, deputy assistant secretary for African affairs, Harvard University, Cambridge, 15 December 1982.

10. Alexandre Mboukou, "Pragmatic Relations: US/Congo," *Africa Report* 26 (November/December 1981): 13.

11. "US Plans a Mission to Southern Africa: Envoys Discuss Ways to Attain the Independence of Namibia," *New York Times,* 29 March 1981, pp. A-1, A-11; and Personal Interview, Alan Keyes, State Department, Washington, DC, 26 April 1982.

12. Lecture, Crocker; and Lecture, Bishop.

13. Philip Taubman, "Shultz Testifies Soviet Conflicts Aren't Inevitable," *New York Times,* 15 June 1983, p. A-11.

14. Kalb, *Congo Cables,* p. 386.

15. Ibid., p. 388.

16. "Bush Ends Africa Tour in Zaire," *New York Times,* 24 November 1982, p. A-3.

17. Interview, Keyes.

18. See Chester Crocker, "South Africa: Strategy for Change," *Foreign Affairs* 59 (Winter 1980–1981): 323–51.

19. US, Department of State, Bureau of Public Affairs, Address by Chester Crocker, "The Grand Strategy for Southern Africa," 29 August 1981, *Department of State Bulletin* 81 (October 1981): 26.

20. On the easing of entrance restrictions for South African military officers see "US Eases Ban on South African Officers," *New York Times,* 12 March 1982, p. A-3; On the adoption by the US of a less critical approach to South Africa in the UN, see "US Abstains in UN Vote Condemning Totalitarianism," *New York Times,* 24 February 1981, p. A-4; Bernard Nossiter, "US Vetoes Rebuke to South Africans," *New York Times,* 1 September 1981, p. A-1; Bernard Gwertzman, "Washington's No Apologies Approach to the Third World," *New York Times,* 6 September 1981, p. E-1; and "UN Condemns South Africa over its Plan for Parliament," *New York Times,* 18 August 1984, p. A-2.

21. George Gedda, "IMF Approves Controversial $1.07 Billion Loan to South Africa," *Washington Post,* 4 November 1982, p. A-7.

22. Crocker, "Regional Strategy for Southern Africa," p. 26.

23. Ibid.

24. Lawrence Eagleburger, "Excerpts from Address on US Policy in Africa," *New York Times,* 24 June 1983, p. A-7.

25. Moose, "Southern Africa: Four Years Later," p. 9.

26. Lecture, Crocker; "US Supports Mixed Race Party on Joining Pretoria Political Plans," *New York Times,* 6 January 1983, p. A-4; and "US Disturbed by Arrests," *New York Times,* 24 August 1984, p. A-4.

27. Joseph Lelyveld, "Pretoria Upholds Ruling on Blacks," *New York Times,* 23 June 1983, p. A-13.

28. Elise Pachter, Interview of Chester Crocker, "Reagan's African Policy," *SAIS Review* 13 (Spring 1983): 88.
29. "US Abstains in Vote Condemning Totalitarianism," p. A-4.
30. "Interview of President Reagan by Walter Cronkite," pp. 10-11; and Gwertzman, "Washington's No Apologies Approach," p. E-1.
31. Lelyveld, "South Africa Struggles to Build Nuclear Industry," p. A-2.
32. Miller "US Easing Nuclear Sales," p. A-7.
33. Ibid.; Judith Miller, "Effort to Halt Spread of A-Arms Said to Falter," *New York Times,* 21 June 1982, p. A-4; "Sale of Nuclear Gear to South Africa Cleared," *New York Times,* 27 September 1983, p. A-5; and William Farrel, "Percy Warned About Fate of Nuclear Curbs," *New York Times,* 2 October 1983, p. A-3.
34. Miller, "US Easing Nuclear Sales," p. A-7.
35. Interview, Keyes.
36. Bernard Nossiter, "At the UN, the So-Called Third World Turns Real," *New York Times,* 3 May 1981, p. E-5.
37. Bernard Nossiter, "US Policy at UN: A Superficial Split," *New York Times,* 17 May 1981, p. A-3; and Interview, McHenry.
38. "UN Unit Renews Call for a Free Namibia," *Boston Globe,* 1 June 1983, p. 8.
39. Joseph Lelyveld, "New Namibia Plan Backed in Pretoria," *New York Times,* 15 April 1981, p. A-11; and RW Apple, "Western Group Will Seek a Revision of UN Plan for South-West Africa," *New York Times,* 23 April 1981, p. A-4.
40. Bernard Gwertzman, "US Favors Alternative Namibia Proposal," 1 April 1981, p. A-1; and Juan de Onis, "Progress Is Reported on Namibia in Haig Talks with South African," *New York Times,* 15 May 1981, p. A-8.
41. Alan Cowell, "Peace in Namibia Misses a Deadline and Despite High Hopes, Pitfalls Persist," *New York Times,* 15 August 1982, p. A-3; and Bernard Nossiter, "US Says Talks on Namibia Made Some Gains," *New York Times,* 26 August 1982, p. A-9.
42. Leslie Gelb, "US Seeks Angolan Compromise as Price of Accord on Namibia," *New York Times,* 1 June 1981, p. A-1.
43. Interview, Keyes.
44. Joseph Lelyveld, "Namibia and the Cubans in Angola: US Linkage Pleases South Africa," *New York Times,* 15 July 1982, p. A-10.
45. US, Department of State, Bureau of Public Affairs, Address by Chester Crocker, "US Interests in Africa," 5 October 1981, *Department of State Bulletin* 82 (January 1982): 26.
46. Lecture, Crocker; "South Africa Seeks Cuban Pullout," *New York Times,* 18 June 1982, p. A-4; Bernard Nossiter, "US Official Defends Policy on Cubans in Angola," *New York Times,* 6 October 1982, p. A-9; Joseph Lelyveld, "South Africa Finding Few Namibian Politicians for an Interim Government," *New York Times,* 30 July 1983, p. A-4; Bernard Gwertzman, "US Moves to End Namibia Deadlock: South African Plan to Pull out of Angola Is Called the Key," *New York Times,* 25 January 1984, p. A-1; and "Crocker Meets Pretoria Foreign Aide," *New York Times,* 26 May 1984, p. A-5.
47. Pachter, "Reagan's Policy," p. 84.
48. Interview, Keyes.
49. Eagleburger, "Excerpts from Address," p. A-7.
50. Mboukou, "Pragmatic Relations," pp. 12-13.
51. Bernard Gwertzman, "US Plans High Level Talks with Angolan Rebels," *New York Times,* 3 December 1981, p. A-17; and US, Department of State, Bureau of Public Affairs, Statement by Acting Department Spokesman Alan Romberg, "Angola," 9

December 1981, *Department of State Bulletin* 82 (March 1982): 34.

52. On attempts to repeal the Clark Amendment see the following sources: Martin Tolchin, "Foreign Aid Bill Clears the House," *New York Times,* 10 December 1982, p. A-1; Steven Roberts, "Foreign Aid Bills Voted in Congress Sent to President," *New York Times,* 17 December 1982, p. A-1; and Interview, Weissman.

53. "Angola Mobilizing after S. Africa Raid," *Boston Globe* 26 August 1981, p. 1; "South Africa Says Army Is in Angola," *New York Times,* 27 August 1981, p. A-1; "South Africans Kill 201 in Angola Raid," *New York Times,* 17 March 1982, p. A-3; "Fifteen South African Soldiers Are Lost in Angola Drive," 11 August 1982, p. A-4; "South Africa Says Angolan Forces Are Fighting Against Its Soldiers," *New York Times,* 29 December 1983, p. A-4; "South African Force Fighting in Angola May Total 10,000, *New York Times,* 3 January 1984, p. A-5; and "South African Troops Pull Out of Angola," *New York Times,* 16 January 1984, p. A-5.

54. "South Africa Says Army Is in Angola," *New York Times,* 27 August 1981, p. A-1.

55. Nossiter, "US Vetoes Rebuke," p. A-1.

56. "US Says Angola Raid Shows Urgency of Namibia Solution," *New York Times,* 15 March 1982, p. A-10.

57. "Angola Reports Advance by South African Troops," *New York Times,* 14 August 1982, p. A-2.

58. Crocker, "US Interests in Africa," p. A-8; Bernard Nossiter, "Angola Sees US Paranoia on Question of Cuban Troops," *New York Times,* 6 October 1982, p. A-8; Bernard Gwertzman, "Shultz to Confer with Namibian Rebel Leader," *New York Times,* 25 May 1983, p. A-12; Alan Cowell, "South Africa Seeks Military Freeze in Angola," *New York Times,* 26 January 1984, p. A-10; "South Africans and Angolans Set up Disengagement Panel," *New York Times,* 17 February 1984, p. A-5; and Bernard Gwertzman, "Cuba Said to Resist Leaving Angola," *New York Times,* 10 May 1984, p. A-3.

59. Pachter, "Reagan's Policy," pp. 84–86.

60. Joseph Lelyveld, "South Africans Attack Rebels in Mozambique Capital," *New York Times,* 31 January 1981, p. A-3; "South African Jets Raid Mozambique in Reply to Rebels," *New York Times,* 24 May 1983, p. A-1; Alan Cowell, "5 Hurt in Mozambique Bombing," *New York Times,* 18 October 1983, p. A-4.

61. Eagleburger, "Excerpts from Address," p. A-7.

62. Interview, Weissman; and Bernard Gwertzman, "US Retaliation Suspends Food Aid to the Mozambicans," *New York Times,* 21 March 1981, p. A-1.

63. "Mozambican Sees Ties with US Improving," *New York Times,* 9 October 1983, p. A-5; and Thomas Henriksen, "Mozambique: "The Enemy Within," *Current History* 81 (March 1982): 113.

64. US, Department of State, Bureau of Public Affairs, Statement by Chester Crocker, "The Search for Regional Security in Southern Africa," 15 February 1983, *Department of State Bulletin* 83 (April 1983): 51.

65. "Reagan to Name Envoy to Mozambique," *New York Times,* 12 July 1983, p. A-5; Alan Cowell, "Mozambique Signs Accord on Rebels with South Africa," *New York Times,* 17 March 1984, p. A-1; and "US Lifts 7-Year Ban on Aid to Mozambique," *New York Times,* 13 June 1984, p. A-11.

66. Interview, Keyes.

67. Mboukou, "Pragmatic Relations," p. 12.

68. Joseph Lelyveld, "Zimbabwe's Guests Pledge $1.3 Billion," *New York Times,* 25 March 1981, p. A-5.

69. Chester Crocker, "The Role of the US Private Sector in Zimbabwe," Speech

delivered at AAI/APA Conference on Zimbabwe, New York City, 26 March 1982.

70. On Zimbabwe's movement toward a one party state intolerant of dissent see Joseph Lelyveld, "Nkomo Ousted in Zimbabwe: Plot is Charged," *New York Times,* 18 February 1982, p. A-1; "Zimbabwe Arrests Deputy Army Chief," *New York Times,* 13 March 1982, p. A-6; "One Party Rule Coming, Mugabe Tells Zimbabwe," *New York Times,* 5 August 1982, p. A-7; "Zimbabwe's Press Like Rhodesia's Is Unadventurous," *New York Times,* 7 March 1983, p. A-3; "Nkomo Takes Exile, Days After Fearing Mugabe Death Plot," *New York Times,* 10 March 1983, p. A-1; and "Six Nkomo Supporters Detained in Zimbabwe," *New York Times,* 29 May 1983, p. A-5. Official expressions of US support for Zimbabwe are contained in Personal Interview, Joseph Segars, State Department Zimbabwe Desk Officer, State Department, Washington, DC, 27 April 1982; and Crocker, "The Search for Regional Security in Southern Africa," p. 51.

71. On tensions between the US and Zimbabwe in the latter half of 1983 see Steven Weisman, "Reagan and Mugabe Explore Disagreements," *New York Times,* 14 September 1983, p. A-6; "US–Zimbabwe Ties Strained," *New York Times,* 4 November 1983, p. A-7; and Sanford J. Ungar, "Foolish Policy on Zimbabwe," *New York Times,* 28 December 1983, p. A-23. On US economic assistance to Zimbabwe see Frank Donatelli, "Why US Aid to Zimbabwe Was Reduced," *New York Times,* 16 January 1984, p. A-14.

72. Pachter, "Reagan's Policy," p. 89.

73. Personal Interview, Curt Kamman, State Department regional director for East Africa, State Department, Washington, DC, 10 December 1981.

74. Alan Cowell, "Guerilla Drive in Somalia Seems Part of a Proxy War," *New York Times,* 16 July 1982, p. A-3; Richard Halloran, "US Flying Arms to Somalia after Ethiopian Raids," *New York Times,* 25 July 1982, p. A-6; and "Somalis Report Vast US Airlift," *New York Times,* 27 August 1982, p. A-5; US, Department of State, Bureau of Public Affairs, Address by Chester Crocker, "US Response to the Challenge of Regional Security in Africa," 28 October 1982, *Department of State Bulletin* 82 (December 1982): 25; and "Somalia Announces Invasion of 2 Areas by Ethiopian Forces," *New York Times,* 17 July 1983, p. A-4.

75. Alan Cowell, "Ethiopian, New Head of OAU Denounces US as Military Peril," *New York Times,* 14 June 1983, p. A-15; and "Ethiopians Expel Part of US Embassy Staff," *New York Times,* 7 February 1984, p. A-9.

76. Interview, Kamman.

77. Ibid.

78. Bernard Gwertzman, "US Pledges to Aid African Countries that Resist Libyans," *New York Times,* 3 June 1981, p. A-1.

79. "Reagan Praises Liberian Leader," *Boston Globe,* 18 August 1982, p. A-13; Crocker, "US Response to Challenge of Regional Security," *New York Times,* p. 25; and Clifford May, "Wary Steps Toward Democracy in Liberia," *New York Times,* 10 June 1984, p. 4E.

80. Gwertzman, "US Pledges to Aid Countries," p. A-1; and Crocker, "US Response to the Challenge of Regional Security," pp. 22–23.

81. Crocker, "US Response to the Challenge of Regional Security," pp. 22–23.

82. Ibid.; and "Haig, Nigerian Discuss US Aid for Chad Effort," *Boston Globe,* 13 December 1981, p. A-10.

83. Piero Gleijeses, "French Skill on Chad," *New York Times,* 29 August 1983, p. A-19.

84. Richard Eder, "Quick Withdrawal from Chad Vowed," *New York Times,* 5 November 1981, p. A-1.

85. "Capital of Chad Reported to Fall," *New York Times,* 8 June 1982, p. A-11.

86. "4000 Rebels Attack Major Chad City," *Boston Globe,* 24 June 1983, p. A-3; "Rebels Surround Town in Northern Chad," *New York Times,* 25 June 1983, p. A-4; "Libyan-Backed Rebels Moving South in Chad," *New York Times,* 27 June 1983, p. A-9; and Drew Middleton, "Pentagon Concerned About Assault on Chad," *New York Times,* 30 June 1983, p. A-4; Alan Cowell, "France to Deploy Troops in Village on Chadian Front: Mitterand Aide Meets Habré—French Now in 2 Towns as New Line is Drawn," *New York Times,* 15 August 1983, p. A-1; Alan Cowell, "Paris's Choices in Chad: Action by France Has Halted Rebel Drive but End to the Conflict is Nowhere in Sight," *New York Times,* 16 August 1983, p. A-2; "France, Forces in Place in Chad, Tries Diplomacy," *New York Times,* 25 August 1983, p. A-3; Clifford May, "Chad Equation: France Plus Libya Equals Division," *New York Times,* 20 September 1983, p. A-2; and E. J. Dionne Jr., "Qaddafi Proposes Accord on Chad: Libya and France Would Pull out Troops under Plan—Paris Is Studying Offer," *New York Times,* 15 May 1984, p. A-5.

87. Bernard Gwertzman, "US Drops Sahara Issue in Arms Sale to Morocco," *New York Times,* 26 March 1981, p. A-15.

88. Bernard Gwertzman, "US and Morocco to Set up Joint Military Commission," *New York Times,* 13 February 1982, p. A-1; and Barbara Crossette, "US and Morocco Reported Near Accord," *New York Times,* 20 May 1982, p. A-3.

89. On Morocco's strategic partnership with the US see Pachter, "Reagan's Policy," p. 92; On the uncertain impact of Morocco's decision in early September 1984 to establish a union with Libya on its relationship with the US see Judith Miller, "Libya's Congress Approves Union with Morocco," *New York Times,* 1 September 1984, p. A-2.

90. "Bush, Casey to Africa in Diplomatic Blitz," *Africa News* 19 (11 October 1982): 1.

91. Bernard Gwertzman, "US Plans a Mission to Southern Africa: Envoys to Discuss Ways to Attain the Independence of Namibia," *New York Times,* 29 March 1981, p. A-1.

92. "Bush, Casey to Africa," p. 1.

93. US, Department of State, Bureau of Public Affairs, "Vice President Bush Visits Africa and Bermuda," November 1982, *Department of State Bulletin* 83 (January 1983): 34–50.

94. "Progress is Reported on Namibia in Haig Talks with South Africa," *New York Times,* 15 May 1981, p. A-8.

95. Joseph Lelyveld, "US Envoy Ends Talks with Botha on the Independence of Namibia," *New York Times,* 12 June 1981, p. A-6.

96. "US Envoy Begins Talks in Angola on Namibia," *New York Times,* 22 July 1982, p. A-5.

97. Nossiter, "Angolan Sees US Paranoia," p. A-8.

98. Bernard Gwertzman, "A Top Angolan Is Said to Meet Shultz in US," *New York Times,* 14 April 1983, p. A-1.

99. "South Africa Lifts Ban on Publication of Namibia Newspaper," *New York Times,* 1 September 1984, p. A-2.

100. Eagleburger, "Excerpts from Address," p. A-7.

101. Juan de Onis, "Strong African Ties Promised by Reagan: Message to Sierra Leone Says He Will Encourage Trade and Increase Assistance," *New York Times,* 12 January 1981, p. A-12.

102. US, Department of State, Bureau of Public Affairs, Statement by Lannon Walker,

acting assistant secretary for African affairs, "FY 1982 Assistance Requests," 24 March 1981, *Department of State Bulletin* 81 (May 1981): 18; and Carol Lancaster, "United States Policy in Sub-Saharan Africa," *Current History* 81 (March 1982): 100.

103. Personal Interview, Phil Christianson, Dirksen Senate Office Building, Washington, DC, 9 December 1981; and Interview, Keyes.

104. Lancaster, "United States Policy," p. 100.

105. Richard Halloran, "US Flying Arms to Somalia After Ethiopian Raids," *New York Times,* 25 July 1982, p. A-6; and Walker, "FY 1982 Assistance Requests," pp. 19–20.

106. "Reagan Praises Liberian Leader," *Boston Globe,* 19 August 1982, p. A-1; and May, "Wary Steps in Liberia," p. 4E.

107. Crocker, "US Response to the Challenge of Regional Security," p. 23.

108. "US to Give Chad More Aid: Libya Said to Strike Deeper," *New York Times,* 15 August 1983, p. A-2.

109. Walker, "FY 1982 Assistance Requests," pp. 19–20; and B. Drummond Ayres, "More Money and Arms Are Sought for Sudan," *New York Times,* 29 March 1984, p. A-4.

110. US, Department of State, Bureau of Public Affairs, Address by Chester Crocker, "The African Private Sector and US Foreign Policy," 19 November 1981, *Department of State Bulletin* 82 (February 1982): 95–96; and Pachter, "Reagan's Policy," pp. 95–96.

111. Pachter, "Reagan's Policy," p. 100.

112. Lancaster, "United States Policy," p. 133.

113. "Panel Backs $10.7 Billion Foreign Aid Bill," *Boston Globe,* 28 May 1982, p. A-6.

114. Barbara Crossette, "US and Morocco Reported Near Accord," *New York Times,* 20 May 1982, p. A-3.

115. Lancaster, "United States Policy," p. 132.

116. Ibid.

117. US, Department of State, Bureau of Public Affairs, Statement by Chester Crocker, "US Policy on Namibia," 17 June 1981, *Department of State Bulletin* 81 (August 1981): 55; US Department of State, Bureau of Public Affairs, Statement on Namibia Issued by Canada, France, the Federal Republic of Germany, the United Kingdom and the United States, 24 September 1981, *Department of State Bulletin* 81 (November 1981): 86; Bernard Nossiter, "Africa Asks West for a Namibia Plan," *New York Times,* 29 April 1983, p. A-3; and Eagleburger, "Excerpts from Address," p. A-7.

118. "France to Airlift Military Supplies to Chad," *New York Times,* 28 June 1983, p. A-5.

119. Middleton, "Pentagon Concerned About Assault," p. A-4.

120. Barbara Crossette, "Portugal Defends Angola on Cubans," *New York Times,* 3 October 1981, p. A-6; "French Official Rejects Namibian-Angola Linkage," *New York Times,* 13 October 1982, p. A-7; and "France Criticizes US on Namibia," *New York Times,* 26 April 1983, pp. A-3, A-7.

121. Bernard Nossiter, "Angola Asks UN Meeting on the South African Raid," *New York Times,* 28 August 1981, p. A-3; Alan Cowell, "State Department Moves to Keep Namibia Talks on Course," *New York Times,* 5 July 1982, p. A-2; and William K. Stevens, "Commonwealth Criticizes US Over Namibia," *New York Times,* 29 November 1983, p. A-12.

122. Nossiter, "Angola Asks Meeting on Raid," p. A-3; and Bernard Gwertzman, "US Doubts Report that South Africa Hits Angola Again," *New York Times,* 4 September 1981, p. A-1.

123. "France Criticizes US," p. A-7.

124. Joseph Lelyveld, "Pretoria Ends Banning Orders on 50," *New York Times,* 2 July 1983, p. A-2.

125. Interview, Weissman.

126. Interview, Kamman.
127. Interview, Keyes; and Smith, "Reagan Forced to Temper Policies," p. A-8.
128. Smith, "Reagan Forced to Temper Policies," p. A-8.
129. Ibid., p. A-1.
130. Leslie Gelb, "Foreign Policy System Criticized by US Aides," *New York Times,* 18 October 1981, pp. A-1, A-8.
131. Leslie Gelb, "Reagan's Foreign Policy Has Lost Many of Its Hard Edges, Aides Say," *New York Times,* 12 May 1982, p. A-10.
132. Gerald Bender, "Secretary of State Helms," *New York Times,* 10 June 1981, p. A-11; and Joseph Lelyveld, "Botha Holds Reagan Aide Liable for South African's Cancelled US Visit," *New York Times,* 17 April 1981, p. A-8.
133. Interview, Weissman.
134. "50 Protest IMF Vote on Loan to South Africa," *Washington Post,* 4 November 1982, p. A-2.
135. Bernard Weinraub, "US Namibia Policy Assailed in Report," *New York Times,* 22 April 1983, p. A-4.
136. Terence Smith, "Companies Fight US Over Angola, Libya: Administration Policy Resisted to Protect Profitable Operations," *New York Times,* 27 June 1981, p. A-37.
137. Rene Loth, "The South African Lobby," *Boston Phoenix,* 14 December 1982, p. 1.
138. "A District of Columbia Law on South Africa is Backed," *New York Times,* 1 February 1984, p. A-6.
139. "Panel Backs Aid Bill," p. A-6; and Crossette, "US and Morocco Near Accord," p. A-3.
140. Interview, Weissman; Anthony Hughes, "Interview of Congressman Howard Wolpe," *Africa Report* 26 (November/December 1981): 7; Tolchin, "Foreign Aid Bill Clears House," p. A-1; and Roberts, "Foreign Aid Bills Sent to President," p. A-1.
141. Interview, Weissman; Personal Interview, Kenneth Zinn, liberal activist, Washington Office on Africa, Washington, DC, 26 April 1982; and Bender, "Secretary Helms," p. A-11.
142. Interview, Christianson.
143. Personal Interview, Chris Chamberlain, Russell Senate Office Building, Washington, DC, 11 December 1981.
144. Miller, "US Easing Nuclear Sales," p. A-7; and "Doing Business with Racists," *New York Times,* 15 June 1983, p. A-26.
145. Bernard Weinraub, "US is Sending African Nations More Arms Aid," *New York Times,* 3 July 1983, p. A-10.
146. For information on Soviet bloc assertiveness internationally see Crocker, "Strengthening US–African Relations,"; and Pachter, "Reagan's Policy," p. 92.
147. Gwertzman, "US Pledges to Aid Countries," p. A-1; Pranay Gupte, "Sudan Seeks Help to Counter Libya: US Is Said to Be Responsive to Request for Equipment and Security Training," *New York Times,* 14 October 1981, p. A-14; "Libyan-Backed Rebels Moving South in Chad," p. A-9; and Middleton, "Pentagon Concerned about Assault," p. A-4; and "Plane Bombs the Sudan Which Accuses Libyans," *New York Times,* 17 March 1984, p. A-4.
148. Lecture, Bishop; Kalb, *Congo Cables,* p. 386; and Henry F. Jackson, "Third World Power," *New York Times,* 27 December 1980, p. A-21; and US, Department of State, Bureau of Public Affairs, Statement by Alexander Haig, "Security and Development Assistance," 19 March 1981, *Department of State Bulletin* 81 (April 1981): A, B.
149. Pachter, "Reagan's Policy," p. 92; Weinraub, "US Sending More Arms Aid," p. A-1; and Alan Cowell, "Peril Seen to US Use of Somali Port," *New York Times,* 1 August 1982, p. A-3.

150. Pranay Gupte, "Split on Polisario Is Threat to OAU: 19 Members Assert They Will Shun Meetings if Western Sahara Rebels Attend," *New York Times*, 14 March 1982, p. A-8; Alan Cowell, "African Parley Disrupted by a Dispute over Sahara Guerilla Group," *New York Times*, 6 April 1982, p. A-3; John Vinocur, "France and 18 African Lands Meet to Discuss OAU Split," *New York Times*, 9 October 1982, p. A-4; Alan Cowell, "Africa at Crossroads: Is OAU Dying," *New York Times*, 27 November 1982, p. A-3; and Alan Cowell, "African Unity Organization Ends Its Summit Gathering in Disunity," *New York Times*, 13 June 1983, p. A-3.

151. Alan Cowell, "Nigerian Official, Warning US, Talks of Oil Curbs" *New York Times*, 27 July 1981, p. A-3.

152. Richard Halloran, "Pentagon Draws up First Strategy for Fighting a Long Nuclear War: 5 Year Plan Gives Insight into Thinking of Senior Defense Official," *New York Times*, 30 May 1982, p. A-12.

153. John Vinocur, "Mitterand Keeps the Lines Open to Africa," *New York Times*, 10 October 1982, p. E-5; and Leon Dash, "Africans See End of French Attempt to Alter Policy," *Washington Post*, 1 January 1983, p. A-1.

154. Interview, Segars; and Weinraub, "US Sending More Arms Aid," p. A-10.

155. Lancaster, "United States Policy," p. 98.

156. Ibid., p. 97.

157. Ibid., p. 98; and Foreign Policy Study Foundation, *South Africa: Time Running Out*, p. 300.

158. Robert Weigand, "Invest in South Africa," *New York Times*, 24 June 1983, p. A-25.

159. Halloran, "Pentagon Draws up Strategy for War: 5 Year Plan," pp. A-1, A-12.

160. Nye, "US Power and Reagan Policy," pp. 401–3.

161. Ibid., pp. 405–9.

162. For information on the narrow popular base of the Mobutu government in Zaire, and its inattention to human rights see the following articles: Barbara Crossette, "Central America Found to Progress in Human Rights: Survey by US Also Criticizes Soviet for Its Activity in Afghanistan and Poland," *New York Times*, 8 February 1982, p. A-10; Alan Cowell, "Superstition Deepens Mobutu's Fear and Isolation," *New York Times*, 19 June 1982, p. A-2; Michael T. Kaufman, "Hard Times for Zaire's President, Are Humbling," *New York Times*, 60 October 1983, p. A-2; and Michael Kaufman, "Life in Zaire, Viewed by Student Critic: ´Les Miserables," *New York Times*, 25 October 1983, p. A-2.

163. References to tensions between the Ethiopians and the Soviets can be found in the following articles: Pranay Gupte, "Ethiopian Links to Soviet Strained," *New York Times*, 21 December 1981, p. A-7; and "Ethiopia Expels 2 As Spies for Moscow," *New York Times*, 8 March 1984, p. A-7; References to divisions within the Angolan government can be found in the following article: Alan Cowell, "Angola's Importance Outstrips Its Strength," *New York Times*, 1 August 1982, p. E-3.

CHAPTER SEVEN

Conclusions and Policy Recommendations

1. Summary and Conclusion

In the late 1950s the vague outlines of an American sub-Saharan African policy began to emerge. The independence process had begun: a process which would accelerate in the 1960s. The early post-independence years would witness a somewhat low-keyed US-Soviet contest for Continental influence. It would be a contest centered on the Congo, but extending in the economic and diplomatic spheres to Ghana, Mali, and Guinea among other states. By the mid to late 1960s Soviet hopes had crumbled. The pro-Western Mobutu Sese Seko was in power in the Congo, and leaders looked upon opportunistically by the USSR in Ghana and Mali had been overthrown. The Soviets could boast of only one governmental ally on the sub-Continent, Guinea's Sekou Toure. Toure's image was not tarnished in Soviet eyes by his resemblance to the charismatic but ideologically suspect deposed leaders of Ghana and Mali, Kwame Nkrumah and Modibo Keita. Enamored with the appearance of leaders hostile to the West, Nikita Khrushchev had declared Africa fertile ground for revolution at the beginning of the 1960s. This was no longer the official Soviet position. The suspicion that the archaic class character of

African societies precluded Marxist breakthroughs in the short-term gained ascendancy. This was accompanied by a Soviet recognition, following probes in the Congo that there were severe limitations on its ability to project its power to Africa. The Soviets turned their attention elsewhere by the latter part of the 1960s. The US, preoccupied with Vietnam and no longer worried about Soviet activities on the sub-Continent did likewise. For a short time Africa became a mere sideshow to East-West interaction in other areas of the globe. The Continent was overtaken by coups and internal turmoil. Marxist revolutions and parliamentary democracy seemed alien to a continent caught in the throes of primeval ethnic struggles. In 1974, sub-Saharan Africa entered an era of re-emergent super-power interest. A coup in Portugal, and a revolution in Ethiopia opened the door to regimes with stronger Marxist credentials than previous governments. The Soviets and their allies attempted to exploit the new geopolitical circumstances. The US hesitated, constrained by self-doubts generated by the Vietnam fiasco. Then in the late 1970s and early 1980s, Western reverses in Iran and Afghanistan served as the chief impetus to a new American presence in Africa. Soviet inroads on the Continent were also a factor.

Looking back at the post-independence period, many analysts have focused on the seemingly ad hoc nature of American actions in sub-Saharan Africa. They assert that it is futile to assess US actions from a regional standpoint. Only an analysis of bilateral contacts yields useful information. While accepting the salience of studies which focus exclusively on US relations with individual states, conclusions can be drawn about American behavior on the sub-Continent as a whole.

An appraisal of American foreign policy in sub-Saharan Africa from the Kennedy through Reagan administrations produces the following findings.

First, underlying assumptions governing American behavior on the sub-Continent can be delineated. Specific policy outcomes cannot be fully understood by reference to them. However, the parameters within which most American initiatives must operate can be identified. When viewed in isolation, American African policy appears amorphous and aimless. When viewed in the context of American global activities, it is somewhat more coherent. Three tenets have influenced US conduct in Africa over the duration of the post-independence era. It is not the contention of the present study that this is an exhaustive list of tenets that have appeared intermittently. Those utilizing a different analytical framework can extract additional premises. Nor is it argued that the configuration of the tenets dealt with here has been uniform over time. They have, however, exerted a more persistent impact on US behavior than other postulates, and their fundamental character has remained intact. They provide at least the beginning of a framework for comprehending US policy in the African labyrinth.

An overriding theme of US foreign policy since the latter half of the 1940s has been containment. It is hardly surprising, therefore, that a principal assumption behind US African policy has been the need to restrict Soviet gains. Corollaries of this have been the desirability of backing pro-Western governments, and ensuring access to minerals. The maintenance of Western financial interests is also an offshoot of this assumption.

According to John Gaddis, the Kennedy and Johnson administrations practiced a near universal (symmetrical) approach to containment. The Nixon and Carter administrations, in his estimation, followed a selective approach.[1] It may be added that following the late 1979 Soviet invasion of Afghanistan, the Carter administration moved toward universal containment. Moreover, the Reagan administration, which falls outside the framework of Gaddis's study, also followed universalism. This study's findings do not conflict with Gaddis's description of US administrations, with the caveat that even in periods of intense activism abroad Africa has not been a core US security interest. Containment during the two decades from the early 1960s through the early 1980s focused intermittently on the Congo (Leopoldville), Rhodesia, Angola, South-West Africa, Somalia, and Chad, among other states. Administrations cannot be distinguished from one another on the basis of intent since all expressed their displeasure with Eastern bloc advances on the Continent. They can be differentiated on the means they advocated and employed to foster "containment."

The Kennedy, Johnson and Reagan administrations took highly circumscribed military steps to discourage penetration by the Soviets and their allies. The former two administrations did so in the Congo and the latter in Chad. Military bases on the Continent were re-established during the Carter and Reagan presidencies. Yet, they were directed largely at non-African security threats. Covert actions to strengthen pro-Western actors were implemented by the Kennedy and Johnson administrations in the Congo. The Ford and Reagan administrations did likewise in Angola and Chad, respectively. The Nixon administration's hopes for containment rested in part with the white regimes of the Continent's southern region. To a varying degree every administration, with the exception of Richard Nixon's, encouraged majority rule as a panacea for the conditions which bred revolution and a reduction in Western authority. Kennedy endorsed it for the sub-Continent. A number of administrations backed it for Rhodesia and South-West Africa.

Reagan officials suggested that a variant of majority rule should be the outcome of the Namibian negotiations. Despite the disparity in means utilized by the administrations to further containment, there were common denominators. Large-scale direct military intervention was considered unacceptable. Massive resource transfers on the order of those elsewhere were looked upon unfavorably. In addition, it was taken for granted that European actors should bear principal responsibility for the Continent. This brings us to the final two presuppositions of America's African policy.

A second tenet was that the human and physical resources channeled toward the Continent would be highly restricted.

High level attention to sub-Saharan Africa has been erratic and crisis oriented. Crisis-provoking high level responses have taken place in Zaire (formerly the Congo/Leopoldville) throughout the 1960s and in the late 1970s, and Angola during the early 1960s and the late 1970s. On a few occasions Rhodesia and South Africa were the objects of high echelon interest for the more than two decades spanning the Kennedy and Reagan administrations. Chad entered the limelight in the early 1980s. There have been efforts to alter this pattern. The early Kennedy and Carter administrations were characterized by an unusual amount of high level scrutiny of Africa. For the Kennedy administration this emanated from the president's curiosity about the Continent and a fear that the hammer and sickle could become emblazoned on its sensitive zones extending from central to western Africa. Top officials of the Carter administration were initially drawn to Africa by the opportunity to display an interest in human rights and developmental issues which were not easily identified as components of the East-West contest. Moreover, Secretary of State Kissinger rediscovered the Continent in the 1975–1976 period, culminating in a trip in 1976 in which he resembled former Assistant Secretary G. Mennen Williams more than Otto von Bismark. The secretary's conversion to the limited ranks of American Africa watchers, however, can be deemed a forced conversion emanating principally from a spurt of disquieting Soviet activities and successes on the sub-Continent.

Apart from these heretical approaches to Africa, the norm has been indifference by the upper levels of the executive branch. This indifference springs from traditional American concern with other regions of the globe. Africa's importance relative to these concerns has been limited.

Administration requests for physical resources to be sent to the Continent have taken a beating.

This can be attributed to congressional and public apathy on African issues, and geopolitical callings elsewhere in the world.

The third postulate underlying US African behavior has been that high salience will be attached to Western European concerns in the formulation of US policy. This is not to be misconstrued as a willingness to allow the Europeans to dictate US actions. It does mean that the US displayed apprehension over following policies which conflicted with those of its European allies. In deference to African sensitivities, American officials made few explicit references to Africa as a European sphere of influence. This was a generally accepted state of affairs, however. Liberia and Ethiopia, states which escaped the colonial yoke, were among the few exceptions to this belief. The retrenchment of English power in the post-independence period diminished its prominence as an actor. It did not erase it as embodied by England's central role in Rhodesia's tortuous passage to independence. France's primacy as an external actor in central and western Africa continued largely unabated. Despite a few anomalies such as Guinea, the French presence was deepseated during the post-independence period. It possessed military and economic dimensions. Even the self-proclaimed Afro-Marxist state of Congo (Brazzaville) was bound to the French economic network. The early 1980s witnessed a resurgence of Portuguese influence in Mozambique, and that of Spain in the mini-state of Equatorial Guinea.

The North Atlantic Treaty Organization's integral role in US security plans, the historical nature of European-African ties, and the existence of US obligations in other regions ensured that each administration would be cognizant of European interests. In the Congo this meant an adjustment to Belgian predilections, and in Rhodesia to those of the British. Nor did the US frequently outpace the caution of the Western Europeans on South Africa. On the Portuguese colonies the administrations did little to alienate the metropole. When differences arose with the Europeans, they were usually followed soon thereafter by a restoration of the equilibrium. Hence, the furor over American support of a UN resolution condemning Portugal for its behavior in Angola during the Kennedy administration did not preclude an improvement in United States-Portuguese relations later as the need for access to the Azores again gained ascendancy.

The principal disparities between the administrations over the third premise can be explained by two factors.

First, the intensity with which the Nixon administration applied its asymmetrical outlook on world affairs to Africa. Africa's peripheral status for the US was embodied by the disdain with which Kissinger initially treated the Continent.

Therefore, with the exception of Rhodesia, the US during the Nixon years deferred to a greater extent to the Europeans in Africa than other administrations during the post-independence era. Hence, Kissinger's acceptance of Portugal's atavistic behavior on the Continent.

A second factor which contributed to an element of discontinuity in the approaches of the administrations to the third pre-supposition were the series of Western setbacks of the late 1970s and early 1980s, including those in Iran and Afghanistan. This precipitated the emergence of a relatively independent policy, particularly in the Horn of Africa: a policy adopted by a centrist to liberal president, and continued by his conservative successor.

Nonetheless, the third premise generally prevailed across administrations of a variety of ideological hues.

The question arises whether containment can be pursued effectively in the absence of a substantial transfer of resources by the US, and an infrequent willingness to adopt independent stances on a wide array of regional issues. This query will be addressed later in this chapter.

A second finding is that bureaucratic and geopolitical variables have had the greatest impact on the configuration of US African policy. Domestic non-bureaucratic and economic factors have had a secondary effect, and that of cultural variables has been tertiary. Bureaucratic and geopolitical forces have sustained their paramount status for the duration of the post-independence era. Domestic non-bureaucratic variables have undergone a gentle rise in importance since the Johnson presidency. The influence of economic factors has been erratic and contingent on the issue being examined. They have been difficult to correlate to policy outcomes.

Cultural forces have remained in the background. Despite their arcane nature they shed light on the policy makers and the process they set in motion.

What lessons can we draw from the use of our models? The chief lesson is that African policy is primarily a creature of the executive bureaucracy. More so than other regions, African policy is largely insulated from the vagaries of public opinion and sustained congressional scrutiny. This is not to argue that public and congressional influence has been non-existent. However, it has been episodic, and only an infrequent determinant of the policy courses adopted.

A related lesson is that while globalists in the upper levels of the bureaucracy have set the tone for African policy, it has been formulated largely by the bureaucracy's middle echelons. The general orientations of the globalists have been influential as reflected in the premises of America's African policy. However, middle level officials practicing the art of bureaucratic conservatism have had chief responsibility for the moderate African policy of the post-independence era. There has been remarkable continuity in US behavior toward Africa since the dawning of post-colonial Africa. The pendulum has not swung wildly in the time honored American tradition between indifference and frenzied intervention. Again, this sets Africa apart from other areas.

Another observation is that fluctuations in African policy are principally a result of two variables. The first is the infrequent intervention of top echelon officials in the policy process. This has only occurred sporadically. The second variable consists of geopolitical developments. For instance, the acceleration of the African independence process in the early 1960s, and the demise of Portuguese rule from 1974–1975. These events altered US treatment of the Continent.

Students of US African policy are advised to focus much of their energy on understanding the dynamics of the executive bureaucracy and the geopolitical factors to which it responds. This approach does not approximate the classical realist model because of its repudiation of the notion that the state is a monolithic actor. An understanding of bureaucratic cleavages is imperative.

Thus, there is room for policy innovation in America's African policy. The lack of large-scale domestic non-bureaucratic input into this policy renders Africa fertile ground for new initiatives. These innovations, however, must come principally in the form of imaginative diplomacy and the skillful use of limited resources. For it is unlikely that the chief premises of US African behavior, and the pattern outlined in this work, will be changed drastically in coming years.

It is evident that the economic and cultural models have only been touched on. This does not constitute a rejection of their utility. The author has found applicable economic data contradictory, and cultural interpretations ambiguous. These models, nonetheless, deserve more comprehensive treatment by other analysts.

A final conclusion is that US African policy has not effectively promoted US security interests. They include lowering the probability that hostile regimes, particularly pro-Soviet governments, will come to power. Another interest is contributing to a stable international system consonant with Western values. US policy shortcomings can be delineated on four dimensions. These shortcomings have been salient in various combinations since the Kennedy presidency.

First, administrations have often misread the domestic American political mood when drawing up African initiatives. Nixon White House staff members exaggerated the significance of Africa to white southern voters. Moreover, by acquiescing to the Byrd Amendment and not firmly backing efforts to repeal it, they allowed companies with interests

171

in Rhodesian chrome to have influence over US policy out of proportion to their objective political clout. The tilt toward Africa's white regimes evolving in part from these stances adversely affected US security needs. Similarly, Jimmy Carter had a distorted view of the importance of Africa to black American voters. Symbolic gestures represented by Vance's call for one man one vote, and an array of dramatic quotes by Andrew Young were sometimes allowed to take primacy over substantive policy measures. This was particularly the case in the administration's early stages. Contrary to the views of some conservatives and liberals, Africa has historically been a blank slate to most members of the general and informed publics.

Beyond a vague commitment to justice on the sub-Continent, the public has had little concern about its internal dynamics. False notions of the salience of Africa to domestic political constituencies should not be allowed to skew policy makers' judgments of what is in the national interest. One concrete belief of Americans about the Continent across racial lines is that we should not get deeply involved militarily in its myriad of conflicts.[2] Those who attempt to violate this maxim risk embarrassment, and a probability that the US may be forced ultimately to back down with negative repercussions for the national interest. Kissinger and Ford, to the consternation of analysts more attuned to domestic realities, learned this lesson the hard way. Their abortive effort to pour military supplies into Angola to avert a takeover by the MPLA in 1975 resulted only in an ignominious loss by US-backed forces, and another blow to US global credibility. A private rejection of massive US military involvement on the sub-Continent need not entail its abandonment to antagonistic elements. US military involvement in Africa need not run aground on the shoals of domestic opinion if it is carefully calibrated and very limited. President Johnson's shipment of three aircraft and one hundred and fifty operating personnel to the Congo in 1967 and the Reagan administration's dispatch of AWACs surveillance planes, and anti-aircraft weapons during the mid 1983 Chad crisis embody such ventures.[3] There will be more on means for promoting US security needs in the absence of a viable option for massive military involvement in the latter part of this chapter.

Another serious deficiency of US African policy has been its indifference to indigenous African political factors. One need not be a victim of regionalitis, a malady rejected by this author, to argue that sound policy must be grounded in a knowledge of local conditions. Knowledge of these conditions does not mean that one is a captive of them. Interestingly, both administrations which attempted to distance themselves from regionalitis and those who claimed they were attuned to African realities have often ignored them. Two conceptual oversights have been prominent. One is a failure to recognize what is happening within individual African states. The other is an inability to predict the probable impact of policy steps on interstate relations among African states.

A reasonable understanding of events within African states need not be the monopoly of a small number of anthropologists or specialists with an in-depth knowledge of the area. A beginning is to keep your intelligence antennae active, a simple principle again violated egregiously by the Nixon administration. It terminated contacts between its intelligence operatives and guerillas challenging Portuguese rule in Angola and Mozambique.[4] This ill-conceived step left Kissinger and other members of the executive foreign policy apparatus with few viable options when the Portuguese junta came tumbling down in April 1974. Similar critiques can be offered of the failure of a number of administrations to maintain adequate ties to opponents of the Mobutu government, and to black South African guerillas. In this realm there have been occasional displays of foresight. Kennedy and Johnson administration contacts with black guerillas in the Portuguese colonies, and the linkages established with black South African liberation groups by Carter officials come to mind. Another missed opportunity has been the refusal of administrations to take advantage of cleavages within ruling cliques in African states. Examples of this phenomenon in post-revolutionary Angola and Ethiopia have been outlined earlier. Carter and Reagan officials alike were slow in following up on the possibility of limiting the dependency of these states on the Soviets.

Nor has the effect of US actions on interstate African relations been factored intelligently into the calculations of many policy makers. Illustrations of this include the tacit support by the Ford administration of South African intervention in Angola in 1975, and its request to Zaire to increase its assistance to the FNLA around the same time. The former incursion delegitimized pro-Western, anti-MPLA guerillas in the eyes of much of the world. The latter action was one precipitant of the invasion of Zaire's Shaba province from Angola in 1977 and 1978. Moreover, it is questionable whether detente actually died in the sands of the Ogaden in the late 1970s. It is a virtual certainty, however, that short term US prospects for improving US relations with the most significant strategic actor in the Horn area, Ethiopia, died there. By moving into a strategic alliance with Somalia, a country of dubious importance for US Indian Ocean and Middle Eastern policy in the late 1970s and early 1980s, the US drove a stake into the heart of its relationship with Ethiopia. It was Dr. Brzezinski who demonstrated an ignorance of US power interests in this case.

To avoid accusations that the author harbors a secret passion for regionally-based judgments, a few comments must be made about the inability of some US administrations to integrate their African policies into a global framework. Again, the phenomenon of the pot calling the kettle black arises. A number of administrations, including those with pretensions of deriving their policy from a coherent sense of global priorities have taken steps in Africa oblivious of long term American global interests. Hence, Kissinger's poorly conceived Angolan gamble. A number of administration insiders told Dr. Kissinger that the Soviets would up the ante if the US sent large shipments of arms. The implication was that the US would not be able to respond correspondingly.

Before proceeding, a brief reference should be made to a US policy success. The success is Zimbabwe. With the exception of the Nixon administration, starting in the mid 1960s officials did not allow a vocal but small minority of US advocates of preserving white rule to deter them from following a policy prudently tailored to internal Rhodesian, inter-African and global variables. It was recognized that the most effective way to preclude the emergence of a pro-Soviet government was not to engage in a futile exercise of regime preservation. Rather, it lay in the support of processes leading to a regime change entailing majority rule. The support of African states was enlisted, and the Soviets were cut out of the action. Both liberal and conservative administrations would promote strong economic and political ties with the ostensibly radical government which emerged. While some may lament the inexorable move of Zimbabwe toward a one-party or one-man rule, the record stands that Western capitalist states (Britain and the US in particular) helped to usher into power an authentic black nationalist with a mass base, and a lack of sympathy for Soviet strategic designs. This was a commendable achievement.

2. Policy Recommendations

We can now turn to the task of policy prescription. The task of drafting guidelines cognizant of Africa's diversity is intimidating. The skeptic may question whether it is possible to formulate general policies for a Continent which encompasses the revolutionary Dergue of Ethiopia, and the traditional tribal rulers of Swaziland. The task of devising recommendations is not impossible, provided that claims are not made as to their applicability in all circumstances. This study's recommendations fall into three areas, each of which relates to a postulate of America's African policy. They are mechanisms for containment, resource allocation and the role of non-American actors on the Continent. These mechanisms must be adopted to the peculiarities of individual states. Additional comments will be made about the Republic of South Africa.

Our first recommendation calls for a multifaceted and prudent approach to containment in Africa. It is incorrect to insist that the West need only sit by quietly, and the forces of African nationalism will inevitably assert themselves on their own accord, defeating external bids for hegemony. This belief ignores the dangers of asymmetry when one side acts assertively on a consistent basis and the other remains passive. It also ignores the acute permeability of most African states. It is not the intent of containment that can be faulted in America's treatment of Africa, but rather its implementation. As mentioned earlier, it has not been founded on an understanding of African societies. Nor has it always used military means wisely. Finally, the non-military dimensions of containment, so essential to the theory of its creator George Kennan, have frequently been neglected.

Having touched on the lack of comprehension by American policy makers of African society, little more need be said here. One point is crucial, however. African governments tend to be highly centralized. They revolve around individuals or cliques whose internal strength is often derived from an ethnic base. Ideology, while a legitimizing tool, is not the main determinant of governmental behavior. The idiosyncratic proclivities of the ruling circle, and ethnicity dictate the actions of governments.[5] South Africa, despite its relative economic development, cannot wholly escape this observation, for ethnocentric Afrikaners steeped in the ethos of another century have a disproportionate amount of influence here. The facile nature of ideological labels in Africa was recognized by David Rockefeller, former chairman of the Chase Manhattan Bank following an early 1982 tour of Africa. "African socialism is no threat," Mr. Rockefeller observed. "I really am convinced that socialism for most of the African leaders I talked with meant a very specialized thing and has little to do with Marxism. One comes to the assessment whether their ideology is that deep and my impression is that it is the other way around."[6] The implication of this factor is that African leaders are often mercurial in their policy choices. The systemic constraints on flexibility in policy postures throughout the developed world are not as applicable here.[7] The disparity between the public and private positions of African leaders must be taken into account in the conduct of American policy on the Continent.

The use of military means by the US to foster containment in Africa has only limited utility. It is perhaps the one sizable inhabited area which has never been considered a vital US security interest. As reflected in the 1975–1976 Angolan debacle, there is little domestic sentiment for

175

large scale military assistance to pro-American elements. Eight years later little had changed as President Reagan declared, following the Libyan invasion of Chad, that the US would not intervene directly under any contingency. Three criteria for an effective African policy bear mention as they relate to US military intervention. Intervention must command domestic support, take into account intrastate and interstate variables on the Continent, and complement US global policy. Few scenarios can be contemplated where it would not be extremely limited and carried out at the behest of a standing government.

This brings us to the non-military dimensions of containment. Subtlety of methodology must be practiced, for the US must not give the impression that its interest in Africa is as a chessboard for the East-West contest. African goals (i.e., economic development, South African liberation) must not be scoffed at. The African predilection for public nonalignment must be respected.[8] Bearing this in mind, in the diplomatic sphere, the US must sustain linkages with groups opposed to prevailing regimes and exploit governmental divisions. These steps have already received attention. Most importantly, the US must attempt to maintain diplomatic contacts with governments across the ideological spectrum. This applies to Angola as well as to South Africa. Withholding diplomatic recognition or terminating diplomatic ties is a futile form of pressure. In the case of Afro-Marxist regimes backed by the Soviets, it eliminates one source of limited US influence.[9]

In the non-military realm, containment can also be facilitated by a transfer of economic resources and a willingness to pursue Continental goals multilaterally.

Proponents of economic aid as a tool of US policy have cited dismal Soviet aid figures and the need of even Afro-Marxist regimes for Western goods and technology. From the early 1950s through the late 1970s Soviet economic assistance to Africa was less than one-half of that of Communist China.[10] By the mid 1970s, the Soviets were among the top five trading partners in only three African states.[11] This state of affairs had changed little by the early 1980s despite the emergence of a number of governments to which the Soviets provided substantial military support.[12] As the 1980s progressed, Afro-Marxist regimes eagerly sought Western technologies and aid unavailable from the Eastern Bloc.[13] Economic transfers can be used as an instrument for increasing US influence and providing openings to states dependent on the Soviets in other areas. Yet, visions of major increases in aid, much less a US Marshall Plan for the Continent, are unrealistic. Objectively, there are greater US interests elsewhere, including Latin America. Moreover, there will not be a powerful domestic constituency in the US arguing on behalf of massive aid transfers in the near term. Sub-Saharan Africa has little choice but to continue to accept circumscribed US economic aid. Restricted aid programs, however, need not be translated into political impotence. US political goals including containment can be realized through a sophisticated use of strategic criteria in determining aid priorities. They can also be promoted through a careful coordination of aid tools.

The use of strategic criteria in determining aid recipients should not involve a narrow definition of the national interest as manifested in the Clay and Korry reports of the 1960s. These reports articulated the view that only a handful of states should be the recipients of US assistance.[14] Nor should crude distinctions between radical and non-radical, or free market and non-free market market states be allowed to dictate aid allocations. A broad definition of US security needs would not foreclose aid to socialist Tanzania in light of its leader Julius Nyerere's Continental influence. It would also facilitate aid to the Southern African Development Coordination Conference. Among the benefits of assistance to this grouping of nine black African states would be lowered reliance by a couple of its members on the USSR. Moreover, even greater Western access to minerals such as Rhodesian chrome could be assured. This would reduce the role of two less desirable sources of strategic minerals, the volatile Republic of South Africa and the Soviet Union.[15] Finally, security conscious aid formulas should not preclude an intermittent focus on the need for humanitarian assistance as a consequence of natural or man-made disasters.

A coordination of aid mechanisms would entail an effort to encourage private assistance in conjunction with a bilateral transfer of public funds. Secondarily, it would incorporate attempts to achieve a minimal degree of coordination between these forms of aid and multilateral sources of assistance.

A policy launched in isolation from other actors pursuing complementary goals would be a failed policy. Hence, the need for multilateralism in US African endeavors. In light of Africa's peripheral status in the American strategic scheme, this tactic is imperative. It is rendered viable by the wide array of national and non-national actors playing a role in Continental affairs. The United Nations undertakes political and economic projects. The Organization of African Unity attempts to mediate conflicts. Morocco sends troops to Zaire. Zaire sends troops to Chad. The Communist Chinese and Saudi Arabians support pet economic projects.[16] The list is long, supplemented by such old African actors as India, and relatively new ones as Brazil and Japan.[17] A rule when the US contemplates military and economic activities on the

Continent is that it should first see if other national or non-national entities are willing to undertake these tasks. A symbolic US role may be adequate. If this is not possible, the US should coordinate its actions with other actors. To avoid an appearance of neo-imperialism, African actors would receive first preference followed by other third world actors and finally Europeans. If all else fails, the US should act alone but this should be only a last resort. Pursuing such a strategy demands a desire to "strengthen international rules," display "flexibility" and foster "alliances."[18]

A failure to deal explicitly with the Republic of South Africa in drafting recommendations would expose this study to charges of negligence. On the other hand cursory treatment of this subject borders on the irresponsible. I will risk the latter in making a few observations. Those who demand an in-depth analysis of policy options for the US toward this troubled nation are urged to consult the fine work of the Study Commission on US Policy Toward South Africa entitled *South Africa: Time Running Out*.[19]

First, after years of studying the issue of sanctions both in an historical context, and as they apply explicitly to the Republic of South Africa, the author has come to the following conclusion.

Comprehensive and sustained economic sanctions would be unenforceable and psychologically counterproductive. They would be unenforceable primarily because of the difficulty of getting such disparate actors as Britain and Japan, among others, to comply. Britain's compliance would be hindered by its extensive economic ties with the Republic. Japan's adherence would be constrained by its traditional refusal to inject overt political considerations into its trading policies. Furthermore, outside of the realm of high technology in a few specialized fields, South Africa is largely self-sufficient.[20] It could withstand sanctions for years, and respond by inflicting unacceptable damage on its economically dependent black African neighbors.[21]

Perhaps even more importantly, it is probable that sanctions would not exacerbate the cleavages among white South Africans significantly, thereby provoking a trend toward liberalization. On the contrary, as exhibited during the period in which Rhodesia was subject to sanctions in the 1960s and 1970s, there would probably be a tendency to close ranks. This would particularly apply to the Afrikaners. In a nation in which the majority of white political dissenters hail from the far right, increasing political repression would probably be the principal outcome of economic sanctions.[22]

There are few signs that the black and colored majority would be able to overcome its deep-seated divisions and military weakness to produce systemic change of a liberal nature. Certainly, the majority of Afrikaners would have few moral qualms about putting down uprisings in a spirit of retribution likely to engender extensive casualties.[23]

The words of one of America's foremost experts on South Africa, Robert Rotberg, deserve mention.

> To isolate [South Africa] is to lose further opportunities to influence a nation on a day to day basis . . . coolness may be preferred to a rupture of relations as a bargaining posture . . . Especially for Americans, the package of incentives may prove much more helpful than a bundle of punishments . . . [24]

This observation does not rule out the potential efficacy of selective and gradualistic economic sanctions and comprehensive military sanctions.

There are economic measures which would be enforceable and not necessarily produce an undesirable counterreaction in South Africa. One would be for the United States to place a moratorium on further investments in the Republic by US companies.[25] Moreover, the arms embargo could be continued and tightened. Multipurpose technology which enhances the coercive capacity of the South African government should not be sent to the Republic.[26]

The complexity of the issue of nuclear transfers precludes much coverage here. However, it is clear that in the realm of nuclear weaponry South Africa has already acquired a limited capacity, or could do so swiftly if it desired.[27] Cooperation by the US in the nuclear area should be based on a strict adherence by the Republic to the Nuclear Nonproliferation Treaty.[28]

The policy steps outlined, while undoubtedly unsatisfactory to South Africa's more militant foes, would serve two purposes. First, they would send a message to the Republic that its political course is unacceptable. Second, it would distance the US a little from the apartheid government in the event of a regime change at some point in the future.

Finally, it behooves US policy makers to speak out forcefully when South Africa destabilizes its neighbors or intensifies internal repression.[29] Silent diplomacy, while occasionally efficacious, is interpreted by South Africa's internal and external foes as acquiescence to its policies. A perception of US complicity with the defenders of apartheid can only enhance the role of America's totalitarian adversaries on the sub-Continent and elsewhere. Nor can we call ourselves a force for justice in the world arena if we shirk our moral duty in the face of blatant assaults on the most basic tenets of human rights.

It has been almost twenty-five years since the Bureau of African

Affairs emerged in the State Department, endowing Africa with a degree of US attention as an independent entity. During that period black Africans, to borrow Nkrumah's phrase, have indeed captured the "political kingdom," with the exception of the Republic of South Africa and the territory of South-West Africa. Over the past quarter of a century there have been a melange of coups, tribal conflicts, and, more recently, revolutions. Despite some cosmetic changes, however, the central character of most African societies has not changed radically. Africa consists of a collection of states relying on agriculture or mineral extraction, where ethnicity prevails over overt class factors. Within these states, individuals or cliques run societies mired between tradition and modernity with only limited success. When formulating policy for the Continent, it is these characteristics which must be taken into account. Though a scourge for the Continent's future political and economic development, they do open the door to an imaginative and flexible US policy.

NOTES TO CHAPTER SEVEN

1. An assessment of the Kennedy administration's approach to containment can be found in Gaddis, *Strategies of Containment*, pp. 198–273. For other administrations Gaddis provides an analysis on the following pages: the Johnson administration, pp. 237–73; the Nixon administration, pp. 274–344; and the Carter administration, pp. 345–52.
2. Fierce, "Black and White American Opinions Toward South Africa," pp. 671-72, 675, 682.
3. Nielsen, *Great Powers and Africa*, p. 322; "US Sends 3 Advisers and 30 Rockets to Aid Chad," *New York Times*, 4 August 1983, p. A-3; and Richard Halloran, "US Sending AWACs and F-15 Fighters to Support Chad," *New York Times*, 7 August 1983, p. A-1.
4. Stockwell, *A CIA Story*, p. 52.
5. For more on the role of ethnicity and ideology in African politics see the following sources: Kilson, "The African Revolution," pp. 6–10; Henry Bienen, "Soviet Political Relations with Africa," *International Security* 6 (Spring 1982): 153–73; and Crawford Young, *Ideology and Development in Africa* (New Haven: Yale University Press, 1982).
6. Pranay Gupte, "David Rockefeller Says Africans Look to US," *New York Times*, 10 March 1982, p. A-6.
7. See Bienen, "Soviet Relations with Africa," pp. 153–73.
8. Young, "Multilateralizing United States Policy," pp. 351–57."
9. Ibid., p. 374.
10. Young, *Ideology and Development in Africa*, p. 275.
11. Ibid., p. 281.
12. On insignificant Soviet economic aid to sub-Saharan African states, see Young, *Ideology and Development in Africa*, pp. 87, 94.

13. Personal Interview, Nick Murphy, State Department regional director for Central Africa, State Department, Washington, DC, 10 December 1981.
14. Young, *Ideology and Development in Africa,* p. 278.
15. Foreign Policy Study Foundation, *South Africa: Time Running Out,* pp. 292-93, 444-49.
16. For references to the Communist Chinese as African actors see Bienen, "Soviet Relations with Africa," pp. 158-59, 161-62; and Young, "Multilateralizing United States Policy," pp. 360, 367-68.
17. Bienen, "Soviet Relations with Africa," pp. 158-59.
18. Nye, "US Power and Reagan Policy," pp. 401-9.
19. Foreign Policy Study Foundation, *South Africa: Time Running Out.*
20. Ibid., pp. 128-46, 420-26.
21. Ibid., p. 422.
22. Ibid.
23. Ibid.
24. Rotberg, *Suffer the Future,* p. 293.
25. Foreign Policy Study Foundation, *South Africa: Time Running Out,* pp. 427-28.
26. Ibid., pp. 413-15.
27. Ibid., pp. 251-53.
28. Ibid., pp. 415-16.
29. John Dugard, "Silence Is Not Golden," *Foreign Policy* no. 46 (Spring 1982), pp. 46-48.

SELECTIVE BIBLIOGRAPHY

I. Books and Theses and Pamphlets

Allison, Graham. *Essence of Decision: Explaining the Cuban Missile Crisis.* Boston: Little, Brown and Co., 1971.

American Enterprise Institute for Public Policy Research. *Africa: US Policy at a Crossroads.* Washington, DC: American Enterprise Institute for Public Policy Research, 1979.

Arkhurst, Frederick S., ed. *US Policy Toward Africa.* New York City: Praeger Publishers, 1975.

Ball, George. *The Past Has Another Pattern.* New York City: W. W. Norton and Co., 1982.

Barratt, John, and Hero, Alfred, eds. *The American People and South Africa: Publics, Elites and the Policy-Making Process.* Lexington, Massachusetts: Lexington Books, 1981.

Barratt, John and Rotberg, Robert, eds. *Conflict and Compromise in South Africa.* Lexington, Massachusetts: Lexington Books, 1980.

Bender, Gerald. *Angola Under the Portuguese: The Myth and Reality.* London: Heinemann Educational Books, 1978.

Bissel, Richard. *Apartheid and International Organizations.* Boulder, Colorado: Westview Press, 1977.

Bissel, Richard E., and Crocker, Chester, eds. *South Africa into the 1980s.* Boulder, Colorado: Westview Press, 1979.

Bowles, Chester. *Africa's Challenge to America.* Westport, Connecticut: Negro Universities Press, 1956.

Brown, Seyom. *The Faces of Power: Constancy and Change in United States Foreign Policy from Truman to Johnson.* New York City: Columbia University Press, 1968.

Brzezinski, Zbigniew, ed. *Africa and the Communist World.* Stanford, California: Stanford University Press, 1963.

Carter, G. M., and Meara, P. O., eds. *Southern Africa in Crisis.* Bloomington, Indiana: Indiana University Press, 1977.

Charles, Milene. *The Soviet Union and Africa: The History of the Involvement.* Lanham, Maryland: University Press of America, 1980.

Claude, Inis. *Power and International Relations.* New York City: Random House, 1962.

Cohen, Barry and El-Khawas, Mohammed A., eds. *The Kissinger Study of Southern Africa, National Security Study Memorandum 39.* Westport, Connecticut: Lawrence, Hill and Co., 1976.

Cohen, Benjamin. *The Question of Imperialism: The Political Economy of Dominance and Dependence.* New York City: Basic Books, 1973.

Cooper, Allan. *US Economic Power and Political Influence in Namibia, 1700–1982.* Boulder, Colorado: Westview Press, 1982.

Cottrell, Alvin and Hahn, Walter. *Soviet Shadow over Africa.* Washington, DC: University of Miami Center for Advanced International Studies, 1976.

Dale, Richard and Potholm, Christian, eds. *Southern Africa in Perspective: Essays in Regional Politics.* New York City: Free Press, 1972.

Davidow, Jeffrey. *A Peace of Southern Africa: The Lancaster House Conference on Rhodesia.* Boulder, Colorado: Westview Press, 1984.

Davidson, Basil. *In the Eye of the Storm: Angola's People.* Garden City, New York: Doubleday, 1972.

Donovan, John. *The Cold Warriors: A Policy-Making Elite.* Lexington, Massachusetts: Heath, 1974.

Duignan, Peter and Gann, L. H. *Africa South of the Sahara: The Challenge to Western Security.* Stanford: Hoover Institution Press, 1981.

Ebinger, Charles. *Foreign Intervention in Civil War: The Politics and Diplomacy of the Angolan Conflict.* Boulder, Colorado: Westview Press, 1983.

Emerson, Rupert. *Africa and United States Foreign Policy.* Englewood Cliffs, New Jersey: Prentice Hall, 1967.

Foltz, William J. *Elite Opinion and United States Policy Toward Africa: A Survey of the Members of the Council on Foreign Relations and its Affiliated Regional Committees.* New York City: Council on Foreign Relations, 1979.

Foreign Policy Study Foundation. *South Africa: Time Running Out: The Report of the Study Commission on US Policy Toward Southern Africa.* Berkeley: University of California Press, 1981.

Gaddis, John. *Strategies of Containment: A Critical Appraisal of Post-War American National Security Policy.* New York City: Oxford University Press, 1982.

Goldschmidt, Walter, ed. *The United States and Africa.* New York City: Frederick A. Praeger Publishers, 1963.

Good, Robert C. *UDI: The International Politics of the Rhodesian Rebellion.* Princeton, New Jersey: Princeton University Press, 1973.

Grieg, Ian. *The Communist Challenge to Africa: An Analysis of Contemporary Soviet, Chinese and Cuban Policies.* Richmond Surrey: Foreign Affairs Publishing Co., 1977.

Halberstam, David. *The Best and the Brightest.* New York City: Random House, 1972.

Harsch, Ernest and Thomas, Tony. *Angola: The Hidden History of Washington's War.* New York City: Pathfinder Press, 1976.

Henderson, Lawrence. *Angola: Five Centuries of Conflict.* Ithaca, New York: Cornell University Press, 1979.

Henriksen, Thomas. *Mozambique: A History.* London: Rex Collings, 1978.

Hodges, Tony and Legum, Colin. *After Angola: The Storm over Southern Africa.* New York City: Africana Publishing Co., 1975.

Hoffman, Stanley. *Primacy or World Order: American Foreign Policy Since the Cold War.* New York City: McGraw Hill, 1978.

Houser, George. *Meeting Africa's Challenge: The Story of the American Committee on Africa.* Pamphlet, New York City: American Committee on Africa.

Howe, Herbert. "Event, Issue, Reconsideration: The United States and the Nigerian Civil War." Ph.D dissertation, Harvard University, 1978.

Jackson, Henry. *From the Congo to Soweto: US Foreign Policy Toward Africa Since 1960.* New York City: William Morrow and Co., 1982.

Jaster, Robert. *Southern Africa in Conflict: Implications for US Policies in the 1980s.* London: American Enterprise Institute for Public Policy Research, 1982.

Jinadu, Adele. *Human Rights and US African Policy Under President Carter.* Lagos, Nigeria: Nigerian Institute of International Affairs, 1980.

Kalb, Madeline. *The Congo Cables: The Cold War in Africa From Eisenhower to Kennedy.* New York City: MacMillan Publishing Co., 1982.

Kaplan, Irving, ed. *Angola: A Country Study.* Washington, DC: American University, 1979.

Kaplan, Irving. *Area Handbook for Mozambique.* Washington, DC: Government Printing Office, 1977.

Kearns, Doris. *Lyndon Johnson and the American Dream.* New York City: Harper and Row, 1976.

Keohane, Robert O. and Nye, Joseph S. *Power and Interdependence.* Boston: Little, Brown, and Co., 1971.

Kitchen, Helen. *US Interests in Africa.* New York City: Praeger Publishers, 1983.

Klinghoffer, Arthur. *The Angolan War: A Study in Soviet Policy in the Third World.* Boulder, Colorado: Westview Press, 1980.

Kornegay, Francis. *Washington and Africa: Reagan, Congress and an African Affairs Constituency in Transition.* Washington, DC: African Bibliographic Center, 1982.

Lafeber, Walter, ed. *America in the Cold War: Twenty Years of Revolution and Response.* New York City: John Wiley and Sons, 1969.

Lake, Anthony. *The Tar Baby Option: American Policy Toward Southern Rhodesia.* New York City: Columbia University Press, 1976.

Legum, Colin. *The Western Crisis Over Southern Africa: South Africa, Rhodesia, Namibia.* New York City: Africana Publishing Co., 1979.

Legvold, Robert. *Soviet Policy in West Africa.* Cambridge, Massachusetts: Harvard University Press, 1970.

Leiss, Amelia, ed. *Apartheid and the United Nations Collective Measures: An Analysis.* New York City: Carnegie Endowment for International Peace, 1965.

Lemarchand, Rene, ed. *American Policy in Southern Africa: The Stakes and the Stance*. Washington, DC: University Press of America, 1978.

Lenin, V. I. *Imperialism: The Highest Stage of Capitalism*. Peking: Foreign Languages Press, 1965.

Libby, Ronald T. *Toward an Americanized US Policy for Southern Africa: A Strategy for Increasing Political Leverage*. Berkeley: Institute of International Studies, University of California, 1980.

Lord, Donald F. *John Kennedy: The Politics of Confrontation and Conciliation*. Woodbury, New York: Barrons Educational Series, 1977.

Losman, Donald L. *International Economic Sanctions: The Cases of Cuba, Israel and Rhodesia*. Albuquerque: University of New Mexico Press, 1979.

Magdoff, Harry. *The Age of Imperialism*. New York City: Monthly Review Press, 1969.

Mahoney, Richard. *JFK: Ordeal in Africa*. New York City: Oxford University Press, 1983.

Marcum, John. *The Angolan Revolution*. 2 vols. Cambridge, Massachusetts: MIT Press, 1969–1978.

Morgenthau, Hans. *Politics Among Nations: The Struggle for Power and Peace*. New York City: A. A. Knopf, 1978.

Myers, Desaix B. *US Business in South Africa: The Economic, Political and Moral Issues*. Bloomington, Indiana: Indiana University Press, 1980.

Nielsen, Waldemar A. *The Great Powers and Africa*. London: Pall Mall Press, 1969.

Nyangoni, Wellington. *United States Foreign Policy and South Africa*. New York City: SCI Press, 1981.

Okuma, Thomas. *Angola in Ferment: The Background and Prospects of Angolan Nationalism*. Westport, Connecticut: Greenwood Press, 1962.

Packenham, Robert. *Liberal America in the Third World: Political Development Ideas in Foreign Aid and the Social Sciences*. Princeton, New Jersey: Princeton University, 1975.

Pelissier, Rene and Wheeler, Douglas. *Angola*. Westport, Connecticut: Greenwood Press, 1971.

Price, Robert M. *US Foreign Policy in Sub-Saharan Africa: National Interest and Global Strategy.* Berkeley: University of California Press, 1978.

Rotberg, Robert. *Suffer the Future: Policy Choices in Southern Africa.* Cambridge, Massachusetts: Harvard University Press, 1982.

Samuels, Michael. *Implications of Soviet and Cuban Activities in Africa for US Policy.* Washington, DC: Center for Strategic and International Studies, Georgetown University, 1979.

Slabbert, Frederick Van Zyl. *South Africa's Options: Strategies for Sharing Power.* New York City: St. Martin's Press, 1979.

Stockwell, John. *In Search of Enemies: A CIA Story.* New York City: W. W. Norton and Co., 1978.

Trautman, William. "Trans-Africa: A Case Study of the Politics of a Black Foreign Policy Lobby in Light of the Development of Black Consciousness and Black Politicization in the US." thesis. Harvard University. 1979.

Weissman, Stephen. *American Foreign Policy in the Congo: 1960-1964.* Ithaca, New York: Cornell University Press, 1974.

Whitaker, Jennifer Seymour, ed. *Africa and the United States: Vital Interests.* New York City: New York University Press, 1978.

Williams, G. Mennen. *Africa for the Africans.* Grand Rapids, Michigan: William B. Eerdmans Publishing Co., 1969.

Yarborough, William P. *Trial in Africa: The Failure of US Policy.* Washington, DC: The Heritage Foundation, 1976.

Young, Crawford. *Ideology and Development.* New Haven: Yale University Press, 1982.

II. Articles

Adelman, Kenneth. "The Black Man's Burden." *Foreign Policy* no. 28 (Fall 1977).

African Policy Information Center of the African American Institute. "African Updates Exclusive Review of Relations between the US and Africa." *Africa Report* 20 (January–February 1975).

Bertolin, Gordon. "US Economic Interests in Africa: Investments, Trade and Raw Materials." In *Africa and the United States: Vital Interests.* Edited by Jennifer Whitaker. New York City: New York University Press, 1978.

Bienen, Henry. "Soviet Political Relations With Africa." *International Security* 6 (Spring 1982).

Butcher, Goler Teal. "US-Africa Relations: America's New Opportunity." *Africa Report* 20 (September–October 1974).

"Carter's U Turn in Foreign Policy." *US News and World Report* 88 (28 January 1980).

Crocker, Chester. "South Africa: Strategy for Change." *Foreign Affairs* 59 (Winter 1980–1981).

Davis, Nathaniel. "The Angola Decision of 1975: A Personal Memoir." *Foreign Affairs* 57 (Fall 1978).

Dugard, John. "Silence Is Not Golden." *Foreign Policy* No. 46 (Spring 1982).

Easum, Donald. "United States Policy Toward South Africa." *Issue: A Quarterly Journal of Africanist Opinion* 5 (Fall 1975).

Emerson, Rupert. "The Character of American Interests in Africa." In *The United States and Africa.* Edited by Walter Goldschmidt. New York City: Frederick A. Praeger Publishers, 1963.

Fierce, Mildred. "Black and White American Opinions Toward South Africa." *Journal of Modern African Studies* 20 (December 1982).

Gilpin, Susan. "Minerals and Foreign Policy." *Africa Report* 27 (May–June 1982).

Hughes, Anthony. "Interview of Congressman Howard Wolpe." *Africa Report* 26 (November–December 1981).

Hull, Galen. "Internationalizing the Shaba Conflict." *Africa Report* 22 (July–August 1977).

Kemp, Geoffrey. "US Strategic Interests and Military Options in Sub-Saharan Africa." In *Africa and the United States: Vital Interests.* Edited by Jennifer Whitaker. New York City: New York University Press, 1978.

Kilson, Martin. "The African Revolution: The Fading of Dreams." *Harvard International Review* 5 (April 1983).

Lancaster, Carol. "United States Policy in Sub-Saharan Africa." *Current History* 81 (March 1982).

Legum, Colin. "The Soviet Union, China and the West in Southern Africa." *Foreign Affairs* 54 (July 1976).

Lockwood, Edgar. "The Future of the Carter Policy Toward Southern Africa." *Issue* 7 (Winter 1977).

Marcum, John. "The Exile Condition and Revolutionary Effectiveness: Southern African Liberation Movements." In *Southern Africa in Perspective: Essays in Regional Politics.* Edited by Richard Dale and Christian Potholm. New York City: Free Press, 1972.

Mboukou, Alexandre. "Pragmatic Relations: US–Congo." *Africa Report* 26 (November–December 1981).

McKay, Vernon. "The African Operations of United States Government Agencies." In *The United States and Africa.* Edited by Walter Goldschmidt. New York City: Frederick A. Praeger Publishers, 1963.

McKay, Vernon. "Changing External Pressures on Africa." In *The United States and Africa.* Edited by Walter Goldschmidt. New York City: Frederick A. Praeger Publishers, 1963.

"Nine Who Helped Shape Carter's Policy." *US News and World Report* 88 (28 January 1980).

Nye, Joseph S. "US Power and Reagan Policy." *Orbis: A Journal of World Affairs* 26 (Summer 1982).

Oudes, Bruce. "The Sacking of the Secretary." *Africa Report* 20 (January–February 1975).

Pachter, Elise. Interview of Chester Crocker. "Reagan's African Policy." *SAIS Review* 13 (Spring 1983).

Peterson, Charles W. "The Military Balance in Southern Africa." In *Southern Africa in Perspective: Essays in Regional Politics.* Edited by Richard Dale and Christian Potholm. New York City: Free Press, 1972.

Young, M. Crawford. "Multilateralizing United States African Policy." In *Harvard University Conference on United States Policy Toward Africa.* Cambridge, Massachusetts: Harvard University Committee on African Studies, 1981.

III. Periodicals and Newspapers

1. Periodicals:

Africa (London).

Africa Confidential (London).

Africa News (Durham, North Carolina).

Africa Report (United Nations Plaza, New York City).

Africa Today (Denver).

African Affairs (London).

The African Review (Dar es Salaam, Tanzania).

Current History (Philadelphia).

Foreign Affairs (New York City).

Foreign Policy (Washington, DC).

Harvard International Review (Cambridge, Massachusetts).

International Security (Cambridge, Massachusetts).

Issue: A Quarterly Journal of Africanist Opinion (Waltham, Massachusetts).

Journal of Modern African Studies. (Cambridge, England).

Newsweek (Los Angeles, California).

Orbis: A Journal of World Affairs (Philadelphia).

SAIS Review (Washington, DC).

US News and World Report (Beverly Hills, California).

2. Newspapers

Boston Globe (Boston).

Boston Phoenix (Boston).

Harvard University Gazette (Cambridge, Massachusetts).

New York Times (New York City).

Washington Post (Washington, DC).

IV. Personal Interviews

Bruce, Bob. State Department regional director for West Africa, Reagan administration. State Department, Washington, DC. Interview, 10 December 1981.

Chamberlain, Chris. assistant to Senator Tsongas (D. Mass.), minority ranking member, Senate Foreign Relations Subcommittee on Africa. Russell Senate Office Building, Washington, DC. Interview, 11 December 1981.

Christianson, Phil. head staff person for Senate Foreign Relations Subcommittee on Africa. Dirksen Senate Office Building, Washington, DC. Interview, 9 December 1981.

Easum, Donald. assistant secretary of state for African affairs, 1974–1975.

African-American Institute, New York City. Interview, 23 March 1982.

Ferguson, Clyde. deputy assistant secretary of state for African affairs, 1972–1973. Harvard University Law School, Cambridge, Massachusetts. Interview, 14 January 1983.

Frank, David. assistant to Congressman Stephen Solarz (D. NY), chairman of the House Foreign Affairs Subcommittee on Africa, latter half of Carter administration. House Office Building Annex One, Washington, DC. Interview, 11 December 1981.

Fredericks, Wayne. deputy assistant secretary for African affairs, Kennedy and Johnson administrations. Ford Motor Company, New York City. Interview, 23 March 1982.

Mr. Irish. staff member, American Committee on Africa. American Committee on Africa, New York City. Interview, 29 April 1982.

Kamman, Curt. State Department regional director for East Africa, Reagan administration. State Department, Washington, DC. Interview, 10 December 1981.

Keyes, Alan. African specialist for State Department Policy Planning Staff, Reagan administration. State Department, Washington, DC. Interview, 26 April 1982.

McHenry, Donald. United Nations ambassador from 1979–1981, Carter administration. Georgetown University, Washington, DC. Interview, 26 April 1982.

Murphy, Nick. State Department regional director for Central Africa, Reagan administration. State Department, Washington, DC. Interview, 10 December 1981.

Newsom, David. assistant secretary of state for African affairs, 1969–1974, Nixon administration. Georgetown University School of Foreign Service, Washington, DC. Interview, 8 December 1981.

Schaufele, William. assistant secretary of state for African affairs, 1975–1977. Harvard University, Cambridge, Massachusetts. Interview, 27 October 1981.

Segars, Joseph. State Department Zimbabwe desk officer, Reagan administration. State Department, Washington, DC. Interview, 27 April 1982.

Weissman, Stephen. staff associate, House Foreign Affairs Subcommittee on Africa, 1979–1983. House Office Building Annex One, Washington, DC. Interview, 26 April 1982.

Zinn, Kenneth. staff member, Washington Office on Africa. Washington Office on Africa, Washington DC. Interview, 26 April 1982.

V. Government Documents and Publications

1. Unpublished and Declassified Documents

    1.1. Documents at John F. Kennedy Presidential Library in Boston.

    1.1.1. Pre-presidential papers of John F. Kennedy.

    1.1.2. 1960 Presidential campaign documents of John F. Kennedy.

    1.1.3. National Security File:

    1.1.3.1. Papers of William Brubeck and Carl Kaysen.

    1.1.3.2. National Security Action memoranda.

    1.1.3.3. Countries and Regions: Africa in general, Congo (Brazzaville), Congo (Leopoldville), Ethiopia, Guinea, Nigeria, the Portuguese colonies of Angola and Mozambique and the Azores, Rhodesia, South Africa, South-West Africa, and the Sudan.

    1.1.4. Oral History Collection:

    1.1.4.1. Attwood, William. ambassador to Guinea. Oral history statement, 8 November 1963.

    1.1.4.2. Bissel, Richard. deputy director of Central Intelligence Agency. East Hartford, Connecticut. Interview, 25 April 1967.

    1.1.4.3. Darlington, Charles. ambassador to Gabon, 1961–1966. Mount Kisco, New York. Interview, 3 December 1971.

    1.1.4.4. Estes, Thomas S. ambassador to Upper Volta, 1961–1966. Washington, DC. Interview, 18 March 1971.

    1.1.4.5. Hilsman, Roger. director of Bureau of Intelligence and Research, Department of State, and assistant secretary of state for Far Eastern affairs. Lyme, Connecticut. Interview, 14 August 1970.

    1.1.4.6. Komer, Robert. senior staff member, National Security Council, 1961–1965. Interview, 18 June 1964.

    1.1.4.7. Nitze, Paul. assistant secretary of defense for

193

international security affairs, and secretary of the Navy. Interview, 22 May 1964.

1.1.4.8. Palmer, Williston. director of military assistance, Department of Defense. Washington, DC. Interview, 5 August 1970.

1.1.4.9. Satterthwaite, Joseph. ambassador to South Africa, 1961–1965. Washington, DC. Interview, 2 March 1971.

1.1.4.10. Williams, G. Mennen. assistant secretary of state for African affairs. Grosse Pointe Farms, Michigan. Interview, 28 January 1970.

1.2. Documents from Lyndon Baines Johnson Presidential Library in Austin, Texas.

1.2.1. National Security File:

1.2.1.1. Countries and Regions: Africa in general, Angola, Congo (Leopoldville), Mozambique, Portugal, Rhodesia, and South Africa.

1.2.2. White House File:

1.2.2.1. Countries and regions: Africa in general, Angola, Congo (Leopoldville), Mozambique, Portugal, Rhodesia, and South Africa.

1.2.3. Head of State Correspondence

1.2.4. Congo (Leopoldville): President Kasavubu, 7 July 1964–6 August 1965.

1.2.5. Oral History Collection:

1.2.5.1. Battle, Lucius. Interview, 14 November 1968.

1.2.5.2. Bohlen, Charles. deputy undersecretary of state for political affairs. Interview, 20 November 1968.

1.2.5.3. Bowles, Chester. Interview, 11 November 1969.

1.2.5.4. Diggs, Charles. Interview, 13 March 1969.

1.2.5.5. Harriman, W. Averell. Interview, 16 June 1969.

1.2.5.6. Helms, Richard. Interview, 16 September 1981.

1.2.5.7. McGhee, Gale. Interview, 10 February 1969.

1.2.5.8. Palmer, Joseph. assistant secretary of state for African affairs, 1966–1969. State Department, Washington, DC. Interview, 8 January 1969.

1.2.5.9. Rostow, Eugene. Interview, 2 December 1968.

1.2.5.10. Solomon, Anthony. deputy assistant administrator for the Agency for International Development, and assistant secretary of state for economic affairs. Interview, 18 November 1968.

1.2.5.11. Williams, G. Mennen. assistant secretary of state for African affairs, 1961–1966. Detroit, Michigan. Interview, 8 March 1974.

2.   Published Government Documents

2.1. Congressional Hearings

2.1.1. US Congress. House. Subcommittee on Africa of Committee on Foreign Affairs. "The Current Situation in Namibia." 96th Cong., 1st sess., 1979.

2.1.2. US Congress. House. Subcommittee on Africa of Committee on Foreign Affairs. "Namibia Update." 96th Cong., 2nd sess., 1980.

2.1.3. US Congress. House. Subcommittee on International Security Affairs, and Subcommittee on Africa of Committee on Foreign Affairs. "Proposed Arms Sale to Morocco." 96th Cong., 2nd sess., 1980.

2.1.4. US Congress. House. Subcommittee on Africa of Committee on Foreign Affairs. "Political and Economic Situation in Zaire." 96th Cong., 1st sess., 1981.

2.2. US, Department of State. Bureau of Public Affairs. *Department of State Bulletin.* January 1961–June 1983.

2.3. US, President. *Public Papers of the Presidents of the United States.* Washington, DC. Government Printing Office. John F. Kennedy, 1961.